The Psycho-Political Muse

Paul Breslin

The Psycho-Political Muse

American Poetry since the Fifties

 The University of Chicago Press
Chicago and London

Paul Breslin is associate professor of English at Northwestern University. His poems, scholarly articles, and reviews have appeared in numerous journals, such as *Poetry, American Scholar,* and *The New Republic.*

The University of Chicago Press, Chicago 60637
The University of Chicago Press, Ltd., London

© 1987 by The University of Chicago
All rights reserved. Published 1987
Printed in the United States of America

96 95 94 93 92 91 90 89 88 87   5 4 3 2 1

Library of Congress Cataloging-in-Publication Data

Breslin, Paul.
    The psycho-political muse.

    Bibliography.
    Includes index.
    1. American poetry—20th century—History and
criticism.   2. Psychology in literature.   3. Politics
in literature.   I. Title.
PS323.5.B74   1987   811'.54'09358   87–10863
ISBN 0–226–07410–2

No doubt the artist is the child of his time, but woe to him if he is also its disciple, or even its favorite.

—Schiller, *On the Aesthetic Education of Man*, Ninth Letter

Contents

Acknowledgments ix

Introduction xi

1 Radical Poetics and Radical Politics 1

2 Allen Ginsberg as Representative Man: The Road to Naropa 22

3 Confessional Poetics: The Poet as Representative Victim 42

4 Robert Lowell: The Historical Self and The Limits of "Conflation" 59

5 Sylvia Plath: The Mythically Fated Self 95

6 Deep Images, Shallow Psychologies: The Unconscious as Pastoral Retreat 118

7 To The Interior and Back: W. S. Merwin 136

8 Ohio and the Collective Unconscious: The Dilemma of James Wright 157

9 Black Mountain: A Critique of the Curriculum 182

10 Warpless and Woofless Subtleties: John Ashbery and "Bourgeois Discourse" 211

Abbreviations 237

Notes 238

Index 255

Acknowledgments

I am grateful to the American Council of Learned Societies, and to the National Endowment for the Humanities, which contributes to the stipend of ACLS grants, for a fellowship during the academic year 1980–81. I did most of the research, and first drafts of the first three chapters, during that period. Part of chapter 6 first appeared in *American Scholar* 47, no. 3 (Summer 1978) as "How to Read the New Contemporary Poem"; part of chapter 9 first appeared in *Poetry* 136, no. 4 (July 1980) as "Black Mountain: A Critique of the Curriculum." In chapter 10, a few sentences survive from "Warpless and Woofless Subtleties," *Poetry* 137, no. 1 (October 1980). I have quoted several short poems in their entirety. I am grateful to Farrar, Straus and Giroux for permission to reprint the following poems by Robert Lowell: "Words for Hart Crane," from *Life Studies*, © 1956, 1959 by Robert Lowell; "Bishop Berkeley" and "Two Walls," from *History*, © 1967, 1968, 1969, 1970, 1973 by Robert Lowell. Atheneum Publishers granted permission to reprint the following poems by W. S. Merwin: "The Night of the Shirts" and "The First Darkness," from *The Carrier of Ladders*, © 1970 by W. S. Merwin; "By Day and By Night," "In the Gorge," and "Finally," from *The Moving Target*, © 1963 by W. S. Merwin; "The Search," from *Writings to an Unfinished Accompaniment*, © 1973 by W. S. Merwin. Wesleyan University Press granted permission to reprint "The Jewel" and "Eisenhower's Visit to Franco, 1959" from *Collected Poems* by James Wright, © 1962 by James Wright. Harper and Row, Publishers granted permission to reprint Robert Bly's poem, "Moving Inward at Last," from *Light Around the Body*, © 1959 by Robert Bly.

Colleagues and friends have been generous with advice and encouragement; I especially want to thank Gerald Graff, Alan Shapiro, and Lawrence Lipking for their help with all stages of the project. Graff's *Literature Against Itself* and several of Shapiro's essays have influenced my approach to the subject in ways too deep-seated to be easily documented in the notes. The debt will be apparent to those who have read their work and so, I trust, will the differences among the three of us.

W. S. Di Piero, Robert Pinsky, and Barbara Foley offered valuable criticism of early drafts. I've also profited from the comments of Steven Gerber, a composer whose sensitivity to modern poetry can be heard in his song cycles; Jeffrey Rice, bookseller and freelance intellectual; and a former Northwestern student, Lynn Laufenberg, now a graduate student at Cornell. But the usual escape clause applies: the faults of the resulting book, be they many or few, are my responsibility, not theirs.

The deepest gratitude, of course, is the hardest to acknowledge in public. People at work on books are notoriously difficult to live with. Of what I owe to my wife Jeanne and my daughter Megan for their love and support, an acknowledgment cannot even scratch the surface.

Introduction

In the preface to the second edition of *The Open Society and Its Enemies*, Sir Karl Popper remarks that "No book can ever be finished. While working on it we learn just enough to find it immature the moment we turn away from it."[1] If that observation is true for someone of his attainments, it must be true several times over for the rest of us, provided we escape the fate of being too dull to learn even that much. When I began working on the present manuscript five years ago, I envisioned a polemical critique of American poetic fashions since the late fifties; it would explain the most widely praised stylistic innovations as diverging from an underlying set of dubious assumptions about poetry and society, and in so explaining them, it would explain them away.

In working at this book over the past five years, I have sometimes had the experience of discovering, against my will, that I liked, was fascinated by, and remembered vividly some poetry that implicitly, or even explicitly, endorsed the dubious assumptions I had uncovered. And I had the experience of being bored by poetry that avoided said assumptions, that had the virtues of solid craftsmanship and intelligence, but lacked the blessing of talent. Finally, I have had the experience of writing poems of my own and finding out how hard it is to do what, from the armchair vantage point of criticism, seems so plainly desirable.

After all of these chastenings, however, I remain convinced that a study of the relations between a style and the way of looking at the world implicit within it can assist in critical judgment as well as historical understanding. Without the gift for sounding the resonances of the language, all the intelligence in the world will not make anyone a poet. And those who have that gift usually find a way to write well, at least sometimes, whatever their limitations in other respects. But assuming the presence of the poet's irreducible gift as shaper of language—and one can assume it, in some degree, for all of the poets chosen for discussion here—there are many possibilities for the realization of that gift, some more promising than others. The kinds of poetry, and ways of talking about poetry, that emerged toward the end of the fifties need more careful, skeptical cross-examination than they have received. Most critics have judged this body of work by the criteria its own creators have advanced; we have reached a point now where we not only can but must begin to detach ourselves from those criteria if the art is to advance. An examination of recent poetry in the context of postwar American history—and intellectual history—provides a way of gaining this detachment. Still-current doctrines of literary taste begin to appear as responses to a particular cultural moment, not as triumphant liberations of truth from the dungeons of the 1950s.

As the manuscript began to take shape, its historical and explanatory purpose seemed increasingly central, the polemical intention increasingly secondary and even dangerous in its temptation to vanity and dogmatism. I now think of this book as a skeptical reappraisal, not a polemical indictment, of some of the most widely admired poetry, and thinking about poetry, during the past thirty years or so, with particular emphasis on the 1960s and early 1970s. Some of the chapters, reworked from earlier articles, still have some of the polemical zeal with which I began; rather than muffle their stylistic energy, I have revised them as little as possible, interfering only where their argument now strikes me as incomplete, flatly wrong, or irrelevant to their present function as chapters rather than essays or reviews.

Critics as well as poets, of course, make underlying assumptions; I should like to be as explicit as possible about my own, or at least about those I am aware of making. First of all, I believe that a poetic style has some sort of coherence which can be described and analyzed. Moreover, I treat this coherence as resulting, at least in part, from the poet's way of trying to make sense of the world and not entirely from the intramural play of language or a Bloomian struggle with literary precursors. I look for relationships between individual poetic styles and the preoccupations of the age in which they are formed (though the relation can be one of rejection or of complex revision as well as of naïve participation). And finally, I assume that some ways of making sense of the world are more tenable than others, and that without claiming to know who is right in any absolute sense, one can tell whether a poet is facing resolutely the problems that trouble his own imagination or trying to will them away.

I am aware that every one of these assumptions is open to question and that a deconstructionist might consider them positively Mesozoic. They owe something to currently fashionable ways of thinking about literature in that they suppose a network of connections linking diverse cultural phenomena and conceive of criticism as a way of disclosing those connections. But they persist in the old-fashioned assumption that the author is not dead, that the poet can be found in the poem, and that the poet found therein is, within historically determined limits, a free intellectual, moral, and aesthetic agent. A poem represents the outcome of *choices* that begin with the first setting of pen to paper and end with the last revision.

What now seems to me the most important part of my argument concerns the cultural circumstances in which the shift in literary taste at the end of the 1950s took place. I have attempted to trace, amid the diversity of American poetry since the late 1950s, the emergence of a common stock of ideas and, to a lesser extent, a shared rhetoric. Although there was not a single dominant period style, several prominent group styles emerged at about the same time. Despite their differences, they share a conception of poetry as engaged in the liberation of human consciousness from a false consciousness imposed by society. This notion of the poet's task can be traced back to Blake, Shelley, and Wordsworth. But the heritage of post-Freudian depth psychology, and its application to the question of how social authority is psychologically internalized, gives contemporary versions of the romantic aspiration a different emphasis and, to some extent, a different content also. The historical part of my argument attempts to show that culturally radical poetry from the late fifties through the seventies typically portrays the relation between self and society much as the radical psycho-political theorists of the same period conceived of it.

It would be folly to assume an all-embracing parallelism between the poetry and the social history of the same period; indeed, just such an assumption is one of the ideas I most wish to question in radical poetics. My assumption is, I hope, more modest: that poets, like most thoughtful persons, are at least casually aware of the public debates of their times, and that psycho-political ideas were at least as prominent in those debates twenty years ago as, say, deconstructionist thinking is nowadays—probably more so, because semiotics has not attracted the notice of popular culture as psychoanalysis did. As Paul Roazen wrote in 1968—the very heart of the historical period under consideration—"the psychoanalytic tenor of our day is one of those aspects of intellectual history that is as obvious as it is hard to document. The difficulty in objectifying the obvious is notorious: for that which we assume is compelling by its very elusiveness."[2]

To be aware of something is not necessarily to understand it in detail, or even to care about it very much. In suggesting that radical psycho-political theory and radical poetics share common intellectual and rhetorical features, I do not mean to imply that poets wrote with copies of *Eros and Civilization* sitting on their desks next to their dictionaries; I only mean to suggest that comparison of the social theory and the poetry reveals that both participate in a style of thought belonging to their place and time. To recognize this is to see the extent to which the often-remarked diversity of recent American poetry can be understood as diverging responses to the same constellation of central problems. When I discuss, in my first chapter, nuances of psychoanalytical or social theories that most poets probably couldn't have cared less about, I do so because the theorists often define problems that emerge, less explicitly formulated, in poetry or in discussions of poetry.

The second, polemical step of the argument proceeds from my conviction that the widely noted "revolution in taste"[3] at the end of the 1950s broke through the limitations of the previous reigning aesthetic at a greater cost than has generally been recognized. Much of what has been praised for its "openness to experience" has been every bit as narrowly "closed," in its own way, as the poetry it replaced. Paul Zweig has described the change as a "plunge away from culture and rationality."[4] That vertiginous dive may have renewed access to the natural and the irrational, but neither rationality nor culture can be got rid of entirely even when one tries; the wish to appear to have done so generates its own forms of artificiality, and these can seem all the more mannered for not candidly acknowledging their artifice.

The evaluative part of the argument is related to the historical part insofar as the historical inquiry can explain why Zweig's "plunge" came to strike many intelligent poets as possible and, however desperate, necessary. Upon finding that highly dubious notions were greeted, twenty years ago, as self-evident truths, one can either congratulate oneself on being so much more intelligent than people were then, or one can ask why people at least as intelligent as oneself and probably more so found such ideas compelling. In general, I believe that while historical explanation is always useful in the study of literature, it becomes especially important in accounting for the uncritical acceptance of art and ideas. If one is going to argue that certain kinds of poems have been overpraised, it helps to show why, given the literary climate in which they appeared, critics were inclined to overvalue them.

Because I deal skeptically with poetry and ideas that have been considered politically and aesthetically "radical," some may hope to find in this book a defense of the positions usually labeled "conservative." I am not sure that these terms ever had much meaning in art, and they have begun to lose what meaning they once had in politics. I shall simply say for the record that in politics, I consider myself neither a radical nor a conservative but a liberal, and that in aesthetics, the important distinction seems to me not between "radical" and "conservative" but between narrow and inclusive. Because of the disproportionate value attached, in our culture, to originality, poets are tempted to exaggerate what is obviously "different" about their work, to the exclusion of everything else. Add to this the fact that contemporary work is usually discussed only in a contemporary context, rather than in the context of a long literary tradition, and one begins to see why American poetry threatens to become locked in an Empedoclean alternation between genteel and neoprimitive forms of narrowness.

Viewed as the liberation of creative energy from the death grip of outworn conventions, the recent history of American poetry is a boring melodrama. It is only credible as literary history if it is viewed as the displacement of one set of conventions by another. Even poetry that seems to come from "experience," or from the unconscious, or from Olsonian "process" has conventions—indeed, it is only by its conventions that such poetry can create the illusion of springing unmediated from those sources.

I hope that the present study will make readers more aware of the conventional nature of various recent poetries of experience. But to object to the notion that certain styles are, in Olson's phrase, "equal . . . to the real itself"[5] is not to endorse the opposite oversimplification, encouraged by deconstructionist theory, that poetry cannot refer to "the real" at all, or that the only knowable reality is the free play of language itself. Inherently unequal to the real itself, poetry nonetheless tries to recover the real through the essentially social mediation of conventions recognized by poet and reader. When it abandons the attempt to point beyond itself, it becomes indistinguishable from elaborate games such as chess—which is pleasurable and requires great skill, but is not like poetry as most readers (quite justifiably) conceive of it.

My premise, then, is that poetry does need to call up the fullness of human experience, but that it does so, inevitably, by artifice. Some forms of artifice are better conjurers of experience than others. Moreover, some are suited only to certain kinds of experience. They seem exceptionally "open" to "experience" only if one defines experience in a narrow and partial way favorable to their preoccupations. No poet, even Shakespeare, encompasses all the possibilities of the art; any style involves choices, and choices involve exclusions. One does better to acknowledge this frankly than to stake out a proprietary claim on "experience" in general. At the same time, since there must be limits, one must try to encompass as much as possible within them. Narrowness that presents itself as such gives shape to inchoate potentiality;

but a narrow mode that claims to have a monopoly on "experience" asks to be taken as defining the range of the possible. It is just when they begin to seem natural that conventions become most artificial; instead of aiding in the exploration of the real, they present themselves as the real already immanent. The contemporary emperor reverses the fable. He proudly claims to be naked, and it remains for someone to cry out: "But he has clothes on, like everyone else!"

A few remarks on the sequence of chapters, and on my inclusions and exclusions, are in order. To some extent, the selections are inevitably arbitrary, since complete coverage would have to be purchased at the cost of brief, superficial treatment for each poet. My selection is influenced by my belief that the labels "confessional," "deep-image," and "projective" poetry, however much they may tempt critics to facile pigeonholing, do represent historically real group styles. Accordingly, the third chapter, on confessional poetics, is followed by studies of Sylvia Plath and Robert Lowell; the sixth, on deep-image poetics, introduces studies of W. S. Merwin and James Wright. My decision to deal with Olsonian projectivism in a single chapter represents, to some degree, a value judgment. It also represents a recognition that projectivist verse, though concerned with the purging of false consciousness, is to some extent antipsychological and, therefore, less intimately connected than the other two group styles to the intellectual history I have traced. Olson proposes a cure of society through a cure of consciousness, but a regenerated consciousness would not be describable in the terms of Freudian or Jungian psychology—although Olson was influenced by Jung to some extent. Unlike Bly, who invokes Jung as the guide to deeper and more natural recesses of the self, Olson proposes an interaction with the surrounding world so absorbing that the awareness of self simply disappears.

Chapters 3 through 9, then, attend to "confessional," "deep-image," and "projectivist" poetics and to representative poets influenced by each of these. Chapter 1 presents the cultural context for the emergence of these group styles. Chapter 2 is a study of Allen Ginsberg, who seems, more than any other poet of significant talent, to participate to some extent in all the fashions of the age; his career is representative. The book closes with a study of John Ashbery, who has emerged as the main candidate for major American poet in the 1980s. Although Ashbery's poetry is less overtly concerned with political matters than that of any other poet considered here, some critics have understood his poetry as implicitly political. Ashbery provides a fitting subject for the closing chapter, because although he has been a respected presence since winning the Yale Younger Poets Prize in 1956, the critical climate of the last five or ten years has been increasingly receptive to his work. A study of his poetry can provide a measure of what has—and has not—changed in our thinking about poetry since the 1960s.

Some readers will doubtless object to the omission of black poets and the sparse representation of women poets (Sylvia Plath gets a chapter, and Denise Levertov receives a third of a chapter.) Of course, in a predominantly negative assessment, omission might be construed as a compliment. Obviously, much of what I say here might be applied to, say, Adrienne Rich or Amiri Baraka. But obviously, too, a fair discussion of Rich or Baraka would have to treat them in the contexts of radical feminism and of black literature, respectively; I do not wish to become any more overextended than I already am. Although, as I have acknowledged, the choices are to some extent arbitrary, the poets chosen for study all have a clear connection to the literary and cultural history I wish to trace, and all have been widely perceived as important contributors to that history.

Radical Poetics and Radical Politics

To begin with commonplaces, which are common ground: between the mid-1950s and the mid-1960s, both American poetry and American politics changed dramatically. A large American left emerged for the first time since the 1940s, and much of the poetry, as has often been remarked, shared in the spirit of the politics. Many well-known poets not only wrote explicitly radical political poetry, but also conceived of poetry, as Shelley and Blake had done, as by its nature opposed to political oppression. Many of the poets who did the most to change the direction of poetry also participated in the protest politics of the 1960s and 1970s—Robert Lowell, Adrienne Rich, W. S. Merwin, Robert Bly, Denise Levertov, Galway Kinnell, Allen Ginsberg, and Amiri Baraka, to name only a sampling of the most famous. What made radical politics and radical poetics more congenial allies than they had been in the 1930s was the psycho-political character of the New Left. Poets had been saying since Shelley's time that social change requires not only a change in outward conditions, but also the cure of consciousness. Yet seldom, if ever, has the political left agreed with them to the extent that it did in the 1960s. The most conspicuously new poetry of the period branches in several directions, and it does not always or even usually proclaim itself as self-consciously political. Nonetheless, much of that poetry can be illuminated by a consideration of the cultural and political radicalism with which it often shares not only rhetorical habits but a way of making sense of the world.

Toward the end of the 1950s, poetry became less detached, less formal, less, as Robert Lowell said, "Alexandrian."[1] Poets and their critics began to talk less about craft and more about "experience." As Donald Hall has remarked, many poets of his generation

went through a movement from a poetry which was formal in its meter and rhyme and which had a rational and external narrative, to poetry which is free verse with improvised forms and improvised resolutions of noise—and which is more intimate, more emotional, and more irrational.[2]

This brief statement contains the central oppositions by which polemi-cists for the new poetry usually defined its rejection of the immediate past. The emotional and irrational were now to be valued rather than the rational, the inward or "intimate" more than the "external." Tradi-tional forms, whether the prosodic exactions of rhyme and meter or the plotting of narrative, belonged to the realm of the external, the rational, and the rigid; it was necessary to break from them in order to have the greater spontaneity of "improvised forms."

Many poets, in taking the direction Hall describes, believed that in doing so they were protesting against a society constricted by excessive devotion to rational order—or to a debased caricature of rational order. In 1966, Robert Bly attacked poetry of "the dead world," which studies the conscious lives of people within society but ignores the uncon-scious and nature, not only as bad art but as a manifestation of national aggression:

Suppose a country's literature never does shed its skin, what will happen to it? Suppose it . . . insists . . . on studying the exclusively human over and over? . . . One can predict first of all that such a nation will bomb for-eign populations very easily, since it has no sense of anything real beyond its own ego.[3]

Galway Kinnell—and he is far from alone in this—equates formality and moral rationality in poetry with acquiescence to repression:

Many people feel one shouldn't poke under the surface—that one shouldn't tempt the gods or invite trouble, that one should be content to live with his taboos unchallenged, with his repressions and politenesses unquestioned; that just as the highest virtue in the state is law and order, so the highest virtue of poetry is formality and morality. . . .[4]

In an interview for the *Ohio Review* (1971), Adrienne Rich agrees with her interviewer that no one needs to talk much anymore about form "or think very much about it," either—formal poetry belongs to an un-usable past, and that past is unusable partly for political reasons: Yeats is a "table-rapping fascist," and the laborious polishing of rhymed stan-zas, presumably, is a pastime for an outmoded authoritarian culture.[5]

The change in poetic taste at the end of the 1950s seemed quite abrupt and rebellious to most observers at the time. Subsequently, we have been able to see that the change was not quite as sudden as it appeared; isolated from the most prestigious cultural centers and broken into local groups unknown to each other, there were a number of poets working in directions undreamed of in *The Kenyon Review*. Some of them, such as Frank O'Hara, Charles Olson, and Robert

Creeley, were to become famous in the 1960s; Allen Ginsberg, notorious in the 1950s, became academically respectable in the 1960s. What has still not been sufficiently recognized is the degree of continuity between the cultural rebellion of the 1960s and some of the best-known social thought of the years from 1945 to 1960. Both the rise of the New Left and the revolt in the arts against reason, culture, and their internalization within the self can be explained partly as a response to events, but also as a belated realization of the full implications of postwar social criticism. A glance at the history of that social criticism makes the urgency of the poetic reaction more intelligible than it would be if considered only in relation to the immediate literary past.

I

The dichotomy between external and inward, rational and emotional, formal and improvisational, figures prominently not only in the judgment passed by the new poetics on the old, but also in the judgment passed by the New Left on the "silent generation" of the fifties. What has not always been remembered, however, is the degree to which social critics in the fifties had already passed the same judgment on themselves. The portrait of the 1950s as a period of conformity in which the inner life was sacrificed to external social codes had already been drawn before the New Left came along. Indeed, the prototypical conformity-critique of the 1950s, Riesman, Glazer, and Denney's *The Lonely Crowd*, was published at the very beginning of the decade. If we break with the current habit of packaging history in decades, we can see that "the fifties" really began in 1945, with the end of World War II, the onset of the Cold War, and the seemingly limitless prospect of economic growth.

In *America in Our Time*, Godfrey Hodgson points out that among the industrialized nations, the United States alone emerged from World War II with its economy intact; for some time thereafter, our country had a lopsided economic and military advantage over every other country in the world—a preeminence that has gradually eroded since the mid-sixties.[6] The strong postwar economy led many liberal intellectuals to hope that before long American prosperity could absorb everyone into the middle class without any political conflict. By the mid-fifties, there was talk of the "end of ideology," a phrase which began as the title of an article by Edward Shils in 1955 and became, five years later, the title of a famous book by Daniel Bell. "In the west," wrote Bell, "there is today a rough consensus among intellectuals on political issues: the acceptance of a Welfare State; the desirability of decentralized power; a system of mixed economy and of political pluralism. In that sense . . . the ideological age has ended."[7]

In retrospect, it may strike us that there was still more poverty in America than was generally supposed[8] and that a prosperous economy cannot automatically solve problems of distribution of wealth. The political consensus, moreover, may have been largely an illusion produced by McCarthyite intimidation of the left. But given the belief that the end of poverty and the end of ideological conflict were at hand, it is not hard to see why social criticism turned from problems of class injustice to problems of cultural malaise. Social criticism of this era shifted its attention from politics as traditionally conceived and tried to describe the social psychology of contemporary life. The dark side of consensus was conformity: the notion that everyone in America had spontaneously come to agree about everything of importance was too comfortable to be true, and all through the 1950s, authors made a good deal of money by pointing out the dangers lurking beneath the placid surface.

Some of the indictments of conformity that appeared in the sixties were aimed at a popular audience. Vance Packard's *The Hidden Persuaders* (1957) and William H. Whyte, Jr.'s *The Organization Man* (1956) became best sellers. Others, such as C. Wright Mills's *White Collar* (1951) and *The Lonely Crowd* itself, were directed to a more intellectual audience, but they were, within that narrower audience, popular reading and were often assigned in college courses. In these writings, a number of themes later associated with the New Left had already begun to emerge: the tendency of Americans to conform to the opinions and manners of their peers; their consequent vulnerability to manipulation by advertising, pressure groups, and government; their tendency to suppress conflict even at the price of denying real problems. Mills, the most radical of these critics, had already begun to attack the ideal of rationality in the social sciences and in corporate management as an excuse for the manipulation of other people as objects and for the blind worship of technological efficiency regardless of its effect on everyday working life. In both *White Collar* (1951) and *The Power Elite* (1956), he made the argument we now associate with the campus revolts at Berkeley and Columbia in the following decade: that the university, while pretending to be a haven for the exercise of reason in the pursuit of knowledge, was becoming a research and development center for big business and the military. Instead of providing a liberal education, Mills charged, the universities were beginning to train technicians, concentrating on the skills demanded by the centers of power.[9] The central thesis of Marcuse's *One-Dimensional Man* (1964) was clearly adumbrated by Mills and Riesman at the opening of the

1950s: within the formal freedom of American democracy, very little real freedom exists. The sinister persecutions of a totalitarian state may be lacking, but a similar absence of real dissent can be induced by social control. Conformity is assured because the individual *internalizes* a distaste for conflict.

Just how close to the radical rhetoric of the next decade these writers often came may be illustrated by comparing a few quotations with parallel texts in the canonical books of the New Left. Consider, for example, this description of other-directed society in *The Lonely Crowd*:

> Approval itself, irrespective of content, becomes almost the only good in this situation: one makes good when one is approved of. Thus all power, not merely some power, is in the hands of the actual or imaginary approving group, and the child learns from his parents' reactions to him that nothing in his character, no possessions he owns, no inheritance of name or talent, no work he has done, is valued for itself but only for its effect on others.[10]

R. D. Laing made essentially the same point when he wrote, in *The Politics of Experience* (1967):

> The others have become installed in our hearts, and we call them ourselves. Each person, not being himself either to himself or the other, just as the other is not himself to himself or to us, in being another for another neither recognizes himself in the other, nor the other in himself.[11]

Similarly, Marcuse argued in *One-Dimensional Man* that contemporary society threatens the very "existence of an inner dimension distinguished from and even antagonistic to the external exigencies—an individual consciousness *apart from* public opinion and behavior." In contemporary industrial democracies there is "an immediate identification of the individual with *his* society and, through it, with the society as a whole." As a result, "there is only one dimension, and it is everywhere, and in all forms."[12]

Both the radicals and the poets of the 1960s sought to recognize an authentic self beneath the inauthentic construct of internalized others. The inauthentic self had already been deplored for at least ten years, to the point where the deplorations had made their way into popular culture. The question was whether an authentic self could still be located, retaining the power to be sharply "antagonistic to the external exigencies."

The resemblance between the conformity critiques of the fifties and the New Left's harsher indictments extends further into particular detail than one might expect. In attributing "one-dimensionality" to a preoccupation with technological means divorced from ends and to an "instrumentalist" or "operational" conception of reason and language, Marcuse departs from the social criticism of the 1950s only in emphasis. *The Lonely Crowd* offers a foretaste of Marcuse's critique of one-dimensional language ("Language itself becomes a kind of consumption product") and even of his paradoxes of "repressive tolerance" and "co-optation." Those seeking autonomy in an other-directed society

> are incapable of defining the 'enemy' with the relative ease of the autonomous person facing an inner-directed environment. . . . Are they enemies, those friends who stand by, not to block but to be amused, to understand and pardon everything? An autonomous person today must work constantly to detach himself from shadowy entanglements with this top level of other-direction—so difficult to break with because its demands appear so reasonable, even trivial.[13]

Mills anticipates the New Left in his tendency to pit the authenticity of feelings against the cold, impersonal "reason" of a bureaucratic society:

> In a world dominated by a vast system of abstractions, managers may become cold with principle and do what local and immediate masters of men could never do. Their social insulation results in deadened feelings in the face of the impoverishment of life in the lower orders and its stultification in the upper circles.[14]

And yet, despite their frequent adumbrations of the radicalism to come, the critics of conformity were not yet New Leftists. Even Mills, who has been called "the father of the New Left," would not deserve that title on the evidence of *White Collar* or even *The Power Elite*. Only in the last few years of his life did he arrive at the threshold of the politics that flourished after his death.

In his essay, "The Orgamerican Fantasy" (1961), Harold Rosenberg had already noted the existence of the conformity-jeremiad as a genre. He criticized the authors of such books for failing to recognize the radical implications of their own indictment: "evoking the sinister concept of man as a tool and as an object, the new writing does so in an oddly disembodied and unpainful way."[15] As Carl Oglesby, a former president of Students for a Democratic Society (SDS), observed, their writing "aches with unliberated conclusions."[16]

Foremost among the "unliberated conclusions" that Oglesby and his contemporaries did not hesitate to unchain was the idea that American society, underneath its democratic exterior, was really totalitarian, scarcely different at bottom from the Soviet Union. Indeed, if the conformity critics saw, or thought they saw, a psychological coercion in American life, they had learned how to name and recognize such coercion from the recent historical lessons of Hitler's Germany and Stalin's Russia. Orwell's *1984* hovers in the wings behind their accounts of American society, as do the writings of Hannah Arendt and Bruno Bettelheim on the social psychology of the German concentration camps. Bettelheim described the German concentration camps as factories for the production of what Marcuse would later call one-dimensionality. It was not enough to dominate or even to kill one's victims; the Nazis wanted, wrote Bettelheim, "*to break the prisoners as individuals* and to change them into docile masses from which no individual or group act of resistance could arise." The victims must consent to their victimization: "The final stage is reached when *the prisoner has adapted himself to the life of the camp.*"[17]

The conformity critics, though they found something resembling totalitarian manipulation in the social psychology of their own country, refrained from making the analogy explicit, let alone taking the large step from analogy to equation. The view of the United States as an aggressive, imperialist empire, the mirror counterpart of its archenemy, the Soviet Union, oppressing its own lower classes at home and the undeveloped nations abroad, arose in response to later developments: the civil rights movement in the American south and, above all, the Vietnam war. By 1964, writes Hodgson, civil rights activists began to suspect that "southern police, southern jails, southern institutions and southern racism might not be medieval extravagancies doomed to be reformed by the march of progress, but mere variants of American police, American jails, American institutions, and American racism." Although the major escalation of the war in Vietnam did not occur until early the following year, "already, young blacks were beginning to make the connection between Mississippi and Vietnam. Already, young whites were getting ready to take that idea back to their campuses with them."[18]

From 1965 onward, the war in Vietnam was the central political issue in American life, whether one supported it or opposed it. Among intellectuals and writers, the opposition was, by the late sixties, almost universal. It seems clear in retrospect that much of what passed for radicalism at the time was really a single-issue, white, middle-class protest. With the arrival of black separatism, whites were no longer welcome allies in the cause of civil rights, and the New Left's attempts to draw support from blue-collar workers, who according to Marxist theory ought to have been the revolutionary class, were notoriously unsuccessful.

At the time, however, the antiwar movement was considered radical, both by opponents and supporters, and its most characteristic rhetoric sounded radical. The hallmark of that rhetoric was its repudiation of the war, not as a mistake, or even as an isolated evil, but as a revelatory crime that laid bare the true nature of American society. "We are living at war," wrote Denise Levertov in 1972, and

the shame and horror of being citizens of the country which, in its ruthless imperialism, is not only ravaging Southeast Asia but, with its military bases, its Polaris submarines, the machinations of its CIA, and the tentacles of its giant corporations, is everywhere the prime force of antilife and oppression—this shame and horror cast their shadow over all we say, feel, and do.[19]

Levertov's statement is notable not only for the melodrama of its rhetoric, but for the assumptions from which that rhetoric distracts us—that political oppression is not directed merely against the oppressed but against life itself ("antilife"), and that "shame and horror" at the actions of our government affects "all we say, feel, and do," even, presumably, in the most private moments of our lives.

Levertov's apocalyptic rhetoric is typical of the period. Such exaggeration may have been partly a legacy of the earlier civil rights movement. In order to get the white majority to support their efforts, the civil rights leaders had appealed to their sense of honor. If indeed they believed in the principle of equality, they would be ashamed to stand idly by while others endured violence and imprisonment to vindicate that principle. The more militant black activists raised the rhetorical ante in the late sixties. They drew not only on the mounting anger and impatience of their black audience, but also on the mounting revulsion among the white, predominantly middle-class leftists against their own class, race, and country. As Eldridge Cleaver wrote in *Soul on Ice* (1968)—required reading among New Leftists—

A young white today cannot help but recoil from the basic deeds of his people. On every side, on every continent, he sees racial arrogance, savage brutality toward the conquered and subjugated people, genocide; he sees the systematic extermination of American Indians; he sees the civilized nations of Europe fighting in imperial depravity over the lands of other people—and over possession of the very people themselves. There seems to be no end to the ghastly deeds of which his people are guilty. GUILTY.[20]

And here is a white radical, Truman Nelson, also writing in 1968. His guilt answers antiphonally to Cleaver's denunciation:

What we do to the black people, daily, makes me want to secede from the white race! It makes me, deep down, hate myself, and my color. All decent whites, especially the young whites, abhor having to bear the burden of racist guilt their fathers have placed on them. . . .[21]

This impulse to proclaim one's shame, guilt, and even outright self-hatred, is one of the most prominent features distinguishing the polemics of the New Left from those of the old. Before joining battle with society, the New Leftists felt compelled to exorcise the socialized part of the self.

II

Already by the 1950s, the Freudian concept of the psyche as divided into conscious and unconscious, ego and id, had been assimilated into the common stock of educated discourse. Moreover, psychoanalytic thinkers had already begun trying to construct a synthesis of depth psychology and social theory; Erik Erikson's *Childhood and Society* (1950), to take a still widely read example, attempted to show how the childrearing practices of a given culture produced the psychological disposition needed for adaptation to its way of life. While most of the book describes tribal societies, parts of it deal with problems in modern Western society. Why, for instance, was Germany so susceptible to the appeal of Hitler after World War I? In his chapter on Hitler, Erikson was asking the kind of question that would trouble Marcuse, Brown, and Laing ten years later: by what process of psychological distortion do people come to accept the unacceptable?

Any psycho-social theory must give an account of social adaptation, which under ordinary circumstances may be treated as "normal." But what about extraordinary circumstances, such as Germany under Hitler—or, so far as the New Left was concerned, the United States under Johnson or Nixon? Was there any higher standard of "normality" by which adaptation to Nazi rule could be considered "deviant"? In an earlier time, one might have appealed to human nature, but cultural anthropologists had been arguing since early in the century that there was no human nature, or that human nature was so malleable it could take any number of forms—in *Patterns of Culture* (1934), Ruth Benedict had thought of human nature as a "great arc" of possibilities, with various cultures ranged along its curve.[22] How could anyone stand outside culture and survey the arc from the central point around which it was drawn? There was a potential conflict in psycho-social theory between the anthropologist's tolerant neutrality, which refuses to prefer the norms of one culture to those of another and treats all as equally valid, and the moralist's recognition that sometimes the group is wrong and the deviant minority quite rightly refuses to adapt. Yet in the absence of a shared religious creed or conception of human nature, on what authority could one speak of "right" and "wrong"?

In Freud's theory, negotiations between self and society were replicated within the mind. The demands of society, primarily as conveyed by one's parents as representatives of adult adaptation, were internalized as part of the conscious self; one's own instinctive desires remained, at the unconscious level, unmodified by all attempts at rational governance. That instinctive desires had been repressed and thus driven unconscious had been part of Freud's theory from the first; what he found in the early 1920s, however, was that part of the ego, the socially adaptive part of the self, was unconscious too, and was as unappeasable and inaccessible to reason as the instinctive desires. Thus he postulated a superego, punitive and "super-moral," distinguished by "its independence of the conscious ego and its intimate relations with the unconscious id."[23] The superego, ostensibly the moral restrainer of the id, was strangely akin to its adversary. The ego, insofar as it was conscious and capable of adjusting the claims of internal compulsion and external demands, had to deal as best it could with the irrational demands of both id and superego, compromising between these demands and what one's actual situation in a world of other people would permit. It was the part of the self charged with making adjustments. Conscience, understood as the Freudian superego, was not a higher rationality that could stand coolly above the claims of adjustment. If it stood against the claims of adjustment, it did so no less irrationally than the sexual, body-centered id. For Freud, the only recourse was to strengthen the conscious part of the ego, allowing it to juggle the conflicting claims as best it could from one situation to the next, without appeal to any transcendent morality.[24]

In the 1930s, such psychoanalytic thinkers as Karen Horney, Harry Stack Sullivan, and Erich Fromm undertook a revision of Freud intended to further the project of strengthening the ego. Taking their cue from cultural anthropology, they argued that much of what Freud had taken to be universal in the human psyche was in fact culturally conditioned. "There is no such thing," declared Horney in 1937, "as a normal psychology, which holds for all mankind."[25] Psychoanalysis, to understand the way the psyche is formed in culture, had to shift its attention from individual psychopathology to the interaction of the individual with other people and to the process by which cultural expectations become internalized. Accordingly, emphasis also shifted from the unconscious to the conscious mind, from the id to the ego, since it is the conscious part of the ego that attempts to mediate between self and environment.

Freud's belief that universally constant libidinal wishes come inevitably into conflict with any form of culture whatsoever gave his thought a conservative implication. He was skeptical about the possibility of radical change in the relations between the individual and society. As Philip Rieff has observed, "for Freud, the more things change, the more they remain the same. Society, as a psychological process, is just what it has always been." [26] To revise Freud by taking into account the malleability of the libido within culture, therefore, might seem to have "progressive" implications—it meant that Freud's *Unbehagen in der Kultur* might be produced by some forms of culture but not others.

There was also, however, a contrary implication in the revisionist position. If there was no such thing as a universal normal psychology, but only adaptation to whatever presented itself as "normal" within a given culture, how could one justify any rebellion by the individual against the cultural norm; for that matter, how could one explain it? Sullivan, especially, was at his most brilliant in describing how, from the very beginning of life, children begin to internalize culturally approved values. He went so far as to call personal individuality an illusion. By their approval and disapproval, and by their "consensual validation" of one's interpretations of the surrounding world, the others install themselves in one's heart so expertly that they are never noticed, but seem to constitute an autonomous "I." [27] Hence Marcuse's charge, in *Eros and Civilization,* that "this psychology has no other objective standards of value than the prevailing ones: health, maturity, achievement are taken as they are defined by the given society." [28]

The revisionists themselves were, of course, aware of the problem. Sullivan, in his nominalist suspicion of concepts such as choice and self, did not profess to recover a standard by which to appeal beyond cultural norms. As Clara Thompson remarks in *Psychoanalysis: Evolution and Development,* "one must conclude that Sullivan thinks that transcending the culture is, at the very least, difficult." [29] But Horney and Fromm defended the possibility—and the value—of quarreling with one's culture. Indeed, they, no less than Rosenberg's "Orgamerican" fantasists, saw excessive preoccupation with other people's expectations as the characteristic problem of their time.

Horney defined neurosis as the failure to adapt to cultural norms, but she also noted that neurotics feel, more than normal persons, a compulsion to comply perfectly with other people's expectations, real or imagined. When adaptation succeeds, norms have been unconsciously internalized, so less anxiety about compliance is necessary. A high incidence of neurosis, with its high anxiety about compliance, means that cultural norms are not being transmitted effectively. "A great frequency of neuroses and psychoses in a given culture is one of the indicators showing that something is seriously wrong with the conditions under which people live."[30] But the "wrong" in question may be only of means rather than ends. One cannot conclude, from Horney's premises, that the norms themselves are "wrong," only that the society in question has done a poor job of acculturation.

When Horney tried to account for the prevalence of neurosis in modern American society, she ascribed it primarily to cultural self-contradictions. American culture emphasizes "competition and success," but also Christian ideals of "brotherly love and humility." One cannot observe either "norm" without violating the other. Advertising stimulates our desire for things we cannot afford; "the psychic consequence for the individual is a constant discrepancy between his desires and their fulfillment." American ideology preaches a doctrine of individual freedom, yet for most people, supposedly 'free' choices are severely limited. And "these contradictions are precisely the conflicts which the neurotic struggles to reconcile."[31]

Without quite recognizing the logical consequences of her own argument, Horney implied that if American culture were only content to encourage competition without hypocritically contradicting itself, if it were frank in telling us that we are not free and should not expect to have what only the rich can afford, we would then have a far healthier society. Yet it would be only the same society grown more crassly explicit, divested of whatever scruples drive us to affirm the pieties of cooperation, freedom, and limitless upward mobility. For Horney, the surest sign of an unhealthy society was the presence of mutually irreconcilable norms—in short, the very sorts of contradictions that a Marxist would welcome as providing some point of entry for the wedge of progressive change. The logic of Horney's argument suggested, however unwittingly, that cultural health is cultural coherence, regardless of the ideological content in question.

Fromm, starting like Horney with a recognition of cultural relativism, nonetheless insisted that there is such a thing as human nature after all. But unlike Freud, he located it not in the ineradicable libido persisting beneath culture, but in the conscious, volitional part of the self. Freud's superego, the punitive, irrational representative of conscience, belongs in Fromm's view only to the authoritarian version of conscience, which "is fed by destructiveness against the person's own self so that destructive strivings are thus permitted to operate under the disguise of virtue." It results from the passive internalization of other people's demands. But the "humanistic conscience," Fromm asserted with surprising confidence, "is our own voice, present in every human being and independent of external sanctions and rewards." This is bound to ring rather hollow when the same author has told us that

The character of the child is molded by the character of its parents in response to whom it develops. The parents and their methods of child training in turn are determined by the social structure of their culture. . . . Genetically, the formation of individual character is determined by the impact of its life experiences, the individual ones and those which follow from the culture, on temperament and physical constitution.[32]

Where, in this welter of determination, could that autonomous voice come from?

The revisionist emphasis on the malleability of human instincts and the plurality of cultures, which at first glance would seem to justify trying to create a better society, on further inspection turned out to deny the existence of any credible standard by which "better" might be defined. And Freud's insistence on the underlying sameness of the instincts, which at first glance seems to have overwhelmingly conservative implications, provided Marcuse and Brown with a way of "transcending the culture." To the extent that adjustment to cultural norms entailed repression of instinct beyond what was indispensable for social cohesion, those norms themselves were illegitimate.

In the eighteenth century and even in the nineteenth, challenges to cultural authority invoked the universality of human reason. If one could show that cultural authority was irrational, then eventually others would be led, by the same inevitable steps of argument, to a conviction of its illegitimacy. Reason, in post-Freudian terms, is an ego function, preeminently social and intersubjective. Freud himself is usually understood (rightly, I believe) as essentially a rationalist, albeit one whose reason teaches him the necessity of acknowledging the power of the irrational.[33] But among the radical Freudians, "reason" had become suspect, at least when it is applied to human affairs rather than the physical sciences. What seems an eminently rational social arrangement in one time and place may seem utterly irrational in another. We can transcend culture not by rising above it through the higher faculty of reason, but by sinking below it to the unconscious and instinctual parts of the self that stubbornly resist socialization.

By thus inverting the hierarchy of reason and instinct, radical psycho-political theory got out of the trap that had snared Horney and Fromm, but it created another. If the part of the self that transcends culture is buried in the inarticulate timelessness of the unconscious, how can its resistance to cultural tyranny be translated into an intelligible critique? The translator must be the acculturated, and therefore suspect, ego, which is by definition the part of the self that has dealings with society. The only part of the self that escapes the encroachment of culture is unable to speak at all except through language, that masterwork of acculturation, which lies in the domain of the ego.

The radical psycho-politics of the 1960s sided with the instincts against the claims of "adjustment." Marcuse recognized some degree of repression as necessary to ensure social cooperation but thought that repressive societies created a needless "surplus-repression." Freud had noted that the superego, rather than demanding only those renunciations of instinct needed for adaptation, exacted also those which were unnecessary and became more rather than less tyrannical as its demands were met.[34] Freud considered this outcome to be inevitable, given the structure of the human psyche; for Marcuse, it was the result of social repression and therefore corrigible. In *Life Against Death* (1960), Norman O. Brown was more sanguine still, hoping to achieve an altogether nonrepressive society.[35]

Marcuse and Brown also depart from the conformity critics in their emphasis on art as an adversary force against repression; the prestige of their writings doubtless contributed to the widespread acceptance of claims for the political efficacy of poetry. Marcuse's views on the political role of art were complicated and to some extent unfashionable. He began with a view of aesthetics derived from Kant and Schiller, in which "the truth of art is the liberation of sensuousness through its reconciliation with reason." To achieve this reconciliation, art must be "sublimated" and maintain an "'indifference to reality' and interest in 'show'"; it must be "non-committing" and must not "engage the human existence in the ordinary way of life; it is 'unreal.'"[36] Nonetheless, much of what he says in *Eros and Civilization* implies that art represents the irrational and the unconscious locked in struggle against technological reason. "Art is perhaps the most visible 'return of the repressed,'" he argues. "The aesthetic reconciliation implies strengthening sensuousness as against the tyranny of reason and, ultimately, even calls for the liberation of sensuousness from the repressive domination of reason." Through the changes in consciousness effected by art, "the aesthetic experience would arrest the violent and exploitative activity which made man into an instrument of labor."[37] In *One-Dimensional Man*, he looks ahead to the day when "rather than being the handmaiden of the established apparatus, beautifying its business and its misery, art would become a technique for destroying this business and this misery." In the meantime,

Contrasted with the fantastic and insane aspects of its [one-dimensional society's] rationality, the realm of the irrational becomes the home of the really rational—of the ideas which may "promote the art of life." If the established society manages all normal communication, validating or invalidating it in accordance with social requirements, then the values alien to these requirements may have no other medium of communication than the abnormal one of fiction.[38]

By the time Marcuse wrote *Counter-Revolution and Revolt* (1972), he had become disenchanted with some of the products of counter-cultural aesthetics; he criticized guerilla theater and other forms of "anti-art" as a "desublimation of culture" that is finally self-defeating. In rejecting "aesthetic form," such art "elaborates anti-forms which are constituted by the mere atomization and fragmentation of traditional forms." Such art attempts "to reduce, if not close, the gap between art and reality," but "precisely its immediate 'life quality' is the undoing of this anti-art."[39] Instead of politically engaged art, Marcuse asks for "an aesthetic form in which the political content becomes *meta*political," so that "the political goal appears only in the transfiguration which is the aesthetic form. The revolution may well be absent from the *oeuvre* even while the artist himself is 'engaged,' is a revolutionary." His concluding chapter opens with the warning that

The common denominator for the misplaced radicalism in the cultural revolution is the anti-intellectualism which it shares with the most reactionary representatives of the Establishment: revolt against Reason—not only against the Reason of capitalism, bourgeois society, and so on, but against Reason *per se*.[40]

Such complexities, however, were lost in the popularization of Marcuse's ideas; in any case, by 1972 Marcuse's influence had already begun to wane.

Brown's position was more extreme, as their exchange of 1967 in *Commentary* clearly shows. Marcuse criticized *Love's Body* (1966) as a mystification of history. In this book, Brown calls for "Fusion: the distinction between inner self and outside world, between subject and object, overcome"[41] (we will meet with a similar yearning in the poetics of Charles Olson and in the critics who claim to find in Robert Lowell a "conflation" of self and history). For Brown, reality becomes entirely metaphorical, and politics is translated into psychology. "Brown's concept of illusion (sleep, dream) covers, undifferentiated, the latent and the overt content of history, or, it de-realizes reality. To him, the political kingdoms are 'shadows,' political power is a fraud. . . ."[42] To this critique, Brown answered:

> From politics to poetry. Legislation is not politics, nor philosophy, but poetry. Poetry, art, is not an epiphenomenal reflection of some other (political, economic) realm which is the "real thing"; nor a still contemplation of something else which is the "real action"; nor a sublimation of something else which is the "real," carnal "act." Poetry, art, imagination, the creator spirit is life itself; the real revolutionary power to change the world; and to change the human body.[43]

Theodore Roszak, in *The Making of a Counterculture* (1969), sided with Brown in this debate;[44] the popularity of Roszak's book suggests the appeal Brown's idealized version of "revolutionary power" had for those who wanted "revolution" without the work of political organizing or the danger of unseemly violence.

Although Marcuse, as a member of the Frankfurt School, belonged to a tradition deeply rooted in Hegelian and Marxist dialectic, and although New Left rhetoric often availed itself of Marxist terminology, I think it fair to say that on the whole, the most characteristic thinking on the New Left was, like Brown's, lacking in real political content. It was closer to the conformity critics of the fifties than to Marxism in its analysis of American society, and closer to anarchism than to either in its recommendations.[45] It located the central evil not in the economic or political domination of one class by another but in the falsification of consciousness in all classes. Conflict arose between the individual (usually, in practice, a middle-class individual) and society, or "the system," as the New Left called it—not between one part of society and another. "The system," while it might serve the interests of another shadowy entity, "the establishment," was not so much anyone's deliberate creation as an interlocking set of illusions, a social embodiment of ideology so complete that it left no standpoint from which it might be recognized as ideological.

What defined people as potentially revolutionary, then, was not, as in Marxist theory, their relationship to the production of wealth, but their relative immunity, often acquired by the liberating therapy of art, to the ideological lie of "the system." Marx's proletariat, the blue-collar workers in factories, were notoriously hostile to the New Left. White New Leftists managed uneasy alliances with blacks and other minorities, who were seen as "outsiders," excluded from the rewards promised by the dominant culture and therefore unresponsive to manipulation. But the main would-be revolutionary class, as Mills had suggested in his "Letter to the New Left" (1961),[46] was not composed of the economically exploited. It was an alliance of students, mostly of middle-class background, with their professors and with various persons in the arts and liberal professions outside the academy.

Despite the talk of revolution, the New Leftists themselves knew that they had to attract a wider constituency, including the working class, if their "revolution" was to become actual rather than purely symbolic. But if the proletariat did not join them, they were ready with an explanation: that was only because the one-dimensional society had brainwashed its victims into assenting to their victimization. Only through a cure of consciousness would an undistorted perception of political reality become possible. The political constituency would be made up of the bearers of newly liberated consciousness. Adversarial politics had to become counter-psychology before it could become politics again.

There was, of course, tension within the New Left between "politicals," who wanted concrete social results, and "culturals," who insisted that psychological transformation must be a precondition of political change. But in general, even the more directly political actions of the New Left were conspicuously theatrical and symbolic. Its leadership could mount attention-getting events—demonstrations, draft card burnings, sit-ins at campuses and draft boards—but fared poorly with the unglamorous tasks of recruitment and organization. Moreover, with the exception of the war, the issues on which the New Left received broad-based support had more to do with alienation than social justice. With the frustration of its political aspirations at the end of the 1960s, the tendency to take refuge in symbolic but politically ineffectual protest increased.

III

Among the ideas current in the sixties, the most suggestive for poets, but also the most problematic, was probably the Marcusean notion that modern American society has only "one dimension," to be met with "everywhere, and in all forms." It was a sort of paranoid version of Whitman's faith in an organic unity binding together the variety of America, connecting each "single, separate person" to all the others and to the nation. Because the one-dimensionality of the system was presumably ubiquitous, reaching even into one's own psyche, the poet had only to look about him, or even into his own soul, to be confronted with the crisis of American society. The private was, as a deconstructionist might say, always already public. But this was a common bond of impoverishment. It was Ginsberg's Moloch; it was what Robert Lowell had envisioned in the closing lines of "For the Union Dead":

> Everywhere,
> giant finned cars nose forward like fish;
> a savage servility
> slides by on grease.[47]

At times, poets exploited the sense of underlying sinister connection to invest the particular details of their poems with a wider public meaning; at other times, they opposed a purer self, and a purer language, to the undifferentiated bleakness that threatened to engulf them.

As Sacvan Bercovitch argues in *The Puritan Origins of the American Self*, the desire to see all of history as the unfolding of a single story, and all individual experience as the replication in miniature of that all-justifying narrative, is deeply rooted in American culture from its outset.[48] Such thinking has survived through the nineteenth century and into our own time, though the principle of correspondence between self and world has been continually reinterpreted. In 1855, Whitman wrote that "the United States themselves are essentially the greatest poem."[49] He installed the others in his heart, to borrow Laing's phrase, quite deliberately, hoping to represent the life of the nation, in all its diversity, within himself. For the American poet of fifteen years ago, the project had become just the reverse: to spit out the all-pervading corruptions of nation and culture, that one's tongue might be clean enough to speak. But since nation and culture reached far into the self, how could they be exorcised without psychological self-mutilation?

All too frequently, contemporary poets have imagined themselves as faced with only two alternatives: to become radical Freudian versions of the *poète maudit*, exhibiting their distorted consciousness as representative of society's distorted consciousness, or to speak from the unconscious, which is untainted by acculturation but, for that very reason, has no language. To give the unconscious a means of representation, some of these poets have resorted to the irrational juxtaposition of images obviously intended to suggest a state of dream or trance. This procedure might seem to be sanctioned by Freud, who wrote that "dreams are the royal road to the unconscious."[50] A closer look at Freud's thinking about dreams, however, leads to serious objections.

In Freud's account, even though dreams are the royal road to the unconscious, the road ends just outside the domain to which it leads. Dream interpretation arrives at the unconscious thought only by inference, working backward through a chain of distortions and substitutions. The unconscious thought cannot emerge directly, since it "has no access to consciousness *except via the preconscious* [Freud's emphasis], in passing through which its excitatory process is obliged to submit to modifications." Therefore, "an unconscious idea is as such quite incapable of entering the preconscious and . . . it can only exercise any effect there by establishing a connection with an idea which already belongs to the preconscious, by transferring its intensity on to it and getting itself 'covered' by it. . . ."[51] Through all of Freud's subsequent revisions of his theory, he did not withdraw this emphasis on the indirectness of relations between the conscious and the unconscious processes and on the need for rational inference in disclosing the unconscious thought. Moreover, dreaming is not in itself liberating. The interpretation of a dream undoes repression, but the dream itself simply replicates it. "When you reject something that is disagreeable to you," said Freud in the *Introductory Lectures on Psychoanalysis*, what you are doing is *repeating* the mechanism of constructing dreams rather than understanding it and surmounting it."[52]

The preconscious associations of which the manifest dream is composed derive from the details of the dreamer's life, and eliciting their latent significance requires knowledge of those details. A poetry of the unconscious, which might seem at first glance to promise release from the ego and its conscious social entanglements, turns out to require extensive representation of those entanglements in order to be intelligible. Joyce, perhaps the greatest writer in the language to be extensively influenced by Freud, understood this. If *Ulysses* were not saturated with realistic social detail, the free associations of Leopold Bloom and Stephen Dedalus would not be intriguingly oblique, but flatly incomprehensible.

If the unconscious was to be the source of an irreducible humanity beyond culture, then any revision of Freud that ascribed to the unconscious some of the "higher" faculties hitherto assigned to the ego had obvious appeal. Probably the most influential alternative to Freud's depth psychology was Jung's, which has been attractive to poets since T. S. Eliot's generation because it locates the origin of art, myth, and religion in a collective unconscious. As I shall argue in discussing the poetics of "deep-image" surrealism, Jungian psychology also conceives of the unconscious in a way that makes it more tractable in language by claiming to discover an underlying universality in irrational associations.

The appropriation of Jung by politically radical poets is a curious development. Marcuse placed Jung "on the 'right wing' of psychoanalysis," and Reich, in 1934, called him "the spokesman for fascism within psychoanalysis." [53] But just as Freud's emphasis on the biological fixity of human nature, at first glance conservative in its political implications, came to provide a court of appeal against the tyranny of culture, so Jung's shadow-community of the collective unconscious provided an alternative to the failed community of contemporary society. What looked to Reich and Marcuse like a flight from material and social reality looks, to Robert Bly, like a defense against the debasement of that reality.

Another psychology of some pertinence to contemporary poetry is the "Gestalt" school, especially as modified by Paul Goodman, radical and man of letters, who taught at Black Mountain College in the 1950s. Charles Olson, and some of the poets influenced by his "projective" theories of composition, shared in the pervasive distrust of the ego and of conscious reflection. But Olson opposed to the ego not the deeper authority of the unconscious so much as a dissolution of the ego's fixities through participation in the continual becoming of the material world. Olson's rejection of interiority, as Paul Christensen has pointed out, [54] is analogous to the Gestalt school's rejection of the Freudian (and Jungian) emphasis on the unconscious and on the persistence of the past. As Richard King concisely, if inelegantly, puts it:

On theoretical grounds Gestalt therapy rejects the Freudian notion of the unconscious as well as an "historical" approach to the etiology of a disturbance. Rather than historical, e.g., what happened when X was 7 years old caused him to . . ., the approach of Gestalt therapy is a phenomenological one; it is interested in how the individual is in the world and deals with it at present. Its concern is primarily with human awareness and how one contacts, senses, responds to, and uses his environment, in the broadest sense. [55]

Finally, there is Wilhelm Reich himself, the first psychoanalyst to try to synthesize depth psychology and radical politics. Although, of the poets considered in this study, only Allen Ginsberg, so far as I know, has professed admiration for Reich, one might easily take Paul Robinson's summary of Reich's position, in *The Freudian Left*, for a paraphrase of something written in the 1960s rather than of arguments advanced in the late 1920s and early 1930s:

Reich did not deny the existence of this [Freud's] unconscious, but it remained for him the distortion of a more basic reality which was essentially healthy. His confidence in the instincts was practically unlimited. He ultimately came to think of the human personality in terms of a three-tiered model. At the deepest level were man's "*natural* sociality and sexuality, *spontaneous* enjoyment of work, [and] *capacity for love."* When these whole-some instincts were repressed, as in our sex-negating culture, a second layer arose, "the Freudian 'unconscious,' in which sadism, greediness, lascivi-ousness, envy, [and] perversions of all kinds" held sway. This layer was in turn covered over and kept in check by the characterological super-structure, "the artificial mask of self-control, of compulsive, insincere so-ciality". . . . [I]n the final analysis, character was itself a disease, all the more pernicious because it was not recognized as such. Thus Reich took as his special mission the denunciation of the ego and all its works.[56]

Whether derived from Reich, Jung, the later radical Freudians, or con-tagion of the *Zeitgeist,* a sentimental greening of the unconscious and a corresponding hostility to "the ego and all its works" pervades much poetry, and discussion of poetry, in the sixties and seventies. In the studies of poets that follow, I shall try to show that their styles can be understood as roads diverging from a common origin in the desire to recover a self disentangled from acculturation and its burden of guilt.

2

Allen Ginsberg as Representative Man: The Road to Naropa

In choosing to begin with Allen Ginsberg, I do not wish to imply that he is the best of the poets considered here, or the most influential, but only that in some rough way, he is the most representative. He participates to some degree in several important movements or "schools," yet belongs to none of them entirely. When "Howl" made his national reputation, he was classified among the "beats," but M. L Rosenthal, in *The New Poets* (1967), included him with Lowell, Berryman, and Plath among the confessional poets. Ginsberg's interest in oral poetry and in rapid, revision-free composition, allies him with projectivist poetics. Ginsberg met Charles Olson in 1946; they later became close friends and admired each other's work.[1] Finally, his fascination with mystical experience, culminating in his discipleship to Chogyam Trungpa at the Naropa Institute, gives him something in common with Robert Bly, Galway Kinnell, and W. S. Merwin. He has attracted the largest readership of any poet who also commands the respect of literary critics: there are, Robert von Hallberg notes, 315,000 copies of *Howl* in print as of 1985.[2] His movement from political activism in the sixties to contemplative withdrawal in the seventies follows the same path taken by the radical students who made up an important part of his audience. He is the man Schiller warned us about, the artist who is not only the child of his time, but its disciple and, to judge by the sale of his books, one of its favorites.

Ginsberg's earliest free-verse poems, collected in *An Empty Mirror*, date back as far as 1947, and his inept formal poetry, of interest only because it is his, dates from his student days at Columbia, spanning the years 1943 to 1948. It is "Howl," completed in 1955 and published the following year, that marks the beginning of Ginsberg as we now know him. "Howl" also presents, in a remarkably complete form, a sensibility (if that Eliotic word will serve for such an un-Eliotic temperament) that we associate with a later time. The title and first line alone, closely considered, are packed with signs of things to come. In the mid-fifties, a poem might have a title such as "Speech for the Repeal of the McCarran Act" (Richard Wilbur, 1956); "The Dancer's Reply" (Howard Nemerov, 1958), or "Argument" (Elizabeth Bishop, 1955). In such poems, the title implies that a voice is speaking aloud, but doing so for a socially defined purpose, or on a socially defined occasion. More commonly, one might give a poem a sharply nominalized title, so as to hold up an object or landscape as a central symbol for contemplation: "The Beacon," "The Sunglasses," "The Bight" (Wilbur, Nemerov, and Bishop again, from the same collections).[3] Titles of that period typically emphasize the act of seeing or contemplating; if they emphasize speech, then it is considered speech, fitted to an occasion. But a "howl" is unconsidered speech, prompted by overwhelming desperation or rage; indeed, it is not speech at all, but pure inarticulate sound as uttered by an animal. Nor can one rule out the possibility that "Howl" is an imperative verb addressed to the reader, in which case it is opposed to the more usual noun-phrase title in form as well as spirit. The conception of poetry as an expression of preverbal states akin to the consciousness of animals or perhaps even matter itself, the rhetoric of expressiveness or exhortation, the preference for titles that invoke actions or processes (often with a nominalizing -ing suffix)—all of these widespread tendencies of poetry in the next decade were curled up, latent, within Ginsberg's title.

It takes the benefit of hindsight to extract all that from Ginsberg's title, but one can hardly make too much of his first line: "I saw the best minds of my generation destroyed by madness, starving hysterical naked . . ." (AG, 126).[4] The opening "I saw" does not startlingly violate period style; as it happens, Lowell's "Where the Rainbow Ends" opens with the same words. But the "I" of this poem, we soon discover, is more literally Ginsberg than the "I" of Lowell's early poem is Lowell. Moreover, Ginsberg is not seeing in the usual sense; one does not "see" minds being destroyed by madness. Even more than Lowell in "Where the Rainbow Ends," which also speaks a language of visionary prophecy, Ginsberg uses seeing as if it meant knowing, as if moral knowledge were as immediate as sensuous intuition, and as self-evident. To say that one believes invites argument, but to say that one sees places the matter beyond dispute.

Like the campus New Leftists of the sixties, (and, as we shall find, like John Berryman and Robert Lowell as well), Ginsberg perceives himself as part of a "generation," victims sharing a collective historical fate. The best minds among them, Ginsberg says in passive voice, were "destroyed by madness"—as if madness were some sort of danger abroad in the world, like a hurricane or a virus, and could descend upon the individual mind to destroy it. Moreover, "madness" seems choosy about its victims, singling out the best minds to destroy; perhaps they go mad *because* they are the best minds. The three adjectives perched on the end of the line—"starving hysterical naked"—may at first seem mere overwriting. But they suggest that these elect "best minds" are "starving" not only for food, drugs, and sex, but for spiritual transcendence, for "the ancient heavenly connection to the starry dynamo in the machinery of night" (AG, 126). Such yearning seems mystical only to a society that represses its own hunger for spiritual (as well as sexual) exploration. They are "naked" not only in their refusal to wear the clothes of social convention, or in preparation for lovemaking, but also in their vulnerability. In refusing all covering, they refuse protection also. The best minds have no Reichian character armor. And although "minds" stands metonymically for persons and emphasizes consciousness rather than the body, these "minds" are presented in predominantly bodily terms: one thinks of the body in connection with the words "naked" and "starving," and even "hysterical" derives from the Greek word for "womb." The hysterias that Freud decided to treat psychologically had previously been considered somatic ailments. The effect of Ginsberg's language is to sexualize the concept of "mind," making it more bodily and instinctive, while simultaneously spiritualizing the body, making its hunger and nakedness into emblems of religious yearning.

The entire first section of "Howl" rushes forward in a single sentence. By line four, it settles into a litany of "who" clauses, each of which gets a long Whitmanian line to itself. Occasionally Ginsberg substitutes another initial word for "who," and he may have intended to signal the approach of closure by breaking the pattern in the last ten lines, only one of which begins with "who." The incantatory syntax, as many critics have remarked, draws attention to the poem as speech rather than as an object for contemplation; the sweep of the enormous sentence encourages the reader not to stop and savor nuances, but to surrender instead to the insistent rhythm. Moreover, the syntactical complexities one associates with nuance are missing. There is little variety of sentence construction and, therefore, little complexity in the relations among words. To say this is not necessarily to condemn the poem, which aims at force, not subtlety. But the effect of the steady accumulation of parallel subordinate clauses goes beyond the suggestion of passionate speech. Like the catalogue passages in Whitman, the first section of "Howl" implies by its syntax a view of reality: the many parts of the world simply exist, next to each other, without conflict and without hierarchy of greater and lesser, and they are unified not by complex relations among the parts, but by a simple and all-embracing relation between any part and the whole.

But if we ask what that whole is, we must return two answers. There is the demonic world, in bondage to "Moloch the heavy judger of men" (*AG*, 131), and an angelic world, in which, as Ginsberg flatly declares in the "Footnote to Howl," "Everything is holy!" (*AG*, 134). The two worlds, moreover, exist in the same place at the same time. We read of "holy Bronx" (*AG*, 126), "the supernatural darkness of coldwater flats" (*AG*, 126) and "Zen New Jersey" (*AG*, 127), and we hear Ginsberg exclaim, "Holy the solitudes of skyscrapers and pavements" (*AG*, 134). Yet we also find the same urban reality treated as the embodiment of the unholy "Moloch whose eyes are a thousand blind windows! Moloch whose skyscrapers stand in the long streets like endless Jehovahs!" (*AG*, 131).

Ginsberg seems aware of this contradiction, and at points scattered throughout the poem, he attempts to resolve it. Although Moloch is demonic, there is nonetheless "the Angel in Moloch," stunned perhaps, but never killed or displaced. In a long letter to Richard Eberhart, later published as a monograph, Ginsberg compared "Howl" to "Sunflower Sutra." Just as, in the shorter poem, the poet recognizes and loves the sunflower beneath its coating of industrial grime, so he recognizes in "Howl" an essential self and an essential world beneath the distortions of Moloch. "The effect is to release self and audience from a false and self-denying self-deprecating image of ourselves which makes us feel like smelly shits and not the angels which we most deeply are."[5]

One could justify this division of the world into two superimposed images by various mystical traditions known to Ginsberg: the Gnostic doctrine of the *pneuma* struggling through a world of darkness toward its home in a world of light; the contradictory higher and lower truths of Buddhism (that all dharmas are empty, yet all dharmas have a conditional existence), reconciled by the middle path; the Hindu belief in the *Atman*, an essential divine self beneath the secular ego. Supplying traditional precedents absolves Ginsberg from the charge of know-nothing anti-intellectualism. But the trouble with Ginsberg's dualism— as with Manichean dualism—is that it creates an utter chasm between secular intelligence and mystical knowledge. Having made his huge repudiation of existing social reality, Ginsberg has little interest in a more particular account of it, or in secular causality.

Although "Howl" anticipates later confessional poetry, including Ginsberg's own "Kaddish," in its equation of personal and collective crisis, Ginsberg's mystical speculations tempt him to solve the confessional poet's problem of engulfment in false consciousness by a leap of faith rather than by secular moral inquiry. Indeed, it may be his extreme version of the problem of false consciousness that makes the mystical way out so appealing to him. Whereas John Berryman thought that "current American society" was enough to drive people mad,[6] Ginsberg seems at times to think that the problem is the unredeemed condition of the world rather than any particular social evil. There is thus, from the beginning, a conflict between Ginsberg as confessional poet and Ginsberg as religious seeker—or religious prophet. After all, the notion that one's vocation as poet is to be destroyed by madness, bearing witness to that destruction in one's poems, is not very encouraging; Ginsberg can hardly be blamed for wanting to escape from it if possible. But the escape from madness, since the entire secular world is saturated with madness, becomes disturbingly akin to a rejection of secular reality altogether.

The only people in the urban landscape of "Howl" are the isolated "best minds," glimpsed in one-line *tableaux* as they jump from fire escapes, wander at midnight, or seek transcendence in drugs or "ultimate visions of cunt and come" (*AG*, 128). The various persons of the opening section are all-but-interchangeable avatars of the Universal Beat, "mind leaping toward poles of Canada and Paterson" (*AG*, 126), who migrates in the course of the poem from New York through New Jersey, Baltimore, Chicago, Kansas, Colorado, the Southwest, Mexico, Tangiers—only to end up back in New York with Carl Solomon in Rockland. These isolated persons are, as Ginsberg put it in "The Green Automobile," "hidden / like diamonds / in the clock of the world" (*AG*, 84). The square or Molochian world is a mechanism like a clock; in "Howl" it appears not in persons but in images of buildings or machinery, or it is abstractly summarized as the "shocks of hospitals and jails and wars" (*AG*, 127). Through this unremittingly hostile environment the "best minds" wander, like awakened Gnostics, looking for a way out, "waiting for a door in the East River to open to a room full of steamheat and opium" (*AG*, 128). Society and its artifacts are but an elaborate prison, and nature, in this overwhelmingly urban poem, does not exist as an alternative. The world offers nothing for loving contemplation except one's fellow angelic victims.

The entire intersubjective realm of culture, and with it the very landscape, has been devoured by "Moloch." The litany against Moloch in the second section of the poem so easily accommodates a wide range of pent-up grievances against society that one might forget to ask the hard question: what, after all that cathartic frenzy, is Moloch supposed to represent? Capitalism ("Moloch whose blood is running money")?

Industrialization ("Moloch whose mind is pure machinery")? Aggression ("Moloch the vast stone of war," *AG*, 131)? Reason ("Mental Moloch") exalted at the expense of feeling ("Moloch the loveless," *AG*, 131)? Or denial of religious transcendence, of "Heaven which exists and is everywhere around us" (*AG*, 132)? Ginsberg's catch-all bill of indictment lacks incisiveness, although it allows him to work up a good rhetorical head of steam.

Peter Michelson, in an article cast in the form of a dialogue between himself and "G. Graph," whom "the reader of critical prose may be tempted to identify . . . with one Gerald Graff," allows "Graph" to argue that Ginsberg's diatribe against Moloch amounts to nothing but "fake" emotion and the sophomoric belief that

> if you walk safely with the light across an intersection it's a sign of moral obtuseness, whereas if you walk against the light and get flattened by the bourgeois steamroller it's a revelation of your exquisite moral sensibility. Everything is levitated to a simplistic war between good and evil, and your medal of honor is insanity. Ginsberg's Moloch, when it's not pure bombast, is just paraphrastic sophistry.[7]

Although I find that "Graph" has the better of his antagonist here (and it's just possible that Michelson intended him to), this summary of the case against "Howl" fails to take into account Ginsberg's uncertain attitude toward the concept of madness. Even though the poem does for the most part regard insanity as a "medal of honor," it also raises, if only fitfully, the question of whether "madness" is only society's name for resistance to Moloch, or whether some "madness" really deserves to be called madness. Insanity in this sense would be undesirable to Ginsberg as well as to the squares and would signify the triumph of Moloch rather than rebellion against him. Ginsberg finds it hard to decide whether madness is the helpless internalization of destructive social norms or the defiant refusal to comply with those norms.

As an example of Ginsberg's equivocal attitude toward madness in "Howl," one might follow the progression of thought in the eighth line of Section Two:

> Moloch in whom I sit lonely! Moloch in whom I dream angels! Crazy in Moloch! Cocksucker in Moloch! Lacklove and manless in Moloch!
>
> (*AG*, 131)

The line begins with a complaint of loneliness. The second exclamation can be understood as arising from this initial thought: nowadays, people who dream angels usually dream alone. But whereas the first exclamation is a cry of pain, the second is more ambiguous. Is it a cry of pain or a cry of triumph? If being lonely is the price of seeking connection to "the starry dynamo in the machinery of night," then perhaps loneliness is better than company. Next comes the thought: "Crazy in Moloch!" To be lonely is bad enough, but to be "crazy" is worse. Is one "crazy" because one dreams angels or because Moloch frustrates the chance of making such a dream into reality? Then the last two exclamations turn to Ginsberg's homosexuality, which in the less tolerant era of "Howl" was itself often considered a form of craziness. The slang pejorative "cocksucker," moreover, reminds us of the contempt with which homosexuality was regarded. In the last of the exclamatory phrases, the loneliness of the first phrase becomes explicitly sexual.

At first glance, this line would seem to be a series of parallel outcries protesting the suffering that Moloch has inflicted. But one can read it in two mutually irreconcilable ways. One might conclude that Ginsberg himself thinks it is a misfortune to be crazy, lonely, and homosexual; he would rather be sane, surrounded by friends, and heterosexual, but Moloch has twisted him. (To make "homosexual" parallel with "lonely" and "crazy" already implies an introjection of the judgment that these adjectives are near-synonyms.) Or one might conclude, with equal warrant from the poem, that to be crazy, lonely, and homosexual is, as Michelson put it, a medal of honor, the sign of one's solitary resistance to Moloch within a subjugated culture. But Ginsberg wants it both ways. He berates Moloch for turning him into a "cocksucker," but he also portrays homosexuality as rebellion against Moloch when he laments, in Section One, that the homosexual contingent of the "angel-headed hipsters"

> lost their loveboys to the three old shrews of fate the one eyed shrew of the heterosexual dollar the one eyed shrew that winks out of the womb and the one eyed shrew that does nothing but sit on her ass and snip the intellectual golden threads of the craftsman's loom.
>
> (AG, 128)

The words "heterosexual dollar" momentarily align heterosexuality with capitalist greed, although Neil Cassady's "innumerable lays of girls" are elsewhere cause for celebration.

Through the eighth line of Section Two, Ginsberg has imagined himself *inside* Moloch, "the incomprehensible prison," but in the ninth, this spatial relationship is reversed with the cry: "Moloch who entered my mind early!" Moloch's "name is the Mind," but he is an acquired mind; one of his other names is culture. In order to "abandon" Moloch, as Ginsberg claims to do at the end of the section, one must first exorcise him from the self. Thus insanity can be understood, in its laudatory sense, as the refusal of acculturation. If Moloch's name is the mind, and one must abandon him, then one must literally go out of one's mind.

The question remains, however, whether abandoning the acquired mentality of Moloch restores one to a natural sanity that Moloch had usurped or leaves one so radically estranged that only an innocent but ineffectual holy madness is possible. In the third section of the poem, we find the poet in the madhouse with Carl Solomon, whose insanity is sometimes presented as an affliction. Ginsberg cannot think it entirely angelic that Solomon imagines he has "murdered [his] twelve secretaries," or that "the faculties of the skull no longer admit the worms of the senses." And no reader of "Kaddish" would wish on anyone that he should "imitate the shade of [Ginsberg's] mother." At other times, however, Solomon's madness becomes a Christ-like redemptive sacrifice, or political revolution, or, as in these lines, both at once:

> I'm with you in Rockland
>> where fifty more shocks will never return your soul to its body
>> again from its pilgrimage to a cross in the void
> I'm with you in Rockland
>> where you accuse your doctors of insanity and plot the Hebrew
>> socialist revolution against the fascist national Golgotha
> I'm with you in Rockland
>> where you will split the heavens of Long Island and resurrect your
>> living human Jesus from the superhuman tomb
> I'm with you in Rockland
>> where there are twentyfive-thousand mad comrades all together
>> singing the final stanzas of the Internationale. . . .
>>   (AG, 133)

Ginsberg's praise for this wisdom of Solomon—in which madness becomes equated with the "living human" in an inhuman world or with the political alienation of revolutionary "comrades"—echoes through the poetry and politics of the 1960s.

The indictment against Moloch is essentially the one that began to emerge in the conformity critiques of the 1950s and was more completely formulated in more radical writings of the following decade. Like Marcuse and Laing, Ginsberg envisions a repressive social determinism so all-embracing that the idea of individual agency is lost. The ego has been totally socialized, and only by abandonment to the involuntary impulses of the unconscious id can we act from our own motives rather than those of one-dimensional society. But in this extreme position, the crucial difference between madness and rebellion is lost. The rebel *chooses* to rebel, being somehow able to make a choice between accepting the demands of society and rejecting them. But the mad go mad because they cannot help it. Madness resists authority only in a minimal way. Once classified as mad, one is no longer held responsible for understanding authority and is therefore excused from compliance with it. The dissenter or revolutionary wants it known that he understands perfectly well what is demanded but does not consent to it. Declare him mad, and you deny the meaning of his resistance. That is why the Soviet government sometimes puts troublemakers in the madhouse rather than in prison. If "madness" could be understood as enclosed in ironic quotation marks, then Ginsberg's affirmation of it as political rebellion might be easier to accept. But sometimes it is madness not only in Moloch's judgment, but in Ginsberg's own. And then it means estrangement from knowledge rather than attainment of gnosis. It becomes an emblem of defeat rather than defiance.

Ginsberg's next long poem, "Kaddish" (1959; published 1961), provides further insights into the ambiguities of his equation of madness with political rebellion. The retrospective note (1975) to his letter to Eberhart begins by declaring that "*Howl* is really about my mother, in her last year at Pilgrim State Hospital—acceptance of her, later inscribed in *Kaddish* detail."[8] We thus have Ginsberg's own sanction for reading "Kaddish" as a discovery of the personal implications of the experience treated in "Howl." Ginsberg's mother, Naomi, was both politically radical and clinically insane; one might speculate that her son, receiving his first impressions of social causation from circumstances within his family, mistook this accidental conjunction for a necessary connection. In any case, the idea of madness as rebellion was from the outset far more than an idea for him; it was bound up with the most complex and difficult relationship of his life, and the one that apparently had the most influence on his sense of his own identity.

Although, as I have argued, the social implications of madness, nonconformity, and marginality are not entirely clear in "Howl," the poem's attitude is on the whole ruefully defiant: the indignities that society inflicts on Ginsberg and his friends only confirm the brutality of society. Madness is a sign of election; the outcasts are proud to have been cast out. In "Kaddish," however, Naomi's madness causes terrible suffering, not only for her but for her entire family. This is not madness as poetic vision or utopian ardor; it is the real thing in all its harshness. The poet tries to understand and forgive his mother's madness rather than affirm it as political rebellion or higher sanity. The confession in "Kaddish" aims at reconciliation—not only between the poet and his mother, but between the poet and the audience as well. The title makes a revealing contrast with "Howl," denoting, instead of a word-less cry, a formal ritual of mourning. And Ginsberg, this once, is content to be a Jew, standing in the temple with his father, rather than a Gnostic or a Buddhist. Although—or perhaps because—the poem gives us considerable insight into Ginsberg's personality, especially the parts of it that would offend the narrowly respectable, the cumulative effect is to soften rather than sharpen Ginsberg's conflict with conventional morals. In "Kaddish" Ginsberg implicitly asks us to understand the origins of his penchant for emotional melodrama and his difficulty in distinguishing radical unmasking from paranoid fantasy. And to understand is to forgive, or to feel that nothing stands in need of forgiveness.

Reading "Howl" and "Kaddish" together, one confronts a recurrent problem for psycho-political poetry: Does psychology explain politics, as in "Kaddish," or does politics explain psychology, as in "Howl"? If psychology explains politics, how can one be sure that one's own political dissent is not, like the politics one professes to unmask, a mere projection of psychological distortions? And if politics explains psychology, how can one avoid becoming what the existing political situation compels one to be? And if explanation proceeds in a circle, with neither politics nor psychology assuming priority, how shall we know where self ends and culture begins? These are, I submit, real problems, which anyone who does not wish to be self-deceived must confront. But most of the time, Ginsberg, while recognizing the difficulty of making distinctions between inner and outer, decides that it is better to do without them altogether. Private experience thus takes on, automatically, a public implication, but at the cost of confusion and fatalism.

One can see the result of psycho-political confusion in a poem such as "Wichita Vortex Sutra," in which Ginsberg views his mother as only one among many casualties of a vast historical violence. Wichita, where Carry Nation started the temperance movement, "began a vortex of hatred that defoliated the Mekong Delta" and

> murdered my mother
> who died of the communist anticommunist psychosis
> in the madhouse one decade long ago
> complaining about wires of masscommunication in her head
> and phantom political voices in the air
> besmirching her girlish character.
> Many another has suffered death and madness
> in the Vortex.

> (AG, 410)

Here we have an easy, scattershot indictment, in which the prohibition of liquor, McCarthyite anticommunism, the use of defoliants in Vietnam, and Naomi Ginsberg's "death and madness" are all the results of a national "hatred." In this passage, Ginsberg treats individual madness as the symptom of political madness, but again, he wants it both ways. By suggesting, even if only for purposes of metonymy, that Carry Nation began "the vortex," Ginsberg identifies a villain whose individual repressions initiate, through social contagion, the repressiveness of a whole country. (Carry Nation's name serves Ginsberg's turn all too conveniently.) In this sweeping equation of any social evil with any other, individuals can be treated either as willing agents or as passive victims, according to one's mood. Ginsberg extends no sympathy to Carry Nation, who presumably was also shaped by her social environment. Those one has singled out as villains are responsible for their actions, while those who have been cast as victims are not.

In "Kaddish," Ginsberg cannot so easily aggrandize his mother's fate. For one thing, the detailed description of his mother's illness, including the suffering Naomi inflicts as well as that which she endures, resists iconographic idealization. For another, Ginsberg's own presence in the narrative as her bewildered adolescent son gives her competition for the reader's sympathy. To the extent that the young poet is damaged by his mother's actions, he preempts her in the role of victim and forces us to regard her as one who does as well as suffers wrong. Ginsberg, looking back on his own suffering, seems ready to forgive, but does not mute the bitterness of his memories:

> Serving me, meanwhile, a plate of cold fish—chopped raw cabbage dript with tapwater—smelly tomatoes—week-old health food—grated beets & carrots with leaky juice, warm—more and more disconsolate food—I can't eat it for nausea sometimes—the Charity of her hands stinking with Manhattan, madness, desire to please me, cold undercooked fish—pale and near the bones. Her smells—and oft naked in the room, so that I stare ahead, or turn a book ignoring her.
>
> One time I thought she was trying to make me come lay her—flirting to herself at sink—lay back on huge bed that filled most of the room, dress up round her hips, big slash of hair, scars of operations, pancreas, belly wounds, abortions, appendix, stitching of incisions pulling down in the fat like hideous thick zippers—ragged long lips between her legs—what, even, smell of asshole?
>
> (AG, 219)

When Ginsberg claims to have been "revolted a little, not much," it is hard to believe him, for the revulsion is overwhelmingly present in his descriptive language. When one remembers that the acceptance of food from the mother is a child's first experience of internalizing what the world has to offer, one realizes how powerful a metaphor this passage provides for the poisoning of the whole process of socialization at its very origins. Naomi herself, in her madness, believes that she is being poisoned; her son, in this passage, expresses a less literal version of the same fear.

Naomi's madness takes the form of paranoia. She continually imagines plots against herself: the doctors "poisoned me, they want to see me dead"; "Old Grandma" lurks outside "On the fire escape, with poison germs, to throw on me—at night—maybe Louis is helping her" (*AG*, 213). Sometimes she imagines conspiracies on a grander scale, "cosmic financial murder plots":

> 'I am a great woman—am truly a beautiful soul—and because of that they (Hitler, Grandma, Hearst, the Capitalists, Franco, Daily News, the 20's, Mussolini, the living dead) want to shut me up—Buba's the head of a spider network—'
>
> (*AG*, 221)

The suspicion of poison, and of her own family conspiring with the dictators of the world against her, is madness by any standard, and Ginsberg as a character in the poem certainly responds to such accusations as if he judged them mad. His mother's paranoia is not a forbidden wisdom, but a barrier that prevents her from recognizing the love her husband and children continue to feel for her.

Despite Ginsberg's different attitudes toward madness in "Howl" and in "Kaddish," only a slightly heightened exaggeration separates Naomi's ravings from her son's own prophetic lamentations in the earlier poem, wherein the minions of Moloch conspire to destroy the world's truly beautiful souls. Moreover, although her fantasies of being poisoned are wild, her fantasies of political persecution have a certain plausibility. Even in the 1930s, communism was not an entirely safe political position, and in the last years before her death in 1956, people of Naomi Ginsberg's political convictions indeed *were* persecuted. But to say, as Ginsberg does in "Wichita Vortex Sutra," that her madness was a direct consequence of political repression is to oversimplify in a way that "Kaddish" will not allow; it is to explain Naomi as she, in her madness, explained herself. For that matter, the suggestion in "Kaddish" itself that sanity is a "trick of agreement" seems too facile to stand as a fair summary of the attitude toward madness that emerges in the poem. Naomi Ginsberg may have her moment of poetry when she writes, in her last letter, that "the key is in the bars, in the sunlight in the window" (*AG*, 224), but for the most part her madness brings only misery to herself and those around her—it cannot be explained away by changing the social terms of "agreement."

"Kaddish" also reveals more clearly than "Howl" Ginsberg's evasiveness about the source of suffering in the kingdom of Moloch. In "Howl," the unredeemed world seems to be that of a particular society. The landscape, so overwhelmingly urban, represents the culture that made it. The inherent value of earthly existence itself is not in question. But *Kaddish and Other Poems* bears an epigraph from Shelley's "Adonais": "—Die, / If thou wouldst be with that which thou dost seek!" This advice amounts to a rejection not only of a particular society, but of life in this world altogether. Early in "Kaddish," Ginsberg ponders on Shelley's elegy:

> —And read Adonais' last triumphant stanzas aloud—
> wept, realizing how we suffer—
> And how Death is that remedy all singers dream of, sing, remember,
> prophesy. . . .
>
> (AG, 209)

The poet imagines his mother not in heaven, but in a state of pure non-being more like the Buddhist Nirvana:

> Ai! Ai! we do worse! We are in a fix! And you're out, Death let you
> out, Death had the Mercy, you're done with your century, done
> with God, done with the path thru it—Done with yourself at last—
> Pure—Back to the Babe dark, before your Father, before us all—
> before the world—
>
> (AG, 210)

Such passages raise once more the question of whether Ginsberg's quarrel is with urban capitalist society as experienced in American cities or with the human condition generally. In "Kaddish" the problem seems less with society than with life itself, or at least with life that has not been freed from craving and attachment, which, according to Buddhist teaching, are the sources of all suffering. One cannot fairly argue that Ginsberg, in finding a deeper source of suffering than Moloch, has absolved Moloch of contributing misery beyond the unavoidable allotment. But one might wish for a clearer distinction, in the poetry that follows "Kaddish," between the rejection of a particular form of society and the rejection of worldliness altogether.

"Howl" and "Kaddish" remain, I believe, the best writing that Ginsberg has done. Afterwards, the urgency of the voice diminishes, without any gain in clarity. Ginsberg's quarrels with himself, instead of provoking him into poetry, gradually lull themselves into mystical quietism as the years go by. In retrospect, one suspects that these two early poems exhausted the possibilities of his method—either he can "prophesy" against society, illustrating from his personal experience, or he can examine personal experience, trusting wider significance to emerge. In either case, the assumption of an almost automatic correspondence between personal and collective experience mars the poetry, although "Kaddish" is relatively free of this problem, since Ginsberg was for the most part content on that occasion to treat private experience as private, without wringing world-historical implications from it.

In Ginsberg's more recent work, the correspondence between personal and collective experience increasingly depends not so much on psycho-politics as on a unity with nature itself. In the title poem of *Mind Breaths* (1977, *AG*, 609–11), he imagines his breath leaving his mouth, being carried around the world, and returning to him again, completing a circle. As early as "Wales Visitation" (1967), he thinks of the wind in a valley as "One being on the mountainside stirring gently / Exquisite scales trembling everywhere in balance," so that "heaven and earth move together" (*AG*, 481). In these poems, opposition to the repressive totality of society comes less from individual rebellion than from a sense of belonging to another totality, the ecological and spiritual oneness of all beings.

But the new Ginsberg, like the old, still conceives of opposing totalities, and the totalities never really engage each other. When it is convenient to treat the social realm as an illusion, Ginsberg does so; at other times, he treats it as a threat to the realm of the natural and the sacred. Ginsberg and his admirers advocate a poetry of "openness," and yet this poetry is in an important sense closed. Although he has traveled widely and has knocked about in many occupations, Ginsberg incessantly reduces the particulars of his experience to a war between Moloch and the Angel, whether the Angel is thought of as the innocent self persisting beneath the socialized ego, as the innocence of nature persisting beneath civilization, or as an innocence to be attained only by joining Adonais and Naomi Ginsberg outside life's dome of many-colored glass. That a middle ground may exist between the divine and the demonic, or that there are worthy souls, lower than the angels, struggling in this middle ground toward self-knowledge and salvation on their own level—these possibilities, if they occur to him at all, interest him very little.

Jane Kramer's book, *Allen Ginsberg in America*, reveals a man who can be tolerant and even ingratiating in his dealings with the unconverted, a surprisingly cagey negotiator who has helped less practical bohemians to survive in the square world.[9] But this side of Ginsberg seldom appears in his poems. One might imagine, in reading them, that this poet had spent all his life in the company of a few friends, living in cheap apartments, driving around the country, and never setting foot in a bourgeois—or, for that matter, blue-collar—household, let alone an office building or a factory. He does not appear to regard American society, beyond his own programmatically marginal selection from it, as worth writing about from the inside. The outsides of its buildings are all he knows, and all he needs to know.

Ginsberg's lack of interest in an "inside" view is especially evident in *The Fall of America* (1972), a long and for the most part excruciatingly dull political sequence. Most of the poems simply record whatever Ginsberg sees out the window as he drives or flies from city to city. Interspersed with the sights of the landscape are newscasts and songs heard on the radio, or the poet's own casual thoughts. The descriptive language is careless; the poet seems content, in the pursuit of spontaneity, to take the first cliché that comes to his mind. Industrial landscapes remind him of "illustrious robots stretched with wires" (*AG*, 429); they contain "grey robot towers" (*AG*, 419); and, in case you weren't paying attention, he adds that someday "the dead material planet'll revolve robotlike" (*AG*, 511). Such language is itself more than a little robotlike. Predictably, Ginsberg juxtaposes innocent nature with ugly civilization:

> Blue morning in Kansas,
>> black lambs dotted in snow
>> Ice gleaming in brown grass at roadside
>> Corn stacks, small
>> lined up around tree groves—
> Kingman Salvage, rusty autos under rusty hill,
> Jodrell Bank reporting Sensational pictures Rocks on the Moon. . . .
>> (*AG*, 391)

The word-painting in the first three lines is rather striking; I am not claiming that Ginsberg never writes well anymore. But one tires quickly of such programmatic contrasts and easy ironies.

The contribution of the radio to the national well-being varies. When it plays the Beach Boys and Nancy Sinatra, it is "the car dashboard vibrating / False emotions thru the Land / Natural voices made synthetic" (*AG*, 468). When it plays prowar topical songs, we are "Lulled into War / Thus commercial jabber Rock & Roll Announcers / False False False" (*AG*, 469). At other times, however, the radio proffers the Beatles or "Angelic Dylan" as he is called in "Wichita Vortex Sutra" (*AG*, 409), and all is well—as if these singers were not marketed in the same way, and by the same industry, as the Beach Boys and Nancy Sinatra. One is tempted to imagine a board game somewhat like "Monopoly": "Hear Dylan sing antiwar song—advance three"; "See robot factory outside window—back two," and so on. Instead of trying to interpret his random impressions, the poet, by means of adjectives or moralizing interjections, tosses them into the Moloch bin or the Angel bin and keeps on driving.

In his *Paris Review* interview (1966), Ginsberg claimed to have experienced a conversion of sorts in 1963, through which he learned to renounce continual "yearning back to a visionary state," so that he could "get back to now."[10] This change of emphasis may explain why so many of the poems in *Planet News* (1967) and *The Fall of America* attempt little more than a passive record of the daily flux of news and noise. Ginsberg wrote a great deal of political poetry in the late 1960s and early 1970s, all of it sentimental in its insistence that the war in Vietnam resulted directly from bad consciousness, and that good consciousness drives out bad. Even in "Wichita Vortex Sutra," the best of these political poems, Ginsberg portrays the war as the work of "inferior magicians with / the wrong alchemical formula for transforming earth into gold." To this black magic, Ginsberg offers his poem as a thaumaturgical antidote. Calling "all powers of imagination" to his aid, he solemnly intones: "I here declare the end of the War! / Ancient days' illusion!— / and pronounce words beginning my own millennium." After this proclamation, the poet notices the newspaper headline "Kennedy Urges Cong Get Chair in Negotiations"; this coincidence shows us that

> The War is gone,
> Language emerging on the motel news stand,
>   the right magic
>   Formula. . . .
>
>   (AG, 408)

It may be that the Pentagon's blind faith in American technological omnipotence amounted to a kind of magical thinking and that such magical thinking compounded the disaster of Vietnam. But the cure for magical thinking is not counter-magical thinking. Moreover, even if the war was in some sense an expression of the consciousness of those who conducted it, as an external and complex event it had a specific character of its own, having more to do with the history of Southeast Asia than with Carry Nation's temperance campaign, urban blight, advertising, racial oppression, or the other evils that Ginsberg lumps together as one. When everything is so relentlessly reduced to its most general and cosmic significance, everything begins to resemble everything else, and the poetry becomes predictable, boring, and impoverished.

When the war finally ended in 1973, the American left had already been in disarray for nearly five years. With the end of the war, the last cause that had given its lingering efforts direction was gone. Like many others, Ginsberg turned his attention inward. In 1974, he and Anne Waldman founded the Kerouac School of Disembodied Poetics, a Buddhist writing program associated with the Naropa Institute, a school of Buddhist religious instruction whose resident guru is the exiled Tibetan lama Chogyam Trungpa.

The once-notorious incident of 1975 involving W. S. Merwin and Dana Naone is now antique gossip, but Ginsberg's response to it still tells us something about what has become of him since the early seventies. *L'Affaire Merwin* provoked investigative journalism by Peter Marin, Tom Clark, and even Ed Sanders' poetry class at the Institute itself. While staying at Naropa to sit in on the Vajrayana classes, Merwin and Naone irritated Trungpa when they left the class initiation party— which had become quite wild—early, retiring to their room. Trungpa sent his "guards" to ask them to return. When they refused, Trungpa ordered his followers to bring them anyway. The door was locked, but the students took Walt Whitman's injunction to "Unscrew the doors themselves from their jambs" quite literally and dragged the couple downstairs, where both were stripped naked before the company. The scandal raised by this incident brought other charges to light: that Trungpa sexually exploited the female initiates; that he extracted donations in unscrupulous ways; that his "guards" intimidated the other students. In short, people began to ask whether Trungpa was a legitimate religious teacher or a dangerous con-man. What concerns us here, however, is not the gossip about Naropa, but the position that Ginsberg, as head of the writing program, took in defending Trungpa and the Institute. His response makes a fitting coda to a discussion of his poetry, for it sheds further light on the conflict between radicalism and mystical quietism in his poetry.

As Tom Clark observes in *The Great Naropa Poetry Wars*, "Allen Ginsberg happens to subscribe to the star system of eternity. Allen has long believed there are certain immortal heroes of art and thought whose genius ought to be religiously revered. He has made a quite literal point of kissing such personages' feet on first meeting."[11] This kind of hero-worship is obviously authoritarian. In Ginsberg's poetry, the mystical experience of dying to be reborn is sometimes assimilated with alarming ease to the idea of being humiliated or dominated by a superior person. In "Contest of Bards," a long poem in *Mind-Breaths*, an aging poet, obviously representing Ginsberg himself, receives a visit from a young man. The youth reveres the "Bard" for the vestiges of prophetic power in him, but his way of renewing the older man's poetic aspirations consists, aside from sexual intercourse, mainly of verbal abuse. "Ungrateful Unimaginative Bard," the young man calls him, and after their lovemaking, the ungrateful one is treated to more invective:

> "Your door's the musty stone door of a tomb, old man, corpses of corrupted loves're buried under the smooth stone bed we lie on, pitted with yr fearful tears! What animal skins you vulgarize your bed with, boorish stained with creepy-handed dream stuff jacked out of your impotent loins in Pain—
>
> (AG, 675)

And then there is "Please Master," a frankly pornographic submission-and-dominance poem in *The Fall of America*. In this poem, Ginsberg hopes that by being dominated, "ordered," subjected to "brutal" and "violent" intercourse, he can release the most deeply authentic passions, "terror" and "delight to be loved." Like Wilhelm Reich and D. H. Lawrence, Ginsberg connects sex, authority, and emotional authenticity in ways that can have disturbing implications, as when Reich justified physical assaults on his patients as a way of making them aware of their bodies, or when Lawrence, in *The Plumed Serpent*, entertained the idea that the sexually or emotionally tepid should simply be exterminated. Ginsberg's defense of Trungpa brings his own authoritarianism to the surface.

That defense, as presented to Clark in an interview in 1979, rests on the premise that in attending the Vajrayana seminar at all, Merwin and Naone had abrogated the right to privacy, because the very purpose of a relationship with a guru is "to get rid of privacy. . . . The entrance into Vajrayana is the abandonment of all privacy." But a few minutes later, pressed for his own deepest feelings about Trungpa, Ginsberg replied: ". . . if you want to know what I think, way back in my closet, well, I wouldn't want to say. I just don't want to—I want privacy in my belief." And Trungpa, who refused to answer any questions about the incident, has "got his right to privacy" too.[12] One's own privacy is apparently harder to renounce than other people's.

The interview reveals Ginsberg's judgment paralyzed in ways similar to those we have traced in his poetry: the sense that all authority is absolute, and is either divine or demonic; the uncertainty whether his own rebellion is prophecy or paranoia; the attraction to wild generalizations. "I accuse myself all the time," he says, "of seducing the entire poetry scene and Merwin into this impossible submission to some spiritual dictatorship which they'll never get out of again and which will ruin American culture forever." [13] Here again is the self-absorbed inflation of particular experience to world-historical generality—as if the fate of American poetry and culture were to be decided by Ginsberg personally from his throne in Naropa, which, to judge from his pronouncements, is the literary capital of the United States.

The interview also makes it clear, if it had not been clear already, that Ginsberg's flight from the authority of the dominant culture is only the first stage of a quest for a higher and stricter authority elsewhere. The man who has been credited with launching the revolt against Eliot turns out to be more of a "royalist in politics" than the Old Possum himself. According to Clark, Ginsberg told students at Naropa that Trungpa was involved in an "experiment in monarchy," and in the interview Ginsberg objects to the charge that Trungpa is undemocratic:

And American culture! "How dare you criticize American culture!" Everybody's been criticizing it for twenty years, prophesizing [sic] the doom of America, how rotten America is. And Burroughs is talking about, "democracy, shit! What we need is a new Hitler." Democracy, nothing! They exploded the atom bomb without asking us. Everybody's defending American democracy. American democracy's this thing, this OOthoon. The last civilized refuge of the world—after twenty years of denouncing it as the *pits!* [14]

Ginsberg here wraps the concept of democracy in the American flag in order to discredit it. Was it American democracy that everyone denounced, or the failure of America to provide more than lip service to the ideal of democracy? Was the point of "Howl" and "Wichita Vortex Sutra" really that we need a new Hitler?

Most curiously of all, the uproar over the Merwin incident forced Ginsberg to entertain, for a moment, a new implication of his old dilemma of paranoia and prophecy. He had often claimed that madness was really holiness, but on this occasion he wondered whether Trungpa's holiness was really madness. "Paranoia" may be a "defense," but "sometimes it's justified. And in the real world, as we know from Guyana, it could be completely justified. Some big guru makes a big mistake, and turns out to have been mad all along." [15]

We leave Ginsberg, then, still struggling with the same problem that preoccupied him in "Howl": How can one distinguish prophetic madness from the common garden variety? Because the conception of the poet as a sensitive being driven mad by a destructive society also informs "confessional" poetry, we find there a similar preoccupation with madness and a similar uncertainty whether to regard madness as an affliction or as transcendence. I therefore turn next to a chapter on confessional poetics, followed by studies of Robert Lowell and Sylvia Plath.

3

Confessional Poetics: The Poet as Representative Victim

Of the styles that emerged in the late 1950s, the first to command wide admiration was that which came to be known as "confessional." M. L. Rosenthal, who may have given confessional poetry its name and was certainly one of its most influential critical supporters, already felt compelled, by 1967, to put the term in quotation marks when he used it in *The New Poets*. "It was," he wrote, "a term both helpful and too limited, and very possibly the conception of a confessional school has by now done a certain amount of damage."[1] Indeed, as we shall see, the term has an appropriateness that extends beyond the obvious, but it has, as Rosenthal suggests, distracted critical attention from other characteristics, apart from self-revelation, in the poetry it names.

Doubtless some of the attention bestowed on the confessional poets has more to do with confession as in *True Confessions* than with considerations of literary merit. Scandal is always interesting, especially when revealed by the scandalous ones themselves. But Rosenthal made for the confessional poets a more ambitious claim. They illustrate, most strongly of any poets considered in his book, his contention that in "the new poetry the private life of the poet himself, especially under stress of psychological crisis, becomes a major theme. Often it is felt at the same time as a symbolic embodiment of national and cultural crisis."[2] The confessional poet, then, does not confess merely to unburden personal unhappiness in verse, but to offer his own suffering as a historical symbol, as we have already seen Allen Ginsberg doing in "Howl" and "Wichita Vortex Sutra." It is through his "psychological crisis" that the poet becomes representative. A. Alvarez stated the relationship a bit more grimly in *The Savage God* (1971): "The nihilism and destructiveness of the self—of which psychoanalysis has made us sharply and progressively aware—turns out to be an accurate reflection of the nihilism of our own violent societies."[3] The poet's individual "destructiveness"—of self and sometimes of others as well—is ours as well as his; by confessing, the poet shocks the *hypocrite lecteur* into recognizing similar impulses within himself. The poet, in short, is a representative victim.

If, as the social critics of the fifties and sixties continually asserted, society had invaded the psyche and displaced the autonomous self, so that, as Denise Levertov put it in her remarks on the war in Vietnam, public crises "cast their shadow over all we say and do," then confessional poetry offered a chance to wrest some aesthetic advantage from this affliction. If the public had invaded the private, then at least the artistic problem of universality was solved. One had only to look at one's own suffering to find a symbol of historical crisis. Some critics have taken just such a discovery of shared experience in private woe as the central achievement of confessional poetry. Steven Gould Axelrod, for instance, praises Robert Lowell for writing poetry in which "'experience' . . . means the sum of the relations and interactions between psyche and environment. It grows from the Cartesian dualism of inner and outer, but through its interpenetrating energies abolishes the dualism." Thus Lowell is able, by "conflating his individual past with the national past," to treat "each as a metaphor for the other."[4]

If, however, there is no dualism of inner and outer, but only a mutual interpenetration, then the poet cannot know whether his sufferings are representative or not. In order to recognize the cultural origin of his own character traits, the poet must be able to distance himself from them to some extent. He must be able to distinguish between local sufferings peculiar to his own unique circumstances and those that can be traced to cultural influences. The moment one does so, one has already begun to separate inner and outer, public and private. Without such a distinction, one could hardly form a judgment either of society or of oneself. The "conflating" of private and public experience, far from being the triumph of confessional art, is rather the problem with which the confessional poet begins. The question for the confessional poet is not how to relate self to society, but how to unravel the tangled determinisms connecting the two.

Not only does a morally intelligent confessional poetry require a distinction between self and other, it requires a division within the self. As with any autobiographical writing, there is a distinction, at least in principle, between the voice of autobiographer as narrator and interpreter of his own life, and the autobiographer as actor within the events. There is always at least a slight temporal division between the immediacy of the situation described and the reflection on it implicit in the act of writing. Such a distinction implies the possibility of acquiring, at the time of writing, a fuller understanding of the significance of one's past experience than one had at the time it occurred. The autobiographical writer discovers a pattern or narrative shape in that experience which can only become visible in retrospect. But to the extent that the confessional poet believes that his experience is history internalized, such discovery becomes more difficult, since it requires not only a transcendence of the past self, but of the cultural assumptions current within one's historical moment.

Apologists for confessional poetry sometimes fail to distinguish between the idea expressed by Alvarez, that the psychological disorder of the poet is that of society internalized, and the idea that the poet risks psychological disruption because of his heroic attempt to encounter the repressed within himself, thereby releasing impulses that society has taught us to condemn as irrational, destructive, or immoral. This second idea logically contradicts Alvarez's formulation. If Alvarez is right in attributing "the nihilism and destructiveness" in Sylvia Plath's life and work to her internalization of society's nihilism and destructiveness, then her biographer, Edward Butscher, cannot also be right when he explains the same traits as "creative madness,"[5] the liberation of an authentic self from the strictures of acculturation. If the latter view is correct, the fierceness of Plath's late poems would be not a replication of the violence of society, but an angry protest against that violence. It must then be understood, in Wallace Stevens' phrase, as "a violence from within that protects us from a violence without."[6] Such a "violence from within" presupposes at least the partial capacity to recognize and resist the "violence from without" instead of internalizing it and displaying its destructive consequences for one's private life.

If confessional poetry sometimes attempts to unlock the repressed unconscious, it nonetheless is more skeptical about the possibilities of transcending the acculturated self than most of the other kinds of poetry to be considered here (the clear exception would be Ashbery's version of process poetry, in which one keeps helplessly longing for transcendence but knows very well that one will not attain it). The implicit psychology of confessional poetry is Freudian, which is to say, historical and contextual. The consciousness of the poet can only be understood within the context of the poet's life. The language of confessional poetry, although it sometimes includes free association, wordplay, or startling juxtapositions of images, is often quite rational, even analytical. This is truest of *Life Studies* but also true intermittently for Berryman, Plath, and even Ginsberg. One must further qualify Alvarez's generalization: not only is there, at times, a nonrational defiance of the "violence from without" by a "violence from within," there is also an attempt to pass rational self-judgment.

The most important technical considerations in confessional poetry, therefore, are those that affect tone, since it is through tone that the poet registers various degrees of detachment from the damaged self revealed in the poem, and thus, indirectly, from the cultural pressures by which that self was shaped. At one extreme is the dramatic monologue, in which the conventions of the poem unmistakeably insist that the speaker is not the poet; indeed, the poet may arrange for the reader to see through the speaker and judge him far more harshly than he judges himself, as in Browning's "My Last Duchess." At the other extreme would be a poem that presented itself as the poet's candid, unmediated speech.

Given the confessional poets' difficult attempt to offer themselves both as representative instances of socially deformed consciousness and as morally detached critics of social deformity, one would expect in their work a pervasive uncertainty of tone, a vacillation between unmediated presentation of the self in all its nihilism and violence and an attempt to achieve a more detached perspective from which that nihilism and violence might be recognized as such and judged. Remarks by the confessional poets themselves betray uneasiness about the abolition, which their poems often invite, of the New Critical distinction between speaker and poet. That uneasiness is both a defense against literal-minded scandal mongering and a recognition of the need for self-criticism along with the self-revelation in their poems. They were unclear and sometimes evasive, however, about the degree and kind of distance they wished to maintain between their poems and literal experience. Against critics who objected to the intrusion of the literal into poetry, they maintained the importance of truth to experience, but they balked when readers began to assume that the poems licensed a presumption of intimacy. John Berryman, in an introductory note to *His Toy, His Dream, His Rest,* insisted that his Dream Songs were

essentially about an imaginary character (not the poet, not me) named Henry, a white American in early middle age sometimes in blackface, who has suffered an irreversible loss and talks about himself sometimes in the first person, sometimes in the third, sometimes even in the second; he has a friend, never named, who addresses him as Mr Bones and variants thereof.[7]

But not only is Henry the same age as Berryman (who was in his forties when he wrote the first volume of Dream Songs), he has the same friends, the same vocation of poet and teacher; when Berryman goes to Ireland, Henry goes too. Henry's father, like Berryman's, "shot his heart out in a Florida dawn."[8] One must finally trust the poems and not the poet's disclaimer, which seems, like the sliding from first to third person in the poems themselves, essentially a defensive gesture. Both the disclaimer and the shift to third person seek to retain a vestige of privacy even while renouncing it, or to resist the temptations of self-pity with ironic detachment. Yet the Dream Songs frequently abrogate this detachment by reverting to the greater immediacy of first person. The deflating irony of the unnamed friend, another device for ensuring detachment, can also disappear without notice, then reappear in the next poem.

Lowell, though not verging on the disingenuous like Berryman, also warned against a too literally autobiographical interpretation of his poetry. Reflecting on *Life Studies* two years after its publication, he explained that even in the most self-revelatory poems,

There's a good deal of tinkering with fact. You leave out a lot, and emphasize this and not that. Your actual experience is a complete flux. I've invented facts and changed things, and the whole balance of the poem was something invented. So there's a lot of artistry, I hope, in the poems. Yet there's this thing: if a poem is autobiographical—and this is true of any kind of autobiographical writing and historical writing—you want the reader to say, this is true. In something like Macauley's *History of England,* you think you're really getting William III. That's as good as a good plot in a novel. And so there was always that standard of truth which you wouldn't ordinarily have in poetry—the reader was to believe he was getting the *real* Robert Lowell.[9]

This statement has troublesome implications. Lowell assumes without comment that any pattern attributed to experience is an imposed fiction, since experience itself "is a complete flux." And the "standard of truth" is a rhetorical standard—the poet is not required to seek the truth but only to sustain the reader's conviction that "this is true." The distinction between the standard of veracity for "autobiographical writing and historical writing" and that of veri*similitude* for "a good plot in a novel" becomes blurred. After all, one does not believe that the events in a good realistic novel are "true" in the same sense one believes that those in a history of England are. (I am aware that defenders of "documentary fiction" think otherwise, but most readers—and most novelists and historians—still observe a distinction between history and fiction. Macauley's account of William III may be "as good as" the plot of a novel, but it is not good for the same purpose; Lowell is comparing apples and oranges.)

Sylvia Plath's way of talking about her autobiographical poetry was usually to pretend that it wasn't autobiographical at all, as if the speakers of even her most ferociously confessional poems were mere personae in dramatic monologues. Introducing "Daddy" for a reading on BBC radio, she said:

Here is a poem spoken by a girl with an Electra complex. Her father died while she thought he was God. Her case is complicated by the fact that her father was also a Nazi and her mother very possibly part Jewish. In the daughter the two strains marry and paralyse each other—she has to act out the awful little allegory once over before she is free of it.[10]

This remark has the tone of a psychoanalytic lecture ("her case is complicated by the fact . . ."), and we are reassured that the sentiments to be expressed, however "awful" they may at first appear, are only the stuff of "allegory," and a "little" allegory at that. After such an introduction, one might expect a sharply ironic dramatic monologue that exhibits its speaker as a case history, and yet, as we shall see in our consideration of Plath, the relationship between poet and speaker in the poem itself is nowhere near that simple.

The uncertain attitude of the confessional poets toward the confessional impulse in their own poems arises, I believe, from the inherent ambiguity of self-disclosure considered as a social act. This ambiguity can be traced in the history of the word "confess" itself. To "confess" means, in its most familiar sense, "to declare or disclose (something which one has kept or allowed to remain secret as being prejudicial to oneself); to acknowledge, own, or admit (a crime, charge, fault, weakness, or the like)" (*Oxford English Dictionary*, 1). Such disclosure is self-accusatory; one renders oneself up for judgment by others. One's status in the eyes of others is lowered by the admission. One makes the admission nonetheless in the hope of repairing one's relations with the community to which one confesses. This implication is clear in the institution of confession in the Catholic Church. The concealment of fault has cut the individual off from the community of the faithful, and only through confession can membership in the community be restored.

The situation becomes more complicated, however, when one does not share society's judgment that what one acknowledges is indeed a "crime" or "fault." In that case, openly revealing what others will condemn becomes a way of asserting one's independence. To "confess" does not always entail an admission of guilt; it can also mean "to own, avow, declare belief in or adhesion to" (*Oxford English Dictionary*, 4). There is also an obsolete reflexive form that means "to make oneself known, disclose one's identity" (*Oxford English Dictionary*, 1b). These forms are self-assertive, or even defiant—one is unafraid to make one's beliefs known or to reveal one's true identity, regardless of other people's response to the disclosure.[11]

Robert Lowell's "Words for Hart Crane" provides a full but compact example of the tension between these two kinds of "confession" in confessional poetry, and of its close relation to the difficulty of choosing between ironic detachment and lyrical endorsement of the speaking voice:

"When the Pulitzers showered on some dope
or screw who flushed our dry mouths out with soap,
few people would consider why I took
to stalking sailors, and scattered Uncle Sam's
phony gold-plated laurels to the birds.
Because I knew my Whitman like a book,
Stranger in America, tell my country: I,
Catullus redivivus, once the rage
of the Village and Paris, used to play my role
of homosexual, wolfing the stray lambs
who hungered by the Place de la Concorde.
My profit was a profit with a hole.
Who asks for me, the Shelley of my age,
must lay his heart out for my bed and board." [12]

This poem, it must be acknowledged, is not directly "confessional" at all. The quotation marks remind us simultaneously that it is not Lowell who speaks, and that it is Lowell who has put these words in Crane's mouth. We are not getting a self-effacing homage to Crane, but an active appropriation of him. The title and quotation marks distance the utterance from the literal "I" of the poet, as in a dramatic monologue, though without the specificity of occasion that a dramatic monologue usually has. At the same time, they also signal a greater degree of identification between poet and speaker than is usual for a dramatic monologue; the poem is thus a sort of compromise between lyrical and dramatic conventions.

Considered as if it were really Crane's utterance, the poem seems at first glance defiant. The American society of Crane's time appears throughout as contemptible. It rewards the poet only when, out of stupidity ("some dope") or complicity ("or screw"), he affirms prudish, middle-class morality. Its "phony gold-plated laurels" reveal not only that it conceives of worth only as money (gold), but also that it cares only for the outward appearance of worth (gold-*plated*). So Crane scatters such prizes "to the winds" and, in programmatic defiance of middle-class morality, takes "to stalking sailors." He speaks of himself as the Shelley of his age, striking the pose of the poet as visionary prophet. Thus far, the speaker would seem to have achieved a more authentic self, a more detached perspective from which to condemn his society.

A closer look forces us to qualify this judgment. For one thing, the "Pulitzers" have not been showering on Crane but on poets he despises. One cannot scatter to the winds what one does not have. Crane is trying to reject American culture partly because it has rejected him. His flamboyant homosexuality, intended (or so the poem would have it) to shock others into recognition of their prudishness, provokes little thought whatsoever ("few would consider why"). Indeed, as the poem tells us, homosexuality is an available "role," a form of rebellion licensed by society as part of the poet's bohemianism. But to indulge rebellion as bohemianism is to rob it of its critical force. The final two lines are especially double-edged: Crane tells us that if we ask for him, we must surrender ourselves completely, lay our hearts out for his bed and board. In a sense, this is defiance—'if you want anything to do with me,' the poet says, 'you must take me on my own terms'—but it is also a confession of weakness. The poet is incapable of securing bed and board for himself. Lowell's Crane, an outcast "stranger in America," asks us to rescue him from his loneliness by understanding him. One can argue that Crane recognizes something hollow and insecure in his own gestures of rebellion, that he is self-critical and divided rather than simply defiant. He is caught in the attitude that Richard Sennett has called "disobedient dependence." [13] Without a philistine bystander for him to shock, his occupation would be gone.

Of course, the words of the poem are really Lowell's, not Crane's. Lowell makes Crane speak of himself in the past tense, as if he were looking back from a detached perspective after his own death. To look at the poem as Lowell's utterance is to raise the question of Lowell's implied relation to Crane. At first, that relation would seem to be primarily one of identification. The title itself suggests that Lowell is speaking through Crane rather than putting him on stage like one of Browning's characters. Coming as it does just before an autobiographical sequence that describes Lowell's recurrent episodes of madness, the poem implicitly links Crane's abnormality to his own. Moreover, by making Crane recite his lineage, his poetic descent from Catullus, Shelley, and Whitman, Lowell tacitly implies that he joins Crane as their inheritor—a defiant, if oblique, proclamation of self-worth in the face of all the humiliation that the autobiographical poems will reveal.

Once again, however, a second look brings second thoughts. For one thing, Lowell himself had won the Pulitzer Prize for *Lord Weary's Castle*, as most of his readers would have been aware. Did he, then, belong among the "dopes" and "screws" rather than the illustrious company of Catullus, Shelley, Whitman, and Crane? Moreover, unlike the financially insecure Crane, Lowell lived in material comfort, whatever his inward torments, all his life, except for his five-month stint in prison as a conscientious objector. In a later poem, "Second Shelley," Lowell would depict himself standing in a luxuriously appointed room with "oak mantel, panels, oak linoleum tiles," imagining what would happen to Shelley in such posh surroundings:

Here, the light of anarchy would harden in his eyes;
soon he starves his genius for denial,
thinks a clink in the heating, the chirp of birds,
and turns with the tread of an ox to serve the rich,
trusting his genius and a hand from his father
will lift his feet from the mud of the republic.[14]

Within *Life Studies* itself, Lowell writes of his residence on "'hardly passionate Marlborough Street'" and wonders whether he has lost his former capacity for defiance. If "Words for Hart Crane" implies Lowell's identification with Crane, it also implies his doubts of his own worthiness to claim that identification. And yet that very hesitancy reinforces the identification, for Crane too harbors self-doubt and even self-contempt beneath his grandiose defiance. The success of this poem, which manages to state the ambivalences of the confessional attitude clearly and strongly, without veering into blurred confusion on the one side or grandiose claims of insight on the other, may well owe something to the fact that it is autobiographical only by indirection. Very few of Lowell's overtly confessional poems have comparable restraint, balance, and compression. The best poems of Lowell and Plath, the most accomplished of the confessional poets, are usually half-confessional only. They deal with extreme emotional states and sometimes with the theme of individual suffering as inner registration of outward turmoil. One can recognize the experience of the poet in them, whether by internal hints or by clues from their context among other poems, but they often leave the literal details unspecified, to be supplied by implication or by other writings. "Words For Hart Crane," a dramatic monologue that strongly suggests analogies between Crane's situation and Lowell's, is a poem of this kind.

As Lowell's attempt to provide his confessional poems with a literary lineage suggests, the confessional idea of the poet as representative victim grows out of earlier modernist conceptions of poetic vocation. One might begin with Ezra Pound's famous remark that "artists are the antennae of the race." "If this statement is incomprehensible and if its corollaries need any explanation," Pound elaborated, "let me put it

that a nation's writers are the voltometers and steam-gauges of that nation's intellectual life. They are the registering instruments, and if they
falsify their reports there is no measure to the harm that they do."[15]
Implicit in Pound's metaphors are two notions: that poets function as a
sort of early warning system, alerting the less sensitive to historical
change as soon as it can be detected; and that the most important poetic faculty is not imagination, in the Romantic sense, but an exceptionally acute receptivity to the movement of the surrounding world.
Poetry attempts to constitute what Charles Hartman has called the
"circumambience," the whole milieu in which the poet lives and
works.[16]

It might seem impossible to arrive, by receptivity alone, at anything
more than raw materials for poetry, an ever mounting pile of fragments
shored against one's ruin. But as Arthur Mizener has observed, Pound
and Eliot have "an almost mystical theory of perception" in which
"every pattern of feelings has its pattern of objects and events, so that
if the writer can set down the pattern of objects in exactly the right
relations, without irrelevances or distortions, they will evoke in the
reader the pattern of feelings."[17] I put aside for later discussion the objection that the writer can never set down "objects," but only words
intended to evoke the objects, and turn to another: that the "right relations" cannot be derived from the original context of the images in experience, or from any shared connotations, whether suggested by convention or by the properties of the object evoked. In *The Use of Poetry
and the Use of Criticism*, Eliot claims that an author's imagery

comes from the whole of his sensitive life since early childhood. Why, for all
of us, out of all that we have heard, seen, felt, in a lifetime, do certain images
recur, charged with emotion, rather than others? The song of one bird, the
leap of one fish, at a particular place and time, the scent of one flower, an
old woman on a German mountain path, six ruffians seen through an open
window playing cards at night at a small French railway junction where
there was a water-mill: such memories may have symbolic value, but of
what we cannot tell, for they come to represent the depths of feeling into
which we cannot peer.[18]

As Eliot had written many years earlier in "Tradition and the Individual Talent," "the poet's mind is in fact a receptacle for seizing and stor-
ing up numberless feelings, phrases, images, which remain there until
all the particles which can unite to form a new compound are present
together."[19] But the feelings, phrases, and images have been shorn of
their original context, and their place in the "new compound" has
nothing to do with the story of how they were acquired in experience.

Now, suppose a poet has been trained up in modernism, which teaches him to draw poems out of images that have mysterious power over him, but has lost Eliot's mystical faith that such images are objective correlatives of inward states. It is likely that such a poet would begin tracing the emotional power of the images back to their context in experience. The fact that one is moved by the recollection of a fish leaping in a certain place and time would no longer be taken as a guarantee that others would also be moved; we all have a private network of symbols, partly shared with others in proportion to our intimacy with them, significant to others only insofar as they know the stories of our lives or can recognize the symbols as corresponding to something in their own experience. Autobiography becomes a way of including the context of such symbols in poetry, of admitting the reader to the degree of intimacy necessary to share the symbolism.

It may be objected that what I describe is metonymy, which, Marjorie Perloff has argued, replaces symbolism in the poems of *Life Studies*.[20] But the distinction between metonymy and symbolism is one of degree rather than an absolute distinction of kind, since even the most elusive symbols finally owe their suggestiveness to contexts in experience. Eliot's "song of one bird" or "leap of one fish" are particular instances of what turn out to be rather conventional poetic symbols. Maybe no one else has heard that one bird or seen that one fish, but there are equivalents in most people's experience—including their experience of poems that use birds and fish as symbols. Eliot concedes as much by using the generic "fish" and "bird," as opposed to, say, "muskelunge" or "nightingale" (which would already begin to specify place as well, since the first is found in America and the second in Europe). In such cases, where the resonance of the symbol arises from its familiar natural properties, and thus has been apparent to many people already, we may forget that the symbolism depends on context, because the context in question is so unproblematic and universally available.

Those "six ruffians playing cards at night at a small French railway junction where there was a water-mill" are another matter; this image calls our attention to the problem of context, since the conjunction of details seems so purely fortuitous. Most people have seen a fish and heard a bird, but even those who have been to France are unlikely to have glimpsed a scene quite like the one Eliot describes. But if one happens to know about Eliot's nostalgia for the organic community of a bygone preindustrial Europe, his choice of this image no longer seems purely arbitrary. It evokes a simpler, less hurried life still partly preserved in a small French town, where the water mill has survived despite the incursion of the railway; the easy comradery of the "ruffians" contrasts with the anomie of the city-dwellers crossing London Bridge in *The Waste Land.* Eliot, more than most poets, needed to prevent the left hand from knowing what the right hand was doing; the depths of feeling are not quite so impenetrable as he would have us believe.

To the extent that confessionalism represented a distrust of absolute mystical correspondences, it pointed toward a poetry of narrative, emphasizing the contextual origins of symbols. It promised a greater density of detail, a more historical mode in which symbolic implications arise gradually out of particulars. Lowell, after criticizing the "Alexandrian" poetry of the fifties for its inability to "handle much experience," remarked that "prose is in many ways better off than poetry," and in his own commentary on "Skunk Hour" he speculated that "the best style for poetry was . . . something like the prose of Chekhov and Flaubert." [21] The idea of reviving narrative poetry, and of developing a poetic style that could handle particular detail and social nuance in the manner of late nineteenth-century fiction, is completely separable from the commitment to autobiography, and yet it is, I believe, the most valuable contribution that confessional poetry had to make. Some of Lowell's best poems, and to a lesser extent, Plath's and Berryman's, succeed in restoring to poetry the sorts of materials formerly ceded to prose. But unfortunately, if predictably, it was the autobiographical impulse that attracted immediate attention. For the most part, "experience" meant in practice the poet's, not other people's, and it was to be actual rather than imagined.

The emphasis on the actual encouraged poets to forget that experience can enter poetry only as it is mediated by language. Lowell, Berryman, and Plath had worked too long and hard at the technical demands of their art to forget this entirely, but in a confessional poet of the second rank such as Anne Sexton, the damage done by such literalism becomes all too obvious. Nonetheless, even the most skillful of the confessional poets spoke disparagingly of technique, as if it meant the pursuit of empty formal ingenuity, and did not include the search for language that sounded the resonances of experience and clarified its significance. For Lowell one must make a partial exception; he remarked that "Almost the whole problem of writing poetry is to bring it back to what you really feel, and that takes an awful lot of maneuvering." But this was also the occasion of his critique of "Alexandrian" craftsmanship and of his declaration that he was no longer able to "get [his] experience into tight metrical forms." He praised Delmore Schwartz for the "revelation" that "the poet who had experience was very much better than the poet with polish." [22]

There is a fine line between redefining craftsmanship to include the adequacy of language to experience and setting up experience and craftsmanship as mutually opposed qualities. Here we return again to the legacy of modernism. Eliot and Pound never tired of praising exactness in poetry, but by this neoclassicizing rhetoric they meant something quite un-classical. They sought exactness in conveying the elusive texture of consciousness itself; already, they come close to Lowell's redefinition of craftsmanship as bringing language back to "what you really feel." The difficulty in such a conception is the lack of anything reducible to an Aristotelian *techne*. What Eliot said of criticism might also be said of poetic composition as he conceived of it: "the only method is to be very intelligent." [23] Hence Mizener's slight oversimplification in taking the stylistic mediation of "objects" for granted in his summary of the modernist doctrine of correspondences. Eliot and Pound at times come close to the idea that right language flows from right consciousness: cultivate a sensibility attuned to the "mind of Europe," be attentive to the elusive stirrings of your own sensibility, and the words will slowly form themselves in the depths, like the pearls and coral of Ariel's song in *The Tempest*. The imagery of "Kubla Khan,"

whatever its origins in Coleridge's reading, sank to the depths of Coleridge's feeling, was saturated, transformed there—'those are pearls that were his eyes'—and brought up into daylight again.

For Eliot, this saturation, though it can create language rich in suggestiveness, is not in itself enough. In "Kubla Khan," the imagery "has not been *used;* the poem has not been written." [24] But in contemporary poetry, the check of traditional formal demands on the language of authenticity is very much attenuated; poets such as Lowell, who benefited from traditional constraints themselves, undervalued the contribution of such constraints to their own accomplishment.

For the confessional poet's assumption that significant experience is painful experience, and that poets must therefore be unhappy if they are to be profound, we may partly blame another legacy from modernism: the conception of the *poète maudit*, wounded for the transgressions of his spiritually disordered society. This conception reinforces all too well the idea we have already traced through the social criticism of the fifties and sixties, that the suffering of the self arises from the internalization of cultural crisis. But it has also the further implication that the poet's experience is more authentic than other people's. If one believes that the poet is a receptor, uncommonly sensitive to the surrounding world, and the surrounding world is in a bad state, it follows with syllogistic precision that the poet ought to suffer horribly and that his suffering is itself a sign of his uncommon sensitivity. It also follows that others, not sharing his extraordinary receptivity, will be smugly insensitive to the true horror of their situation. Lowell, Berryman, and Plath often appear to assume, like Ginsberg, that madness singles out the "best minds" for destruction.

In 1952, before confessional poetry was dreamed of, Allen Tate declared that when a poet such as Blake, Poe, Baudelaire, or Eliot gives us a version of hell,

his hell has not been "for those other people": he has reported his own. His report upon his own spiritual condition, in the last hundred years, has misled the banker and the statesman into the illusion that they have no hell because, as secularists, they have lacked the language to report it.[25]

When Tate saw the manuscript of *Life Studies* late in 1957, he was repelled much as his banker and statesman would have been repelled by Baudelaire, had they read him; he urged Lowell not to publish the book.[26] Lowell might well have replied that he was taking his old mentor at his word, reporting his own hell in the approved modernist manner. If Tate did not recognize his own hell in Lowell's, that was because he wanted the report rendered *alter idem*, in symbols or objective correlatives. Lowell was giving it to him straight, finding a "secularist" language for hell after all by stripping away the essentially religious faith in symbolic correspondences. What he had left was himself as metaphor, the poet as representative man only by virtue of his representative suffering.

The idea that the poet's suffering is in and of itself desirable, as a sign of election, can occasionally be found in the writings of the confessional poets themselves. Lowell, in a letter to John Berryman (15 March 1959), speculates that

there's something curious twisted and against the grain about the world poets of our generation have had to live in. What troubles you and I, Ted Roethke, Elizabeth Bishop, Delmore, Randall—even Karl Shapiro—have had. I hope your exaustion [*sic*] is nothing very drastic; these knocks are almost a proof of intelligence and valor in us.[27]

In that last sentence, one hears the fatal temptation of the confessional poet: a lyrical desire for suffering, as if suffering were a muse to be wooed, a destiny to be courted—the source or proof of poetic sensitivity rather than an unfortunate by-product of it. And there is something curiously naïve, for a poet as steeped in history as Lowell, about the assumption that his own time was uniquely difficult, for poets or for anybody else. Nonetheless, these remarks were off the record, in a letter to a friend in the art; they were not intended as a public statement. And in hoping that Berryman's exhaustion was "nothing very drastic," Lowell stopped short of wishing for still more "proof of intelligence and valor"; the suffering one can't avoid will suffice.

By 1972, thirteen years and many volumes of confessional verse later, Berryman himself, speaking on the record in an interview for the *Paris Review*, was hoping that his troubles would prove as drastic as possible. An artist, he claimed, must desire to be "presented with the worst possible ordeal that will not actually kill him."[28] And in an earlier interview for the *Massachusetts Review* (1970), his version of the argument that society causes the poet's troubles has an oddly petulant tone:

You ask me why my generation [by which, incidentally, poets of Berryman's generation usually mean poets only, not the rest of their contemporaries] seems so screwed up? . . . it seems to me that they have every right to be disturbed. The current American society would drive anybody out of his skull, anybody who is at all responsive; it's almost unbearable. . . . From public officials we expect to get lies, and we get them in profusion. . . . Perhaps Sylvia Plath did the necessary thing by putting her head in the oven, having to live with all those lies.[29]

Again, as in Lowell's letter of 1959, there is a naïve sense that one's own time is uniquely terrible—as if public officials had not been lying since the dawn of history. Had Berryman never read Thucydides? But the unwittingly revealing word here is "right": They have every *right* to be disturbed, as if "disturbed" were what we all wanted to be, if only we had the courage to claim the disturbance to which we are entitled.

When the vocation of poetry requires the courting of "ordeal," the poet must try to suffer as much as possible, in order to have "experience" for poems, without actually dying—after all, death would mean no more poems. Poetry becomes less an art than a melodrama of risk or, as Robert Lowell described it in his "Foreword" to *Ariel*, a form of "Russian roulette with six cartridges in the cylinder, a game of 'chicken,' the wheels of both cars locked and unable to swerve."[30]

Looking at the poems that Lowell, Plath, and Berryman have left us, I am inclined to believe that the confessional impulse turns out to have been most fruitful for poems that are not themselves especially confessional. Such public poems as Lowell's "For the Union Dead" and "Waking Early Sunday Morning" do not include autobiographical revelations, and they do not offer personal crisis as a metaphor for national crisis. And yet their use of particular social detail (especially in "For the Union Dead") and plain diction would not have been conceivable without the confessional poems in *Life Studies*. There are also a number of poems in which the private is content to remain historically unrepresentative. Harriet Winslow's death in "Soft Wood," for instance, does not represent anything moribund in America, capitalism, or the New England tradition. Her death acquires shared meaning without psycho-political forcing, as the occasion of a meditation on the brevity of human life amid the apparent permanence of nature (the seals that "must live as long as the Scholar Gypsy") and of inanimate objects ("the possessors seldom outlast their possessions, / once warped and mothered by their touch"). It is true that without the lifting of the taboo on direct autobiographical revelation, parts of this poem could not have been written, especially the opening of its last stanza: "Harriet Winslow, who owned this house, / was more to me than my mother."[31] But it is not a confessional poem.

With Plath, too, the most ostentatiously confessional poems, such as "Daddy" and "Lady Lazarus," are not necessarily the ones that wear best, although without the biographical context they provide, more oblique lyrics such as "The Moon and the Yew Tree" or the bee-keeping sequence would fail to release some of their resonance. Now that all of Plath's poems have been available for some while, in approximate chronological order, one can see the extent to which the poems gradually build a context for each other. Plath kept returning, with almost obsessive insistence, to a constellation of central motifs; her use of these in one poem often enriches its implications in another. But by the same token, the self-revelatory poems lose their centrality; most of what we need to know about Plath's life for an understanding of her poetry can be inferred gradually from the cumulative testimony of her work.

With Berryman, the adoption of "Henry" as a persona mitigates the bluntness of self-disclosure. So does his self-deprecatory wit. Lowell and Plath are seldom funny, and even when they are, theirs is a muted, saturnine humor. Already by the fourth Dream Song, Berryman has struck a comic note never sounded in their poetry:

> and only the fact of her husband & four other people
> kept me from springing on her
> or falling at her little feet and crying
> 'You are the hottest one for years of night
> Henry's dazed eyes
> have enjoyed, Brilliance.' I advanced upon
> (despairing) my spumoni.[32]

Much as I like Berryman at his best, I have omitted detailed discussion of his work, because he seems less "confessional," in the sense defined by Rosenthal and Alvarez, than Lowell and Plath. Although

Berryman occasionally claimed representative implications for his private suffering (as in the *Massachusetts Review* interview quoted earlier), the poems seldom draw the sorts of parallels between personal and social history that one finds in those of Lowell and Plath, who, between them, define a polarity within the confessional mode. Lowell's poetry as a rule is more anecdotal, socially detailed, and topical than Plath's—the recovery for poetry of a socially populated world, like that of the nineteenth-century novel, was important to him. And although there are many poems which, like "Soft Wood," are content to rest in an essentially personal occasion, Lowell usually peered intently past the details of his life, hoping to glimpse just behind them the shadow of history. Far more than Plath, he consciously sought historical ramifications within autobiography. If this quest sometimes gave his poetry greater range and ambition than hers, it also could result in forced connections and bombast. Plath's art is narrower than his, but purer; less intelligent, but also less calculating. And if one may say of Lowell that he tried to use the events of his life to illuminate history, one may say of Plath that she tried to discover in history analogies sufficient to the almost incommunicable strangeness that she found in her own life.

4

Robert Lowell: The Historical Self and the Limits of "Conflation"

Of all the poets considered here, Robert Lowell has proved the hardest to place in context. He did more than any other poet to raise the confessional mode to critical respectability, and yet the relationship of his work as a whole to confessional poetics is extremely complicated. After Allen Ginsberg, he was the poet most visibly connected to the antiwar movement of the late 1960s. And yet Lowell's political activism is shot through with misgivings and criticism of the New Left's excesses. If Alan Williamson could portray him in 1974 as a poet whose "political vision" had much in common with the radicalism of Marcuse and Norman O. Brown, Robert von Hallberg could find in him, ten years later, a "liberal" and "centrist" persevering amid extremists.[1] Both portraits contain a measure of truth. The question to be asked about Lowell, then, is this: To what extent did his skeptical intelligence enable him to escape being the disciple of the age and become its critic as well as its inheritor?

Lowell's skeptical intelligence was one of his strengths, but the accompanying weakness was diffusion, complexity so nuanced or fraught with self-canceling tension as to paralyze all sympathy and judgment. Characteristic of Lowell is an ambivalence about ambivalence. At times, this poet wanted to be a visionary prophet, writing from inspiration that admits no doubt, in sonorous language and numinous imagery; at other times (or at the same time, within the same poem), he suspected that this visionary impulse was a trap, analogous in its seductive delusion to the manic episodes that repeatedly threw his personal life into chaos and to the longings for omnipotence and splendor that tempt the powerful. He often presents himself as torn between the promptings of imagination, sexual impulse, or the longing for an earthly paradise (three things that are, for him, closely related), which he cannot think of as compatible with stability, and the competing attractions of self-distrust, irony, and skepticism, unseductive to be sure, but productive of sanity, continuity, and domestic peace. Lowell felt himself to be faced with a choice between a liberating but also destructive assertion of pure desire, or a clarifying but also withering sanity. "Cured," he wrote in "Home After Two Months Away," "I am frizzled, stale and small."[2] The choice of allegiance between the eruptive id and the socialized ego, so absolute for Ginsberg, cannot be absolute for Lowell, though he shares with his contemporaries the yearning "to break loose," as he puts it in "Waking Early Sunday Morning," from restraints.

"Bishop Berkeley" (*H*, 72) shows the dialectic of desire and self-distrust with unusual completeness, revealing its connection to literature, politics, and sexual morals:

> The Bishop's solipsism is clerical,
> no one was much imperiled by his life,
> except he sailed to New England and was Irish,
> he wasn't an Attila or Rimbaud
> driven to unhook his skull to crack the world.
> He lived with quality, and thought the world
> was only perceptions that he could perceive. . . .
> In Mexico, I too caused my private earthquake
> and made the earth tremble in the soles of my feet;
> a local insurrection of my blood,
> its river system saying: I am I,
> I am Whitman, I am Berkeley, all men—
> calming my feet in a tub of lukewarm water;
> the water that scalded one foot froze the other.

Berkeley's "clerical" solipsism derives from an epistemological skepticism; the more dangerous kind of solipsism, by which other people are "imperiled," arises from certainty rather than doubt. Attila and Rimbaud, the brutal conquerer and the visionary poet, occupy the same category of dangerous solipsist. Each "unhooks his skull"—frees it, that is, of fastenings and constraints—with an aggressive intention "to crack the world." Unlike Berkeley, for whom "the world / was only perceptions that he could perceive," these aggressive solipsists imagine that the world is more, rather than less, than it seems to most people. For Attila, the world was space he had to dominate; for Rimbaud, it was a realm of mystical transformation by the alchemy of the word. Berkeley "lived with quality" (a pun, surely, combining the social and philosophical meanings of this word); his solipsism is more accommodating.

Halfway through the poem, Lowell turns to his own experience, making the oft-invoked connection between public and private, self and history. But he does it in a different and more complicated way than Ginsberg, Plath—or the Lowell, it must be said, of certain other poems. The "private earthquake" is presumably the love affair chronicled in the sequence "Mexico" (*N II* 101–7), though the reassignment of the sequence, revised and trimmed from twelve poems to ten, to *For Lizzie and Harriet* rather than *History* separates the allusion from its source. An illicit love affair, like the project of visionary poetry or of world conquest, belongs in the category of dangerous, or aggressive solipsism. In the cases of illicit love and conquest, it is easy to see why. Both of these activities favor the id rather than the ego, the pleasure rather than the reality principle—they are solipsistic in the sense that they value one's own desire absolutely, ignoring the pain of the conquered enemy or abandoned wife. But why is the visionary poet like them?

We have already seen a partial answer to this question in "Words for Hart Crane," where the visionary poet's faithfulness to an intimation of absolute reality unrecognized within the quotidian social world compels him to reject the claims of ordinary responsibility to others. In "Bishop Berkeley," the poet does not so much reject others as appropriate them. His "private earthquake," beginning as "a local resurrection," spreads from the simple assertion of identity ("I am I") to a grandiose claim of oneness with "all men," but there is an intermediate step. "I am Whitman," Lowell says, asserting identity with the poet most famous for such assertions: "In all people I see myself, none more and not one a barleycorn less."[3] As Whitman, Lowell can become Bishop Berkeley, the subject of the present poem, or anyone else. Whitmanian identification with the other risks solipsism in assuming that by seeing oneself in others, one discovers an identity within difference. Perhaps, instead, one turns the world into a huge vanity-mirror.

Whitman, like Crane and Rimbaud, provides Lowell with a figure of the visionary poet, "driven to unhook his skull to crack the world." The momentary sense of identity with "all men" is exciting but, in the end, untrustworthy. The poet describes himself in the closing lines "calming [his] feet in a tub of lukewarm water; / the water that scalded one foot froze the other." The image of soaking one's feet is self-deflating to begin with (cf. the ending of "Ezra Pound": "'I began with a swelled head and end with swelled feet'" [*H*, 140]), and the choice of "lukewarm" makes the irony sharper. In the last line, the poet who was a moment ago claiming identity with "all men" has disintegrated to the point where his own two feet do not share a common perception of the same reality. The water, he knows, is "lukewarm," but neither foot experiences it that way, as each errs in a different direction. The visionary poet's claim of absolute intuition, far from leaping over the gap between subject and object, uniting all in an intuitive unity, may result in a complete disunity of experience. A poem such as "Bishop Berkeley" shows how much the view of Lowell as conflater of inner and outer, or of private and historical realities, needs to be cross-examined, for on this occasion at least, Lowell wrote as if such identifications were not a solution but a problem, a source of illusion and self-deception requiring investigation. Although one voice in Lowell's poetry calls for visionary collapsing of distinctions, another mutters suspiciously against such grandiose presumptions.

This internal debate had been quite fully pursued by the time Lowell came to write "Bishop Berkeley," but its dialectic began with the visionary thesis, which only gradually called forth its skeptical antithesis. The poet of *Land of Unlikeness* (1944) and *Lord Weary's Castle* (1946) presents himself as a religious visionary, prophesying against the nations for the sin of World War II. The problems with that visionary stance are manifested by the poems but not addressed in them; R. P. Blackmur seems aware of them in his famous, if oracular, remark about *Land of Unlikeness*—that "in dealing with men," Lowell's "faith compels him to be fractiously vindictive, and in dealing with faith his experience of men compels him to be nearly blasphemous."[4] To some extent, the voice of the earlier poetry imitates that of Old Testament prophecy; Lowell sets up as Isaiah or Jeremiah. These prophets are at one and the same time representative victims of the Lord's anger and instruments of it; they share the suffering of Israel but understand that suffering as others do not.

In some of the early poems, Lowell similarly views himself as representative of a collective "we," a violent and sacrilegious people that does not foresee, as he does, the retribution that awaits it—and himself:

> O Christ, the spiralling years
> Slither with child and manger to a ball
> Of ice; and what is man? We tear our rags
> To hang the Furies by their itching ears
> And the green needles nail us to the wall.
>
> ("Christmas in Black Rock," LWC, 6)

The poet, presumably, is nailed there along with the rest of us. More characteristically, however, he denounces society from higher ground, claiming the authority of religious faith; at times he indulges in a most un-Christian enjoyment of the wrath he expects God to visit on the rest of us, as in the magnificent but sadistic peroration of "The Quaker Graveyard in Nantucket":

You could cut the brackish winds with a knife
Here in Nantucket, and cast up the time
When the Lord God formed man from the sea's slime
And breathed into his face the breath of life,
And blue-lung'd combers lumbered to the kill.
The Lord survives the rainbow of His will.

(*LWC*, 14)

Even in this, however, Lowell does not depart entirely from prophetic tradition; the literary imagination of Jeremiah and Isaiah often reaches fullest stretch in its depiction of divine vengeance. The difficulty arises when we consider what Lowell is prophesying against. The main target of his zeal in *Lord Weary's Castle* is not hedonism or religious lassitude, but an alternative form of Christian zeal. He holds Protestantism, and in particular American Puritanism, responsible for a fanatically violent strain in American culture, and even for American participation in World War II. The violent religious certainty he denounces in his Puritan ancestors resembles too closely the violent religious certainty of his denunciation. What the poems ask us to take as a prophet's quarrel with his sinful nation looks more like the spectacle of a man shouting at his own image in the mirror. He unwittingly imitates the Puritan in his own nearly blasphemous assumption of rectitude, his own fractiously vindictive attack on those who fail to meet the standards of that rectitude.

One might view the apocalyptic rhetoric of *Lord Weary's Castle* as literary contrivance, a calculated attempt, as Irvin Ehrenpreis put it, "to produce a heat wave in a cold climate."[5] But Lowell's account of his mental breakdown in April 1949 shows how closely this imagery is tied to his own experience; the visionary symbolism of the poems resembles the delusions of his manic episodes. Although these episodes did not begin until after the early poems were written, their symbolism must have been deeply rooted in Lowell's imagination:

The night before I was locked up I ran about the streets of Bloomington Indiana crying out against devils and homosexuals. I believed I could stop cars and paralyze their forces by merely standing in the middle of the highway with my arms outspread. Each car carried a long rod above its tail-light, and the rods were adorned with diabolic Indian or Voodoo signs. Bloomington stood for Joyce's hero and Christian regeneration. Indiana stood for the evil, unexorcised, aboriginal Indians. I suspected I was a reincarnation of the Holy Ghost, and had become homicidally hallucinated.[6]

The sentences about Bloomington and Indiana could easily be spun into a parody of a New Critical commentary on one of the poems. The materials of poetic and psychotic imagination, moreover, are strikingly similar. While in the grip of his delusion, Lowell resembles both the Puritan ancestors he denounces in "At the Indian Killer's Grave" and the speaker of "Where the Rainbow Ends," who claims, like an Old Testament prophet, to be "a red arrow on this graph / Of Revelations," the chosen "victim" standing before "the lion, lamb, and beast / Who fans the furnace-face of IS with wings" (*LWC*, 69). Accuser and accused are united in a common rhetoric of self-righteousness. Self and other, inner and outer, are indeed "conflated," as Axelrod put it, in this early poetry—so much so that the conflation is seldom recognized self-consciously in the poems themselves. It is through his later attempt to avoid resigning himself to destructive illusions as if they were necessity, and flying in the face of necessity as if it were an illusion, that Lowell became aware of the unclear boundary between inner and outer as a problem.

Life Studies, of course, has been almost universally regarded as the most important turning point in Lowell's career and the book in which, as Ehrenpreis claimed as early as 1965, the poet's autobiography "became the analogue of the life of his era; the sufferings of the poet became a mirror of the sufferings of whole classes and nations."[7] In 1983, Mark Rudman was still arguing, similarly, that *Life Studies* "is a microcosmic portrait of American society in a time of crisis."[8] Most critics, from Ehrenpreis to Rudman and down to the present day, have understood this book as Lowell's unveiling of himself as historically representative man; they have praised it as a daring exploration of painful experience and as an ambitious, secular restatement of the prophetic claims of the earlier poetry. But, as Williamson has been virtually alone in recognizing, *Life Studies* is also, in some important respects, a work of retrenchment. Although it narrates emotionally violent experience, the manner of the poetry often seems designed to "hold the chaos of experience at a distance."[9]

Life Studies begins the work of separating and clarifying experience without which it is hard to imagine Lowell continuing to progress as a poet. This analytic emphasis on distinctions concerns technique as well as theme; as Stephen Yenser remarks in discussing "My Last Afternoon with Uncle Devereux Winslow," "the peculiarity" of the style "seems at first almost opposite to that of Lowell's earlier poetry, where the images were welded to one another and the problem was separating them in order to understand what was going on. Here the images are laid next to one another like bricks, and the difficulty is discovering what relationship they have to one another."[10] Morally, the emphasis has shifted from emphatic judgment to inquiry, from prophetic self-asser-tion to ironic self-questioning. Until he could prevent the self from thinking it *was* history, the mediating transactions between history and the self remained invisible to him. Axelrod's "conflation," Ehrenpreis's "mirroring," and Rudman's "microcosm" all suggest an immediate and perfectly transparent translatability of public and private experience into each other. To the extent that the poems really do imply such inter-changeability, they participate in a form of sentimentality characteris-tic of their age; to the extent that they pose the relationship in more complex terms, they escape a disabling trap.

The attempt at disentanglement in *Life Studies* does not always suc-ceed, nor is there any reason to suppose that it was uppermost in Lowell's hierarchy of intentions as he wrote. That it was among his in-tentions, however, seems clear from a remark near the beginning of "91 Revere Street," the prose memoir that prepares the reader for the autobiographical sequence at the end of the volume. Lowell says that the Revere Street house of his childhood is

a setting now fixed in the mind, where it survives all the distortions of fan-tasy, all the blank befogging of forgetfulness. There, the vast number of re-membered *things* remains rocklike. Each is in its place, each has its function, its history, its drama. There, all is preserved by that motherly care that one either ignored or resented in his youth. The things and their owners come back urgent with life and meaning—because finished, they are endurable and perfect.

(*LS*, 12–13)

If the poet's memory summons the immediacy of experience, "urgent with life and meaning," it does so by a displacement that protects against both the pain of that experience, making it "endurable," and "the distortions of fantasy." "The things" stand between "their owners" and the poet; like the shield of Perseus, they make it possible to look at something too disturbing to be seen directly. Moreover, they constitute *evidence* by which "the blank befogging of forgetfulness" can be overcome: "each has its function, its history, its drama." In contrast to Sylvia Plath, who elaborates from "the distortions of fantasy" a myth of her own fate, Lowell clings to the things, and what he knows of their "history," as a check on subjective misperception. The emphasis on things, as I noted in discussing Ginsberg's "Howl," is common in the fifties formalism *Life Studies* supposedly repudiates. But whereas the earlier kind of poem, as Charles Molesworth observes, makes the "gesture of holding up an object taken from its context,"[11] Lowell (like Elizabeth Bishop, whose influence on *Life Studies* is not limited to "Skunk Hour") uses the object to reconstruct a context.

Consider, as an example of Lowell's autobiography through things, the poem "Father's Bedroom," in which the poet's father is represented entirely by the interior of a room. When the poet was a child, we are told in "91 Revere Street," his parents would withdraw to the bedroom to argue; listening through the wall, he "felt drenched in [his] parents' passions" (*LS*, 19). After his father's death at Beverly Farms, he can enter the inner sanctum of those passions and return unscathed. (Doubtless the fact that this is not literally the same bedroom as the one on Revere Street also lessens the anxiety.) Once the locus of marital conflict, the bedroom now has an aura of almost exaggerated calm: the color-coordinated, fine blue threads of the bedspread, the "blue dots on the curtains," the "blue kimono," the "sandpapered neatness" of the floor. The room is in effect the father's deathmask. But if the "Chinese sandals" and the kimono contribute to the impression of austere calm prevailing in the room, they also are linked to the volume of Lafcadio Hearn's *Glimpses of Unfamiliar Japan*. As Lowell says, each object has "its function, its history, its drama"; the history of the Lafcadio Hearn book is revealed by its two inscriptions. It is a gift from mother to son, reminding us of the poet's problematic relationship to his own mother, and of the late owner's timidity; in a sense he remained, throughout life, mother's "Robbie," while vainly trying to assume the role of Siegfried assigned to him by his wife (*LS*, 18) or the role of "Commander Lowell" assigned to him by his son. The later inscription, "This book has had hard usage / on the Yangtze River, China," recalls the elder Lowell's moment of glory when, at "nineteen, the youngest ensign in his class, / he was 'the old man' of a gunboat on the Yangtze" (*LS*, 72). It is a memento of a more exciting life that opened briefly and then closed. The other oriental objects suggest the depth of the father's regret for this road not taken; in context, they no longer appear as exotic decorative touches, but as hints of a thwarted dream of adventure. "It was left under an open / porthole in a storm," the inscription continues, bringing the poem to its end. By these words, the father may have meant to express devil-may-care bravado, but the reader, having witnessed his ignominious carving lessons (*LS*, 34), may find instead pure bumbling incompetence—the skipper didn't even have the presence of mind to move the book or shut the window.

"Father's Bedroom" is an effective but slight poem, one that indeed borrows much of its force from the context of other poems and the prose memoir elsewhere in the volume. But it shows, compactly, the degree to which Lowell conceived of autobiography as analysis rather than cathartic expression, and of experience as something that needs to be recovered historically, rather than as something immediately and completely given in the moment of the event. And it shows that Lowell often pursued such analysis quite far without recourse to analogies between public and private experience. In many of the poems in *Life Studies*, Lowell seems confident that his private experience is not so inscrutably different from other people's as to require buttressing from public analogues.

There are, nonetheless, a number of poems that do compare public and private history, and the arrangement of the sections dramatizes such comparisons. The book opens with four nonautobiographical poems; these are concerned with madness, violence, and spiritual decay in history, not in the self. Then comes the autobiographical memoir, "91 Revere Street." The third section contains four poems about writers (including "Words For Hart Crane"). By the time we reach the autobiographical sequence of Part IV, Lowell's attention has rested first on American and European history, then on his own family history in its most private sense. The poems on writers mediate between the poet's sense of himself as the the biological son of his parents and his aspiration to be reborn, in his public role as poet, as the son of Ford Madox Ford or the brother of Delmore Schwartz. Before one even begins comparing public and private history, there is a tension between public and private implicit when one begins to write autobiography in the first place, because one brings private experience into the public domain of literature.

The poems that make the analogy of public and private most explicit are also, by and large, the ones that have attracted the most attention, and one of these, "Skunk Hour," is widely regarded as the finest of all. I am not ready to argue that "Father's Bedroom" is a better poem than "Skunk Hour" (perhaps the more ambitious "My Last Afternoon with Uncle Devereux Winslow" would provide a fairer comparison), but it does seem to me that "Skunk Hour" has been overpraised and that it pays for its greater ambition with intellectual and emotional pretentiousness. Lowell's attempt to reconstitute the "objective correlative" as a social correspondence between individual and collective suffering is finally less interesting, if more influential, than his simultaneous attempt to make individual experience intelligible by tracing the history of accidental details until they take on symbolic resonance.

In "Skunk Hour," the confessional mirroring of public and private is expressed formally in the poem's symmetrical division into four stanzas about the social environment and four about the poet's "dark night" of voyeurism and incipient madness. Lowell, in an essay on the composition of the poem, revealed that he had written the stanzas about himself first, later adding the other four because he "found the bleak personal violence repellent. All was too close. . . ."[12] But if the process of composition led from self to environment, the reader experiences the reverse order: the speaker perceives symptoms of deterioration in his surroundings and then turns to examination of himself. *Post hoc ergo propter hoc* may be poor logic, but it is sound rhetoric. By putting the stanzas about his surroundings first, Lowell reinterprets the private suffering as only one more symptom of a pervasive cultural breakdown. His account of the composition of this poem, however, points to its central problem. As evidence that "the season's ill," that the surrounding world is falling apart, the first four stanzas simply aren't convincing. They sound like what Lowell admits they are, a calculated attempt to confer on "repellent personal violence" the redeeming general significance of a social theme.

What, after all, are the social analogues of the personal crisis in "Skunk Hour"? There is a slightly dotty "hermit heiress" who "buys up all / the eyesores facing her shore, / and lets them fall" (*LS*, 89). Her son, moreover, is a bishop. If he is her only son, and if he is a Catholic rather than Episcopal bishop, the family line will presumably end there; otherwise, this detail has no discoverable significance. What else is wrong? The "summer millionaire" has died, and his "nine-yacht yawl" has been "auctioned off to lobstermen" (*LS*, 89). Not only that, the "fairy / decorator" has painted the once-functional "cobbler's bench and awl" a garish orange for his shop display, and despite his homosexuality, he is willing to marry for money (*LS*, 89). One would be grateful if these were the worst problems in one's own neighborhood. The sinister language of illness ("the season's ill") and contamination ("A red fox stain covers Blue Hill") does not rest on a convincing portrayal of anything sinister in the environment; it is only intelligible as the projection of the poet's internal sense of foreboding.

In his commentary on "Skunk Hour," Richard Wilbur entertains just such an interpretation, only to reject it for the more conventional view:

"I myself am hell" (the one literary echo in the poem) is what Milton's Satan says "in prospect of Eden," and Lowell surely means us to think not only of Satan's imprisonment in self but also of his envious spying in the scenes of Book IV which immediately follow. Does the quotation aim to suggest that the poet's emotional imbalance makes him see the world falsely, that like Satan he "sees undelighted all delight"? I think not; the first four stanzas have seemed not a prophetic vision, but a dour review of certain facts. . . . The diseased world is really there; the point is that the poet shares in a measure its addlement, "illness," deadness and aloneness, and cannot shuck off the self which the world has thrust on him." [13]

Because "Skunk Hour" fails to satisfy as a portrait of a sick society inflicting a sick self on the poet, I take up again the suggestion that Wilbur dismissed.

The line "I myself am hell" would seem, in isolation at least, to tell us that hell is within rather than without. And if "nobody's here," the hermit heiress and the fairy decorator have in effect disappeared. Our attention is shifted from them to the self that saw in them, as in everything else, only its own misery. If so, then the poet has proposed the external analogues of the first four stanzas only to turn on himself and reject them as rationalizations. The plot of "Skunk Hour," so interpreted, is one of self-recognition.

Much as one might wish to construe the poem thus, it will not quite support such an interpretation. There is a curious, and as it turns out, crucial slippage of tense in stanza five. The "dark night" is recounted, for five lines, in the past tense. Then comes an ellipsis and the declaration, in present tense, that "my mind's not right." The poem continues in present tense, although the events are recollected, all the way to the end, implying that the encounter with the skunks occurred when the speaker returned from his voyeuristic prowl among the "love-cars." It makes a great deal of difference whether the recognitions expressed in "my mind's not right" and "I myself am hell" occur in the narrative past, as realizations already made during the dark night and now recollected, or whether they now strike the poet unexpectedly for the first time in the moment of recollection. For if the speaker of the first four stanzas has already had these insights, one cannot suppose that he catches himself in a self-deception as a new interpretation of the recollected experience suddenly dawns on him. The blurred boundary between recollected experience and the process of recollection makes it impossible to decide whether the analogues in the first four stanzas should be taken as reliable or not.

Some of Lowell's poems avoid the rigged rhetoric of "Skunk Hour" by relatively modest ambition, as in "Father's Bedroom"; others make the frustration of the quest for correspondence between self and other part of their theme. And there is at least one justly celebrated poem that takes a third and simpler way: "For the Union Dead."

One virtue of "For the Union Dead" is its restraint of analogies between public and private experience. For once, Lowell treats his public theme as precisely that and not another thing. Although, as Rudman points out, its landscape, the Boston Common, "is a ten minute walk from 91 Revere Street,"[14] many thousands of Bostonians have "passed it every day" besides Lowell. As the very name of the Boston Common implies, the poem is set in a public space. Although Lowell does recollect his childhood visits to the aquarium, he mutes the theme of his own unique relationship to the setting and concentrates on its shared meanings. In contrast to "Skunk Hour," the focus shifts away from self and toward environment. The landscape of the Boston Common, far more densely inscribed with cultural signs than that of Castine, Maine, offers readily what Lowell had to force on his surroundings in "Skunk Hour": a storehouse of symbols that reveal the consciousness of the inhabitants, past and present. This landscape, because it is urban and man-made, contains objects that testify, by their very existence, to what the people who made them value—and fail to value. The determinate historical origin of the surrounding objects provides a firm check on the tendency to treat self and environment as mutual reflections. The Shaw Memorial, the Statehouse, and even the unwittingly macabre Mosler Safe advertisement have a public meaning before the poem gets hold of them. "For the Union Dead" stands out in Lowell's work for its unusually firm resistance to solipsism and to conflations of public and private.

Not only does the landscape provide artifacts that were deliberately invested by their makers with public symbolism, it offers a full historical range from colonial times (the State House, the "old white churches") through the nineteenth century (the Shaw memorial itself) to the contemporary Mosler ad, which evokes both the historical present and the immediate historical past ("Hiroshima boiling"). The poem, one might say, is organized by archaeological strata (as Lowell may have wished to suggest by speaking of the "excavation" of the garage).

The two main symbolic artifacts in the poem are the aquarium and the Shaw Memorial, and the relationship between them is crucial to its interpretation. Given the title, the opening of the poem surprises by its obliquity. Lowell opens not with the Civil War monument but with his recollection of childhood visits to the aquarium, and it takes him five stanzas to come round to Colonel Shaw. The connections between the aquarium and the monument only emerge later, but the transition between the two begins in the third stanza. The statement "My hand draws back" signals also a drawing back from recollection into the present. "I often sigh still," the speaker admits, "for the dark downward and vegetating kingdom / of the fish and reptile" (*FTUD*, 70). The fascination with the fish is linked both with a desire to escape from human consciousness into the lower phyla (cf. Eliot's Prufrock: "I should have been a pair of ragged claws / Scuttling across the floors of silent seas") and with regressive nostalgia for childhood or, in later stanzas, the historical past. The fish and reptile "kingdom" is the lowest stratum visible in the "excavation" the poem undertakes—it is our prehistory, the residuum of the animal within the human. The city has been built above it, yet never altogether covers or effaces it. The topmost strata appear mainly in images of mechanism, frantic activity, and ever more rapid change: the steamshovels threaten the Shaw monument, "propped by a plank splint against the garage's earthquake," and even the Statehouse requires bracing. The aquarium has been closed down, presumably to make way for new construction. And yet the surface and the depths are linked, since Lowell renders his images of mechanism in fishy and reptilean language—"dinosaur steamshovels," or the "giant-finned cars" of the last stanza.

Williamson finds, in the persistence of the fish and reptile, a critique of the very desire to build cities and monuments. He reads "For the Union Dead" as an indictment of civilization much like Norman O. Brown's in *Life Against Death*. "Man creates cities and technologies partly in order to . . . escape his two greatest fears, his animal instincts (purged in the cleanness of mechanical processes) and animal mortality (denied in the seeming permanence of steel and stone)." The closing of the aquarium becomes emblematic of our repression of the fish and reptile within, and the persistence of the fish and reptile in descriptions of steamshovels, cars, and the monument itself (which "sticks like a fishbone / in the city's throat") hints at a Brownian return of the repressed, "more pervasive and uncontrollable in direct proportion to the intensity of the repression. . . . Denied a fixed locality in the scheme of man's city or man's mind, the fish suddenly appears everywhere."[15]

Williamson's remarks need to be qualified by the recognition that the aquarium, though it once gave the fish and reptile the "fixed locality" they are now denied, is nonetheless a public building, no less an example of civic architecture than the Statehouse or the Shaw Memorial. Indeed, one might argue that the aquarium is itself a monument, parallel in symbolic function to these other buildings. Just as the Statehouse recalls vanished ideals of government and the Shaw Memorial recalls an ideal of heroism we prefer to ridicule as sentimental, the aquarium, while it remained open, had held up a mirror to our animality. The point is not, in that case, that building monuments and cities denies our animality; on the contrary, the earlier society that still took monuments and civic virtue seriously also found it easier to accept the connection between human and animal nature. If, as Lowell remarked in introducing the poem at a reading in 1960, "we've emerged from the monumental age,"[16] so much the worse for us. Instead of Colonel Shaw, leading the first black regiment into battle, we have the nonheroic speaker reduced to spectatorship, watching the civil rights struggles of his own day on television, where "the drained faces of Negro school-children rise like balloons" (*FTUD*, 72).

In "For the Union Dead," the denial of "animal instincts" and "animal mortality" as part of the human condition is not expressed in the desire to attain immortality through monumental architecture; rather, this denial is akin to the denial of history expressed in the destruction of the aquarium and the near-destruction of the war memorial. It is a failure of memory. To endanger the Shaw Memorial for the sake of a garage is to forget the meaning of Shaw's death or to deny that this meaning still matters. And yet, the presence of those "Negro school-children" on television proves that it still does. To close the aquarium is to forget a more distant past, the common evolutionary origins that bind us to the fish and reptile. To advertise a safe as impervious to a nuclear explosion is to forget a very recent past, the atomic bombing of Hiroshima and Nagasaki only fifteen years before the poem was written. The forgetfulness of the present is symbolized by the hectic urban renewal everywhere visible in the landscape; the lack of purpose to this activity is symbolized in the fact that the destruction of the landscape will bring forth only a parking lot for the "giant finned cars" of the last stanzas. These cars, too, are monuments in a debased sense, expressing their owners' preoccupation with acquisition and mobility. But here, the representation is unconscious; the society that builds and buys the cars reveals its values without having intended to do so. The cars are a means, not an end: they will take their passengers to any destination. The garage, then, is a means serving a means, and the steamshovels digging the garage are a means serving a means twice removed. Lowell's judgment on monuments, mechanisms, and cities in this poem is finally closer to Allen Tate's than to Norman O. Brown's:

what we build reveals what we desire, and only when we desire worthy ends do we build well. "A society of means without ends, in the age of technology," wrote Tate,

so multiplies the means, in the lack of anything better to do, that it may have to scrap the machines as it makes them; until our descendants will have to dig themselves out of one rubbish heap after another and stand upon it, in order to make more rubbish to make more standing room. The surface of nature will then be literally as well as morally concealed from the eyes of men.[17]

Lowell's "civic sandpiles" are a version of Tate's "rubbish heap." But Lowell, more pessimistic even than Tate, fears that we will not be able to keep digging ourselves out but will slide into the ever-nearer "ditch" of extinction.

With the question of Lowell's attitude toward monuments goes that of Lowell's attitude toward heroism. Axelrod argues that Lowell "praises the military valor of Shaw, but also suggests dark, mixed motives beneath that valor"; Philip Cooper finds a "death-wish" in Shaw's acceptance of his commission; Jonathan Crick finds in Shaw the embodiment of "the Puritan virtues" that "also produced the commercial greed that has devastated Boston, and the destruction of war." Williamson observes that the Massachusetts 54th was exploited for propaganda purposes and "trained with a hastiness that suggests no high regard for the value of black lives"; Shaw was thus "wholly committed to a morally dubious, though seemingly idealistic, enterprise."[18] It is worth remembering that Crick, Cooper, Williamson, and Axelrod were writing during or soon after the war in Vietnam, a historical circumstance that would dispose them toward a cynical view of military heroism like Shaw's. It is hard, from the vantage point of the mid 1980s, to discover irony in Lowell's praise for Shaw:

He is out of bounds now. He rejoices in man's lovely,
peculiar power to choose life and die—
when he leads his black soldiers to death,
he cannot bend his back.

(*FTUD*, 71)

The stanza seems all the more unequivocal in the context of Lowell's other work. The "power to choose life and die" must have seemed especially "peculiar" to a poet of futility and divided will, for whom "the simple word," as he later put it, was always becoming "buried in a random, haggard sentence, / cutting ten ways to nothing clearly carried" (*H*, 132).

What troubles Lowell's meditation on Colonel Shaw is not the possibility that Shaw's heroism is an illusion but rather the possibility that such heroism can no longer exist. For one thing, as the Mosler advertisment reminds us, the individual act of courage has little consequence in a war fought with modern techniques of mass destruction; for another, the problem that Lowell discovers in contemporary Boston is not one that can be solved by a dramatic and clear-cut action like Shaw's. One can't die in battle against the forces of forgetfulness and commercial greed. Even the civil rights movement, which did produce a hero in Martin Luther King, is treated unheroically, from the perspective of a concerned but passive witness for whom participation in events is unimaginable—for a brief moment, one sees the anxious children on television. Like the fish in the aquarium, they are separated from the speaker by a wall of glass. Implicitly, Lowell proposes this way of experiencing public reality as typical of our time.

In "Waking Early Sunday Morning," which Lowell read before the march on the Pentagon in 1967, the sense of being able to suffer public experience without being able to participate in it receives more extensive exploration. This poem (especially when taken in the context of the sequence, "Near the Ocean," to which it belongs) offers a devastating critique of the idea that private suffering embodies the historical suffering of the age; rather, the attempt to transcend private suffering tempts us to inflate private desires into historical ambitions—a harmless enough fantasy for most of us, but ruinous when it seduces a king or a president. "Waking Early Sunday Morning" meditates on the futility of escaping imprisonment in the private. Public reality appears not as diseased consciousness replicated in individual madness, but as the power of the state, dragging its citizens into "small war on the heels of small / war," deaf to their modest desire to persist in their unquiet privacy.

The poem begins with an expression of desire:

O to break loose, like the chinook
salmon jumping and falling back,
nosing up to the impossible
stone and bone-crushing waterfall—
raw-jawed, weak-fleshed there, stopped by ten
steps of the roaring ladder, and then
to clear the top on the last try,
alive enough to spawn and die.

(NO, 15)

To "break loose" is to affirm, like Colonel Shaw, "man's lovely, peculiar power / to choose life and die." That choice is "peculiar" to "man" because what the poet in his self-consciousness must will himself to do, the salmon does by instinct. The image of the spawning salmon implies membership in a continuity of generations; faith means not only overcoming "impossible" obstacles to accomplish an individual purpose in life, but transmitting a heritage from the present to the future, forming part of a collective identity. And yet the rest of the poem relentlessly undercuts the hope of such continuity. What if there is no future and no collective identity except a common susceptibility to self-destructive illusions?

The second stanza pulls back from the necessity enjoined by the first. The leap up the waterfall can be postponed, or perhaps avoided altogether; to "break loose" may require us to reject necessity rather than to accomplish it:

> Stop, back off. The salmon breaks
> water, and now my body wakes
> to feel the unpolluted joy
> and criminal leisure of a boy—
> no rainbow smashing a dry fly
> in the white run is as free as I,
> here squatting like a dragon on
> time's hoard before the day's begun!
>
> (NO, 16)

These lines express a wish to escape from mutability altogether, to remain in a state of untrammeled potentiality like that of childhood, prior to experience, limitation, and loss. But in their language, they also express the untrustworthiness of the wish. The "leisure of a boy" is "criminal" because the speaker who claims it is an adult. And the freedom of the rainbow salmon "in the white run" is illusory, for the "dry fly" is a fisherman's lure. Like Mr. Edwards' spiders, who "purpose nothing but their ease" and yet unwittingly hasten their own destruction, the salmon cannot escape the law of its own being. The image of the poet "squatting like a dragon on / time's hoard before the day's begun" reveals another impossibility in his wish: although both time and treasure can be "spent," only the latter can be hoarded.

The third stanza considers yet a third response to the problem of how a time-bound, mortal being may act, and it is the most unattractive of all: "in some dark nook a fieldmouse rolls / a marble, hours on end, then stops." This is arbitrary activity continued out of habit, ceasing as arbitrarily as it began. From the ennobling comparison of human activity to that of the salmon, Lowell descends to a more sinister analogy with "Vermin." To fieldmice, termites, and other "creatures of the night," dawn is a "daily . . . blackout"; their activity takes place in a moral darkness or blindness. But most of our activity is like theirs and takes place in a similar darkness: "business as usual in eclipse / goes down to the sea in ships," we read in the fourth stanza. And the ninth begins: "When will we see Him face to face? / Each day, He shines through darker glass." Exiled by his human consciousness from the salmon's instinctive sense of purpose and by his skeptical age from belief in a purpose derived from religion, the poet is left with activity for activity's sake, the "business as usual" he sees around him. ("Business as usual" was a politically charged phrase when the poem was written, deriding the idea that one ought not to disrupt routine in order to protest the war.)

Turning outward from himself to see the ships in the harbor outside the window, the poet describes them in language that evokes their traditional symbolism of pilgrimage (the biblical "morning watch," the allegorically freighted name, "Good Hope") and adventure (the Homeric "wine-dark hulls"). But in our modern, un-biblical, un-Homeric world, the symbolism proves empty. The ships are at the disposal of "business as usual," and they trail a "wake of refuse, dacron rope." All voyages have been made, all destinations long since mapped.

Since the harbor offers only another image of exhausted possibilities, the poem veers off again in the reactive, discontinuous manner that the reader has already begun to expect. It meditates on a glass of water—as if the turbulent river of the opening stanzas or the expanses of the harbor could somehow be tamed, their essence caught in a transparent container small enough to be held in one's hand, still and available for contemplation. The glass of water becomes a metaphor for individual being, thus suggesting that the self is formed of the same substance as the world around it (the river in which the salmon swims, the ocean on which the ships sail) and that the nature of both is fluid, indeterminate, Protean. Lowell also suggests this Protean nature by an optical metaphor: the glass of water, in its transparency, takes on the colors of the objects refracted through it. One might think of the glass of water as an ideal analogue for the poet's being. It is completely receptive to the surrounding world and is yet unstained by the images that pass through it. "O that the spirit could remain / tinged but untarnished by its strain," the next stanza begins; but the spirit cannot escape "strain" in its transactions with the world; what it contains alters it. The metaphor makes, obliquely and delicately, the observation that the apologists for confessional poetics made crudely. There is a risk in being receptive to experience, especially when what one experiences is likely to be painful. The emphasis, however, is not on the special hardships of the poet, but on the universality of the "strain."

The next sudden turn, though it occurs within stanza six rather than between two stanzas, marks the sharpest division thus far. Lowell moves from analysis of his predicament to consideration of traditional modes of transcendence: religion, work, and (in stanza ten) empire. The Sunday morning church bells ("new electric" ones) and hymns with "stiff quatrains shoveled out four-square" are the last vestige of a faith that once "gave darkness some control / and left a loophole for the soul." For Lowell, at least, that loophole is now closed.

The alternative to religion is the attempt to build something out of what religion rejected:

> No, put old clothes on, and explore
> the corners of the woodshed for
> its dregs and dreck: tools with no handle,
> ten candle-ends not worth a candle,
> old lumber banished from the Temple,
> damned by Paul's precept and example,
> cast from the kingdom, banned in Israel,
> the wordless sign, the tinkling cymbal.
>
> (NO, 19)

This stanza not only proposes carpentry on the sabbath, it proposes the building of an anti-Temple from discarded materials. These objects strike me as symbols of triviality and lost function (and not, as Williamson argues, of proscribed sexuality[19]). They are worthless, not threatening. Why then have they been "banished," "damned," "banned," and "cast from the kingdom," rather than casually thrown aside? Perhaps it is because they contradict the religious vision of a cosmos in which all objects speak the intention of their Maker in His creation; there must not be a "wordless sign" or a "tinkling cymbal [symbol]." The project of the anti-Temple is not so much the Prometheanism of Blake or Rimbaud, trying to liberate the forbidden energies of the body from repression, as the patient bricolage of a Stevens or a Williams, trying to cobble something together from the rubble of the Christian cosmos.

But the attempt to raise an anti-Temple from the discarded scraps of the old fails. Instead of finding a way to invest the banished materials with the significance that was once attached to religious symbols, the poem reduces the religious symbols to the level of the "dregs and dreck," consigning both to a common marginality: God's "white spire and flag- / pole" are one with the china doorknob. If the doorknob can "calm the mad," it cannot cure them. Even its modest power to calm derives not from its function as a symbol but from its very meaningless-ness, which makes it an emotionally neutral focus of concentration. If there is an implicit reference, moreover, to Lowell's own recurrent madness, the effect is nonetheless different from that of "Skunk Hour." Madness does not provide a principle of correspondence between self and world; rather, the world, by refusing all correspondence, threatens the interpreting self with madness.

Having abandoned the hope of replacing religion with some sort of hand-built alternative, the poem turns, again without transition, to a stanza on "Hammering military splendor," finding here too "little re-demption." This passage moves the poem from its middle section, pre-occupied with the loss of religious faith, to its closing meditation on the bleakness of contemporary history. Lowell writes of Roman and bibli-cal warfare, of "elephant and phalanx" and of Goliath, but in anach-ronistically contemporary language, pointing up the analogy to our own war in Vietnam. The last line, alluding to the slaughter of the Shechemites,[20] also reminds one of Auschwitz: "a million foreskins stacked like trash. . . ." The word "trash," moreover, recalls the "dregs and dreck" in the woodshed of stanza eight. It reminds us that among the things the great religions consigned to insignificance were the bodies of those outside the faith; and it reminds us, too, that religious chauvinism has survived the cooling of religious zeal.

"Sing softer," the poet tells himself, much as he had instructed him-self to "Stop, back off" after longing to "break loose" like the salmon. He will neither celebrate nor denounce "Hammering military splen-dor"; instead, he will seek the private virtues of "tenderness" and "san-ity." Even in proposing this alternative, however, he questions it. The attempt to scale down manic aspirations leads only to "restlessness," "self-deception," and a "caution" that is "reckless" because it is bound to trigger some reactive outburst. The return of the church bells and the line "anywhere, but somewhere else" from stanza six underscores the poet's impasse; in the eleventh stanza, he is quite literally back where he started. The twelfth stanza begins by repeating the first words of the poem: "O to break loose."

The twelfth stanza draws on the familiar psycho-political idea that hunger for political power is a distorted form of balked erotic desire, but Lowell's use of this commonplace is unconventional. "All life's gran-deur / is something with a girl in summer," he says, becoming sud-denly pastoral. Perhaps "to break loose" would be to accept this private happiness. But "something with a girl in summer" is inevitably transitory. There are the other three seasons to be considered, and the boy and girl have to become man and woman. Moreover, the public realities of the war, and the still-worse danger of nuclear war, have power to dissolve the lovers' idyll. "Life's grandeur," then, is a momentary fling, a brief escape from necessity.

The elation of the lover enjoying "something with a girl in summer" is compared to that of

> the President
> girdled by his establishment
> this Sunday morning, free to chaff
> his own thoughts with his bear-cuffed staff,
> swimming nude, unbuttoned, sick
> of his ghost-written rhetoric.

(NO, 23)

The surprise in this passage comes in its sympathy with President Johnson as man of power, free only "this Sunday morning" from his usual constraints. His nudity evokes the innocence of boyhood expeditions to the swimming hole and makes a frank avowal of the body possible only when the protective weekday clothing has been "unbuttoned." Whereas Marcuse imagines a "one-dimensional" society in which false consciousness cannot possibly be recognized as such, Lowell's Johnson knows that the speeches he delivers, "ghost-written" for him by his staff, are not the utterance of his true self. But "sick" of them as he is, he is stuck: the presidency, which might seem to be the very center of power, turns out to be more restrictive than enabling. It is a role, and Johnson is trapped in it; even in his moment of freedom, he is "girdled by his establishment"—with all the implications of confinement and concern for appearances that the verb suggests. Unlike Bly and Duncan, who around the same time were depicting Johnson as an inhuman monster, Lowell resists the temptation to easy villification.

The last two stanzas remind one of the apocalyptic endings in *Lord Weary's Castle* in their attempt to deliver summary judgment of the world, present and future. But instead of a dramatic judgment, the future brings only an indefinite prolongation of the present, with its anxiety and war of attrition; wars continue to "flicker" on and off, there is "no advance." In Eden, where "the tree of life" stood, Adam and Eve were closely watched over by their creator; but now, man can go on "thinning out his kind" unreproved by God, who has disappeared—or just possibly, reappeared as "the pruner."

The end, as the last stanza envisions it, comes with neither a bang nor a whimper but as a condemnation to eternal vigilance despite the exhaustion of "all joy"; wars continue though there is nothing to be won by them, policing continues though there is nothing to be protected. The chasm between public and private experience appears once more in the lines, "peace to our children when they fall / in small war on the heels of small / war." In this elegaic wish, "our" identifies speaker and readers as parents, each with children to care for. But all we can wish for "our" children is that they find "peace" as they go to their inevitable deaths; the hope that "we" might be able to prevent the small wars in the first place is too sanguine, presupposing as it does an actual sense of participating in a shared public world that can be understood and controlled.

When the word "our" appears again in the last line, it identifies "us" more publicly but also more ambiguously; the last phrase of the poem has a tenuous grammatical connection to the rest of the stanza:

> until the end of time
> to police the earth, a ghost
> orbiting forever lost
> in our monotonous sublime.
>
> (NO, 24)

The infinitive "to police the earth" does not have a subject, but it sounds like an ironic description of American foreign policy. "A ghost" at first seems, because of the line break, to describe the policing agent, but it turns out to be appositive to "earth." Our children, the Americans of the future, are doomed to police an earth that has become "a ghost," in the sense that "all joy," all hope, and all value have departed from it. (That things have already reached this culmination is suggested by the verbal connection with Johnson's "ghost-written rhetoric" in stanza twelve.) The earth continues in its course "forever lost / in our monotonous sublime." What does this second "our" mean? It may refer either to ourselves as a nation or to the entire human race. In either case, it is our dreams of transcendence or conquest, already present in the religion of King David's Israel and the "Hammering military splendor" of his Philistine enemies, that have finally led to the desolation of the present. These "sublime" aspirations (and perhaps there is a glance at the Freudian concept of "sublimation" in this word as well) are finally "monotonous" as they collapse, again and again, into disillusionment and defeat.

The theme of "Waking Early Sunday Morning" is the failure of the meditative consciousness itself to find an alternative to "our monotonous sublime." It does not portray the self as inhabited by contaminating social forces, but as clinging vulnerably to private happiness. We bring "our children" into a world that we expect to be brutal to them; as Lowell put it elsewhere, in "Fall 1961," "A father's no shield / for his child" (*FTUD*, 11). Looking for transcendence—whether through religion, philosophical contemplation, or the leaping salmon's blind animal faith—one is balked at every turn, and there is not even the consolation of feeling representative in one's suffering, as there was, perhaps, in "Skunk Hour." The poem's lurching abruptness of movement, its lack of an easily located center, performs a mimetic function yet does not sink to the imitative fallacy, since there is an implicit logic beneath the apparent randomness of its progression. It begins, in the stanzas devoted to the salmon and the glass of water, with consideration of individual transcendence, then turns to the shared but no longer tenable "Faith of our fathers," and ends by considering the failure of secular faith in nation and culture. It stands out from most other political poetry of the 1960s for its pessimism, its complexity, and its rejection of an easy universality through "conflation" of public and private materials. Indeed, it is so pessimistic that it verges on the apolitical; it not only makes no recommendations, it provides no way of imagining any. It is political only in its recognition that incomprehension of the political situation is itself a political situation. But it does not claim adversarial power in the way that Ginsberg's poems do; it has no thaumaturgy to practice against the war.

From 1967 to 1973, Lowell wrote what eventually became three sequences of unrhymed sonnets, beginning with *Notebook: 1967–68*, which was revised and expanded in 1970; in 1973, Lowell broke *Notebook* into two volumes, *History* and *For Lizzie and Harriet*, bringing out in addition a new sequence, *The Dolphin*. These poems met with a mixed reception;[21] if some of the negative criticism seems, in retrospect, the expression of a change in taste rather than a change in Lowell, some of it responds to the opacity and uncertainty of impulse in many of the poems themselves, especially in the earlier *Notebook* settings. The revision of these sequences shows Lowell in uneasy dialogue with the fashions of the age. In the late sixties, the emphasis on the irrational, the surreal, and the improvisatory gained its widest acceptance. The very title *Notebook* suggests that Lowell was attempting to join in the spirit of improvisation; as the fact of two subsequent revisions in public shows, he couldn't resist second thoughts. As Kalstone remarks, "the *Notebook* of 1969 begins in a craving for immediacy," but then, "having risked disorder," Lowell "decides that the composition of *Notebook* seems to him haphazard."²² In his brief "Note" to *History*, Lowell strikes the pose of craftsman: "I have cut the waste marble from the figure" (*H*, 7 [extrapolating backwards from numbered pages]). The important question, of course, is the value of the poems, not the indecisiveness that presided over their making. *History*, as the "public" part of *Notebook*, concerns us more, in a discussion of psycho-politics and poetry, than the two domestic sequences. Von Hallberg has proposed it as Lowell's masterpiece, "a major imaginative embodi-ment" of "American liberalism," and "one of the most successful book-length poems" of "the last thirty-five years." Apart from the question of evaluation, von Hallberg raises the question of accurate description. Is he right to read *History* as "a thoroughly centrist book" written against the grain of the late sixties, when it was common to "assume that the center was uninhabitable"?²³

It may be that *History*, as von Hallberg says, "embodies nothing so systematic or impersonal as an ideology,"²⁴ but that does not mean that it is "liberal" or "centrist"—after all, liberalism is an "ideology" like any other. Williamson is more precise, I think, in characterizing the relationship of this poetry to "ideology" (he writes of the second *Note-book* rather than *History*, which appeared when his book was about to go to press, but the generalization remains just). He finds in it a "sus-pension of judgment" that permits "a purely phenomenological ap-proach," in which the truth claims of ideologies are, in Husserl's sense, bracketed:

Lowell allows his impulse or fantasy of the moment, whether radical or re-actionary, to work itself out to its conclusion, not without internal irony, but without any externally imposed judgment. Lowell will acknowledge the strange distance and nonresponsibility toward one's own opinions that this method entails. . . . His justification would be the universality and irre-ducibility of the conflicts of value he finds within himself. . . . The method's great advantage is that it allows Lowell to write about his politics as a partly irrational psychic event.²⁵

When we compare *History* with other political poetry of the same period, such as Ginsberg's or Bly's, "the method's great advantage" may seem absolute. But the method's great disadvantage is its risk of triv-ializing political response altogether. Political (and moral) judgment threatens to evaporate into the mist of "psychic event"; one has opin-ions as one has moods. Nor is Lowell himself blind to this problem—as we have already seen in discussing "Bishop Berkeley," which depicts an ambivalence about the claims of certainty as opposed to those of skeptical doubt and also Lowell's sense of the ambivalence that skeptical doubt itself brings. The poet, having skeptically undercut his moment of visionary assertion, cannot even get his own two feet to agree about the temperature of the water. If the danger of liberalism is paralysis through ambivalence as one tries to mediate conflicting moral imperatives, Lowell has invented a more elaborate fate. He is ambivalent about ambivalence itself, vacillating between the desire to mediate between irreconcilable imperatives and the desire to yield himself to passionate certainty. The Lowell of *History* is not a liberal; rather, liberalism itself is a choice among others, and all choices exact a cost, a diminishment of one kind or another. Yet he suspects the melodramatic oppositions posed by radical psycho-politics: the bondage of the conscious ego or the freedom of the unconscious id, the puritanical cruelty of power or the innocence of unfettered sexuality. *History* certainly concerns the relations between psychology and politics, sexuality and power, but it does not always, or even primarily, construe those relations as the radical Freudians did or even as Lowell himself sometimes did in his earlier poetry.

The first two poems in the sequence, "History" (*H*, 24) and "Man and Woman" (*H*, 24), seem to pose alternatives: the public realm of history, the private realm of sexuality. "History," the first begins, "has to live with what was here, / clutching and close to fumbling all we had." To live in history is not only to experience "what was here" as an encumbrance within the present, something one "has to live with"; it is also to know the possibility of loss, of awakening to find that what was here is here no longer. And it is, finally, to learn that in the very act of "clutching" the past to prevent it from vanishing, we are apt to lose it, "fumbling all we had." For Lowell, historical consciousness means a heightened fear of death, an awareness that the energy of the "cows crowding . . . against high-voltage wire" or the "baby crying all night like a new machine" drives toward change, and that change means violence, loss, eventual extinction: history begins with Cain and Abel. The "skeptic" tries to remain aloof from this process, but it "electrifies" him; his innocence is "terrifying" because it is untenable.

The violence of history, moreover, seems to begin with fulfilled rather than repressed desire: the "skeptic" owns a herd of cows, so he does not lack wealth; he has a baby, the fruit of sexual consummation. The gratification of desire is aggressive, as suggested in the description of the "white-faced, predatory, / . . . beautiful, mist-drunken hunter's moon," likened at the close of the poem to the poet's own visage. (It seems pompous to attribute the conversational voice of *History* to a "speaker," although of course here too "the poet" as he appears in the poem cannot be "the real Robert Lowell" in any literal sense.)

"Man and Woman" begins with another meditation on loss, and it continues the lunar imagery of "History":

> The sheep start galloping in moon-blind wheels
> shedding a dozen ewes—is it faulty vision?
> will we get them back . . . and everything,
> marriage and departure, departure and marriage,
> village to family, family to village,
> all the sheep's parents in geometric progression?
>
> (H, 24)

As if blinded by the moon (figured, in the first poem, as a predator), the sheep (the proverbial victims of predators) begin scattering in circles, "shedding a dozen ewes." "Will we get them back," the poet asks, and immediately extends the question to "everything": the past and the people from whom we have been parted. But the way the itemization of "everything" proceeds is instructive. To restore "everything," not only would villages have to be brought back to families that have left them (or vice-versa), but the irreconcilable choices of "marriage and departure" would also have to coexist in a simultaneous present: one would be married, divorced, and remarried all at the same time. One's consciousness would get too crowded, trying to take in "all the sheep's parents in geometric progression."

"It's too much heart-ache to go back to that," Lowell decides,

> not life-enhancing like the hour a student
> first discovers the unblemished Mother
> on the Tuscan hills of Berenson,
> or of Galileo, his great glass eye
> admiring the spots on the erroneous moon. . . .

Not the effort to stem mutability by conserving the past, but the moment of first discovery, is "life-enhancing." And yet, the student discovers what the art connoisseur Berenson has taught him to discover, and the poet, looking for an image of youthful discovery that opens the future to the unexpected, can only turn to an example he has found in history, to Galileo 350 years earlier. Even the decision to live in the present or the future, rather than trying to rescue the past, evokes the simile of the student—and what is this figure, for a middle-aged poet, but an attempt to restore an earlier self? One cannot imagine the future without the analogies supplied by the past; nonetheless, it makes a difference whether one goes to history with the intention of "clutching" the past as it vanishes or of finding analogies by which to imagine the future. At the end of the poem, the poet is able to say: "I watch this night out grateful to be alone / with my wife—your slow pulse, my outrageous eye." For the time being, "this night," the present, is enough, and being alone as "man and woman" is enough, without the crowd of presences summoned from the past.

A closer look at the significance of the "eye" in this poem, however, shows us how unstable this contentment is likely to prove. Looking means discovery, whether for the student discovering "the unblemished Mother" or for Galileo, whose "great glass eye" discloses "the spots on the erroneous moon"—a much-blemished and mutable "mother." The lust of the eye for discovery creates the possibility of adventure into the unforeseen rather than the frightened "clutching" of the past. But discovery is in the spirit of "departure," to borrow the antithesis in the first poem, not of "marriage." The speaker's "outrageous eye" will not be long content with domesticity, with the calming rhythm of a wife's "slow pulse." The eye is libidinous, adventuristic, predatory.

One can understand Lowell's conception of the relationship between desire and power by looking at his portraits of the powerful in myth and in ancient history. Whether they are oppressors, heroes, or a mixture of both, Lowell's men and women of power tend to be figures of untrammeled libido. Rather than distorting sexual desire into a will to dominate or a will to destroy gratification for others, as the worshippers of Ginsberg's Moloch do, they burn the candle at both ends, reveling in excess. "Like Henry VIII," one poem begins, "Mohammed got religion / in the dangerous years, and smashed the celibates, / haters of life, though never takers of it." Here, the repressed are the victims, not the aggressors, while

> the boys of the jihad on a string of unwitting camels
> rush paradise, halls stocked with adolescent
> beauties, both sexes for simple nomad tastes.
>
> ("Mohammed," *H*, 52)

The "boys" who ride into "the jihad" also "rush" a fleshly paradise of polymorphous sexual gratification.

Violence, for Lowell, is more commonly an expression of megalomania than of repression. The great figures of history have, like the poet who chronicles them, an "outrageous eye." They place themselves, gigantic, at the center, and see everything and everyone else as insignificant: "The eye that cannot size up the Bosphorus / in a single drop is an acorn, not the eye of a man," says Timur, and behaves accordingly ("Fame," *H*, 52). "I am become the eye of heaven," says Clytemnestra, "and hate / my husband swimming like vagueness, like a porpoise, / in the imperial purple of his heart" ("Clytemnestra 2," *H*, 34). Having assumed a godlike vantage point, she claims the godlike power to dispose of Agamemnon's life. Alexander's "numinous eye is like the sun" ("Death of Alexander," *H*, 40); it provides the light by which all else becomes visible. And in the light of such suns as these, all else exists that it may be conquered, appropriated, consumed: Hannibal "found the plains of Africa too small"; if "nature blocked his road," then "he derricked mountains ("Hannibal 2. The Life," *H*, 42). "One world was much too small for Alexander," and when Xerxes led his army across the land, "breakfasting Persians drank whole rivers dry" ("Xerxes and Alexander," *H*, 39). Like Emerson's poet, Lowell's conquerer stands at the center. He reduces all he sees to raw material for the realization of his will, like Caligula who wishes "the Romans had a single neck," that he might throttle all of them at once ("Caligula 2," *H*, 48).

Many poems, to be sure, reveal Lowell's compassion for the victims of power; although most of these are found in the later pages dealing with modern events, even his treatment of antiquity includes poems such as "Sheep" (*H*, 37), a meditation on our

> forerunners bent in hoops to the broiling soil,
> until their backs were branded with the coin
> of Alexander, God, or Caesar.

But Lowell's indignation on behalf of the dominated is undercut by the suspicion that perhaps they have allowed themselves to be mastered too easily. Though Lowell was far too self-analytical to give way to it (except during his breakdowns, which were often signaled by apologetics for Hitler[26]), his temperament included a streak of fascist power-worship. Moreover, from his own manic episodes he understood the seductiveness of self-aggrandizement; his poems often describe megalomania as a solipsistic exaggeration of the common desire for pleasure, recognition, and respite from the fear of death, more to be pitied than censured. Even at his moments of greatest sympathy for the murderous powerful, however, Lowell usually remains aware that the consolations of the tyrant are illusory. Since one world is too small for him, and the distractions afforded by that world finally limited, the tyrant at last hurls himself against his own finitude. "A grave was what he wanted," says Lowell of Alexander the Great: "Death alone / shows us what tedious things our bodies are" ("Xerxes and Alexander," *H*, 39).

Lowell includes at least one other kind of violence, best exemplified, among his portraits from early myth and history, by Orestes in "Clytemnestra 3" (*H*, 35):

Orestes, the lord of murder and proportion,
saw the tips of her nipples had touched her toes—
a population problem and bad art.
He knew the monster must be guillotined.
He saw her knees tremble and he enjoyed the sight,
knowing that Trojan chivalry was shit.

The violence of Orestes responds, of course, to his mother's killing of Agamemnon. It is an example of reactive rather than primary aggression, and it has a rather different style. Instead of killing in the quest of limitless gratification or limitless self-aggrandizement, Orestes angrily responds to Clytemnestra's overextension of her own prerogatives; he claims to restore "proportion," to force limits on those who acknowledge none. The queen's "nipples had touched her toes"—the grotesque image suggests not only the sagging of the body with age (she is said to be sixty years old), but an obscene aggrandizement of her own sexuality, symbolized by her breasts that hang the length of her body. Orestes is youth telling age to step aside; he is moderation telling desire to acknowledge its limits; he is even neoclassic good taste rebuking romantic excess. Williamson argues that a cycle of violence and retribution links the Orestes figure to his tyrannical victim;[27] I wish to insist, however, on their essential difference: the tyrant and the tyrannicide act from opposing impulses, polarities between which those who would balance the claims of desire and the claims of justice must uneasily steer.

One familiar advocate of balance, obviously, is the liberal, whose portrait Lowell draws in "Life and Civilization" (*H*, 75). Not only the allusions to Locke and Voltaire, but the location of the poem in the sequence, place it in the eighteenth century—the next two poems take up Mozart, Robespierre, and Saint-Just. Liberalism, then, must be understood through its historical origin, as part of the Enlightenment attempt to govern life by reason. Interestingly, Lowell does not define liberalism in any usual political sense—as belief in individual freedom, as tolerance of conflicting ideologies, or as belief in social progress. He defines it, rather, as renunciation of instinct, synonymous almost with Freud's "civilization" in *Civilization and Its Discontents* (which Lowell's title recalls). The poem opens with a description of the woman, dressed in a short skirt, "black mesh tights" and a "figured [patterned, but also figure-revealing] sweater." She is no classic beauty, but despite the "birthmarks" visible through the mesh of the tights, the poet is aroused: "I see your legs as perfect legs." He affects disdain; "who would want to finger or approach / the rumination in your figured sweater," he asks, but as the rest of the poem admits, he wants to very much.

With the turn from the woman's attractions to the poet's resistance to them, the problem of "the Liberal" makes its unlikely entrance:

> Civilization will always outdo life,
> if toleration means to bear and hurt—
> that's Locke, Voltaire; the Liberal dies for that,
> bites his own lip to warm his icy tooth,
> and faces all vicissitudes with calmness.
> That's why there are none, that's why we're none,
> why, unenlightened, we shiver once a moon
> whenever Eros arcs into the Virgin—
> as you, no virgin, made me bear myself.

The assumption "the Liberal dies for" is that "toleration means to bear and hurt." The word "toleration" is of course familiar in definitions of liberalism—but what has it to do with forgoing the charms of the un-virginal woman in the short skirt? The liberal must "tolerate" not only other people's beliefs and actions, but his own passions. These, one might suppose, must be restrained in order to prevent encroachment on the liberty of others; we recall Lowell's gallery of libidinous despots, unleashing their passions on everyone within reach. But the woman in this poem seems more than willing to oblige her reluctant admirer. The problem, then, is that to preserve a disinterested liberalism, one must face "all vicissitudes with calmness." To be mastered by passion is to lose one's disinterestedness.

But no one can face *all* vicissitudes with calmness—even though he has not yielded to his desire, the speaker has lost his "calmness" with the first glance. "The Liberal," as Lowell's upper-case L emphasizes, is at best an ideal figure, to be imitated, like Christ, in the knowledge that the imitation must fail: "That's why there are none, that's why we're none." At worst, he is an imposter, feigning Olympian calm when in fact he "bites his own lip" with frustration. Two centuries after the Enlightenment, Voltaire and Locke notwithstanding, we remain "un-enlightened," ruled by the cycles of the moon and by the recurrent victory of Eros over the virginity that the Liberal would like to pre-serve intact. One sees in this speaker not von Hallberg's poet as liberal, "seeking the center," but a poet for whom the center, however desir-able in theory, is an untenable position. We know—from the poems

themselves, without Ian Hamilton to tell us—that Lowell often yielded
to the kind of temptation this poem describes.

If liberalism won't quite do, neither will radicalism. Lowell prefers
the New Left's "casually defined / anarchists' faith in playing the full
deck" to the "monochrome socialism" of the old ("West Side Sabbath,"
H, 180). The New Left's casual habits of definition, however, come
under satirical attack in "The Revolution" (*H*, 155), in which a stereo-
typical Californian brings news from the front:

> "We're in a prerevolutionary situation
> at Berkeley, an incredible, refreshing relief
> from your rather hot-house, good prep-school Harvard riots.
> The main thing is our exposure to politics;
> whether this a priori will determine
> the revolutionary's murder in the streets
> or the death of the haves by the have-nots, I don't know;
> but anyway you should be in on it—
> only in imagination can we lose the battle."

As the last line, with its caustic double meaning, tells us, this fool need
not fear defeat. His pretentious use of "a priori" and his empty statement that "The main thing is our exposure to politics" give him away,
and yet his position is a caricature of Lowell's own: that it is better to
plunge into experience for the splendor and intensity of it than to be
overfastidious in judgment, that it is better to be Alexander the Great,
trailing his crimes behind him, than his "mean, obscure, and dull" critics ("Death of Alexander").

Not only did Lowell recognize the banality of much New Leftist
rhetoric, he recognized that the myth of the student left as a party of
eros did not always correspond to the reality. His portrait of Mark
Rudd, the most prominent leader of the Columbia student strike in
1968, recognizes "blind ambition" on the left as well as on the right.
Like Mussolini and Hitler, "blind mouths shouting people into things,"
Lowell's "Leader of the Left" (*H*, 150) is a demagogic rhetorician:

> His voice, electric, only burns low current;
> by now he's bypassed sense and even eloquence—
> without listening, his audience believe.

The New Left was supposed to stand for authenticity in contrast to the
false front of American society, yet this New Leftist is all facade:

> his whole face took on a flesh of wood,
> a slab of raw plastic grafted to his one

natural feature, scars from demonstrations
borne like a Heidelberg student for the New Left . . .

Elsewhere, Lowell's treatment of the student leftists is sympathetic but also a bit condescending. In "Small College Riot" (*H*, 153), a "half-moon of students" is "coughing disk-hymns to pot." The students have set two bonfires, and as firemen move in to put them out, "we professors— / fans of the Colosseum—wipe our glasses / primed for the gladiatorial matinee." The poet is a spectator, rooting for the Christians against the lions, perhaps, but not a participant. Nonetheless, he has not become so much the entrenched academic as to share the blindness of "Our guest speaker on Shelley" who "says, 'If I met a student, I might have to kill him'"—forgetting which side Shelley himself would certainly have taken. In "Thanksgiving 1660 or 1960" (*H*, 160), "the young are mobile, friends of the tossed waste leaf [cf. Shelley, "Ode to the West Wind"], / bellbottom, barefoot, Christendom's wild hair." But they are also inarticulate ("words are what get in the way of what they say"), and their sexual promiscuity, unlike the poet's, is casual and impersonal, a Heraclitean flux in which "none sleeps with the same girl twice."

In many of the poems, the representation of political substance becomes curiously displaced. The two poems about the march on the Pentagon (*H*, 148–49) and the dramatic monologue "Women, Children, Babies, Cows, Cats" (*H*, 199) are the most content-oriented of the lot, and they are concerned with the war. But the poems about the Columbia strike, for instance, never touch on the students' objectives, only on the style of their behavior. For reasons noted in the opening chapter, the New Left emphasized political process rather than political goals, style and symbolic gesture more than results. Lowell appears to have accepted the New Left's reversal of priorities: his political poetry shares this preoccupation with manner. Although he is critical of the radicals' style, it does not occur to him to criticize them for being too concerned with style to begin with. At times, Lowell appears to consider the substance of political conflict too simple or obvious for any but the most vulgar representation and therefore fit to be recognized only by a tacit understanding or glimpsed at the margins of the poem with one's peripheral vision. Even the assassination of Martin Luther King, a figure whose identification with the civil cights movement is virtually iconographic, elicits from Lowell an eerily oblique response (*H*, 169):

Two Walls
(1968, Martin Luther King's Murder)
Somewhere a white wall faces a white wall
one wakes the other, the other wakes the first,
each burning with the other's borrowed splendor—
the walls, awake, are forced to go on talking,
their color looks much alike, two shadings of white,
each living in the shadow of the other.
How fine our distinctions when we cannot choose!
Don Giovanni can't stick his sword through stone,
two contracting, white stone walls—their pursuit
of happiness and his, coincident. . . .
At this point of civilization, this point of the world,
the only satisfactory companion we
can imagine is death—this morning, skin lumping in my throat,
I lie here, heavily breathing, the soul of New York.

Given the parenthetical reference to King, one may connect the references to whiteness and "color" with race, but the connection seems
arbitrarily allegorical. Without that directive, I doubt it would occur to
anyone to read this as a poem about race, much less about the death of
Martin Luther King. One would still be invited to read it as a poem
about "this point of civilization" and to take the opening lines as emblematic of a cultural impasse. But one would be more likely to come
up with a theme something like Marcuse's "one-dimensional" society
(here, Marcuse's rather clumsy metaphor of "one-dimensionality" would
be replaced by that of monochromaticism). A white wall is featureless,
blank, death-pallid (Melville's chapter on "The Whiteness of the Whale"
and Frost's "Design" come immediately to mind). Although the walls
are opposite each other, they are "much alike," each symbiotically
"burning with the other's borrowed splendor," "living in the shadow of
the other." If the speaker is the citizen enclosed in the four walls of his
nation, then the room in which he lives is a whited sepulchre. There is
an illusion of dialogue (the walls "are forced to go on talking") and an
illusion of choice ("How fine our distinctions when we cannot choose!"),
but in reality, the choices are all one: whiteness and blankness. Don
Giovanni appears as thwarted libido, the man of desire meeting the
negation of the white wall, which is like the white marble of the Com-
mendatore's statue.
    Yes, but what has all this to do with "Martin Luther King's Murder"?
If one tries to read the poem as directly *about* King or the struggle for

civil rights to which he gave his life, one must resort to the most contrived sort of allegorical substitution. One makes more headway by reading it as a poem about Lowell's meditation on American society, *prompted by* the shock of King's death. Here is one sense in which Lowell really does conflate public and private. The focus is often on his response, on some train of thought set in motion by events and only secondarily on events themselves. But this is a very different matter from the abolition of distinctions between public and private experience.

If, in many of the poems of *History*, Lowell avoids the clichés of psycho-politics and of confessional identification of self with history, in many others he does not. In "Che Guevara" (*H*, 145), for instance, he opens with an account of the

> Week of Che Guevara, hunted, hurt,
> held prisoner one lost day, then gangstered down
> for gold, for justice—violence cracking on violence,
> rock on rock, the corpse of our last armed prophet
> laid out on a sink in a shed, revealed by flashlight. . . .

The scene then shifts to Central Park, where the poet walks among New York's own "poor Latins much too new for our new world," and where "our clasped, illicit hands / pulse, stop my bloodstream as if I'd hit rock." The echo of "violence cracking on violence, / rock on rock" connects the suddenly introduced illicit love affair to the revolutionary heroism of Che the "armed prophet." The poem ends: "Rest for the outlaw . . . kings once hid in trees / with prices on their heads, and watched for game." The poem hastily constructs a community of the illicit, in which the poet and his mistress, the hunted revolutionary, and the deposed Charles I are all in the same predicament. One wants to reply, 'What is your extramarital affair (in which you have the company of millions of guilty husbands) compared with the success or failure of a revolution?' The poem is held together by ideological balingwire, by the assumption that sexual and political repression are connected.

Finally, however, the most serious reservation to be raised about *History* is that, in its attempt to be of its time yet skeptical of its time, to cover all the territory while avoiding all the traps, it tries to be too many things at once and lacks a center.[28] Williamson has noted that Lowell could be conservative and radical at once; von Hallberg praises *Notebook* for its "encyclopedic grandeur."[29] But to be always seeing each issue from all sides, qualifying each position with its corrective opposite, can become self-canceling rather than inclusive. One is left with the sense that history, for Lowell, finally operates on the Great Man principle—so many of the poems are named for someone and are at least predominantly concerned with an estimate of that person's place. The great artists, political leaders, conquerers, and tyrants blaze out for a moment in their individuality, subsiding into loss, death, disillusionment. Political roles—revolutionary, tyrant, liberal—are in essence dramatic roles, and history is a star vehicle. In rare instances, like that of Lincoln, who "may have loved underdogs and even mankind" (*H*, 88), someone may achieve historical immortality in a way that also commands moral admiration. For the most part, however, history poses the choice of being anonymous and good or illustrious and ruthless. As man and moralist, Lowell preferred, as he put it in "The March 2" (*H*, 149), to be "weak" and "right" rather than powerful and guilty. In two poems, "Can a Plucked Bird Live?" (*H*, 148) and "Non-Violent" (*H*, 200), he explicitly repudiates violence as a means to power. And yet, the bent of the imagination in these poems leads to another conclusion. Lowell is fascinated by Alexander, Caligula, Stalin, and Hitler, and palpably bored—as a poet, at least—by Abraham Lincoln or Eugene McCarthy. The important thing is to achieve a vivid individuality, to be (as Lowell says, not very convincingly, of Robert Kennedy) a figure "out of Plutarch" (*H*, 174).

If *History* is not the masterpiece that von Hallberg claims it is, it remains, centerless though it finally may be, far more searching and intelligent in its response to the events of the late sixties than other poetry of the period. And if the style, like the political stance of the author, seems uneasily caught between the desire to admit the inspiration of the *Zeitgeist* and the desire to resist it, nonetheless it achieves distinction, maybe even greatness, at its best moments. If there are many bad poems in *History*, there are, after all, a *great* many poems to begin with, enough to absorb considerable failure.

Of Lowell's career generally, I am forced to a similarly uninflammatory, measured assessment. There are disappointingly few poems that impress one as fully sustained and fully integrated throughout, and of these, many are in the minor mode of "Father's Bedroom" or "Soft Wood." There is a lot of slack writing and posturing in the late poetry especially, as Donald Hall has unsparingly noted.[30] And yet there are a great many lines that burn themselves into one's memory; the range and ambition of the lifework as a whole commands admiration; the complexity of the moral intelligence, the gift for writing the resonant line, set him apart from most of his contemporaries. There is simply more to him than there is to the rest of the poets I have considered here. When the smoke clears, some poet like Elizabeth Bishop who simply resisted the whole pull of the age may seem the best of our time. But if that doesn't happen, I think that Lowell, warts and all, will have to do.

5

Sylvia Plath: The Mythically Fated Self

If the prestige of Lowell's example made confessional poetry respectable, Sylvia Plath's suicide and posthumous volume *Ariel* gave it a martyr, a poet who had explored the "nihilism and destructiveness of the self" so fearlessly that she became lost in the interior and died there. Lowell's introduction to *Ariel*, in which he made the comparison between the poems and "Russian roulette with six cartridges in the cylinder" or "a game of 'chicken'" with "the wheels of both cars locked," contributed to the mythical aura surrounding Plath, as did such remarks as Berryman's speculation that she might have been "right to stick her head in the oven," given the unbearable evils of contemporary society. According to confessional hagiography, Plath was a dull poet before *Ariel*; toward the end of her life, she managed to release her imagination from the fetters of academic formalism, but in so doing, she also released her desire to die, which sprang from the same source as the late poems.

Plath's most nakedly confessional poems are also the most famous, but not necessarily her best. For Lowell, the discovery of the confessional mode led to a new directness of diction and to a more casual sort of public poem than he had been able to write before. Public and private converged in immediate experience and could be found there, tangled together. And yet, for the sake of artistic and moral clarity, Lowell found it necessary to disentangle them once again, reinstating distinctions between the two. He did not always succeed in doing so, but, as I have argued, the intention is often evident, and at times, the accomplished fact as well.

Critics such as Jon Rosenblatt and Judith Kroll have tried to correct the exaggerations in the Rosenthal-Alvarez view of Plath by arguing that her poems must be separated to some extent from the life and must not be read as a teleological journey toward her eventual suicide.[1] Kroll quite justly remarks that Plath, unlike Lowell or Sexton, seldom presents autobiography in much literal detail. Rather, she treats the events of her life as the plot of a myth, turning the key persons—her-

self, her father, her children, and her husband—into archetypal figures, transposing the story into a language of recurring symbols. "In
Plath—although many narrative details of her mythic system are
drawn from her life—the emphasis is more on expressing the structure
of her state of being."[2] But the mythical interpretation of Plath's work
can be turned around to confirm the conventional wisdom, since it
shows that Plath constructed the posthumous myth herself, within the
poems. Her suicide enacts the myth on the literal level, closing the gap
between art and life, myth and biography.

And yet, Plath's conception of her life as mythically fated was inherently self-destructive; it may indeed be held accountable for some of
the suffering dramatized in the autobiographical myth itself. To view
one's life as enacted myth is to embrace a determinism as strict as that
of Calvinism. The story is already written, the role already there to be
performed, and once one becomes conscious of the role, there is no
alternative but to play the story out to its end. Unlike Lowell's sort of
autobiographical poetry, which implies a constant attempt to change,
to heal the self by insight and confession, Plath's mythmaking seems
otherwise motivated. It offers the consolation that one's suffering may
have the dignity of fate rather than the triviality of accident. But in
return, it demands that one must not question the necessity of that
suffering.

Moreover, the conception of one's life as an unfolding myth is ahistorical; it pays no attention to the shifting circumstances in which one
lives, or to the unforeseen impingement of other lives upon one's own.
Sooner or later, the script of the myth is bound to conflict with the
imperatives of one's life as a social being. Plath's continual perception of
other people as threats to her integrity, their smiles or voices as "hooks"
on which she might be snared, may have something to do with her re-
sentment of their intrusion on her mythical fantasy. It is hard to be the
moon goddess with a husband, two kids, and literary friends who drop
in without notice.

Finally, in addition to these essentially moral objections to autobiography conceived as myth, there is a more purely technical problem.
Traditional myths are shared, prior to the individual poem, by poet
and audience alike. It is the poet's treatment of the myth that matters.
But an autobiographical myth comes to the audience only through the
poems themselves, which thus have the burden of converting private
history into a shared mythical pattern. Plath's poems sometimes bring
off this transformation, but at least part of her appeal is to readers who
treat the mythmaking of the poems as a sort of code to be penetrated;
nor can such readers be dismissed lightly as philistines, since many of

the poems invite such an approach. The most widely read of Plath's books nowadays is not *Ariel*, but *The Bell Jar*, which is an inferior work of art but also a better source of thinly veiled autobiography than the poems. There is, in short, a hazy boundary between transmuting autobiography into myth and teasing the reader with veiled half-revelations.

To the extent that Plath's work transcends these difficulties, it does so, I believe, by mitigating its ambitions. The strongest achievement of her poetry is its preternaturally vivid imagery, which she uses to convey a sense of what "the structure of her state of being" looks like from the inside. She does this in ways that are familiar from earlier symbolist and visionary-irrationalist poets—Mallarmé, Rimbaud, Hart Crane, and even T. S. Eliot. In her attempt to transcend the particular in the archetype, she sometimes resembles Kinnell, Merwin, Bly, or Wright, although her conception of archetypal symbolism is more complex than theirs. In general, she is least convincing when she is claiming cultural or mythical universality for her experience, most convincing when she is simply conveying the inward quality of that experience.

In her attempt to transform her life into myth, Plath seems to have been torn between two plots. There is an often-remarked discrepancy between the Plath of the journals and, still more, the Plath of the letters to her family, and the tragic Plath of the poems. The Plath who had to function socially as her mother's daughter seems caught up in a myth too, but her destiny in that myth is the opposite of the one in the poems. It is essentially a highbrow (and sexually transposed) version of the Horatio Alger success story, with a self-made woman rather than a self-made man and with poetic rather than monetary fortune-making as its goal. She was to be happy, industrious, constantly improving herself. Being a woman complicated success still further: one had to be a literary golden girl while also becoming a wife and mother. "I am made to be busy, gay, doing crazy jobs and writing this and that—stories and poems and nursing babies," she wrote in her journal entry for 19 July 1958. And then, with characteristic willfulness: "How to catapult myself into this?" Other entries contain exhortations to self-improvement: learn French and German, work up botany, the stars, the Tarot deck; try to be more cheerful ("Joy: show joy & enjoy: then others will be joyful. Bitterness the one sin. That and the ever-prevalent sloth"). She did not think of writing as a game of chicken but as a way to happiness. In the fall of 1959, when she was trying her hand at short stories, she wrote: "If, IF I could break into a meaningful prose, that expressed my feelings, I would be free. Free to have a wonderful life. I am desperate when I am verbally repressed." The mood of the journals oscillates between days when she can say "I am now a calm, happy writer" and days when she can only long for "the right state of mind like a never never land ahead of me."[3]

The letters are even more insistent in their dogged will to happiness. One would not expect them to be as candid as a private journal, but when, in the letter of 27 August 1962 announcing her separation from Ted Hughes, she insists that she is on the brink of "a wonderful life," she is not merely keeping up appearances for mother, but speaking in a voice we immediately recognize from the journals:

> I do not believe in divorce and would never think of this [the separation], but I simply cannot go on living the degraded and agonized life I have been living, which has stopped my writing and just about ruined my sleep and health . . .
>
> . . . I feel I need a legal settlement so I can count on so much a week for groceries and bills and the freedom to build up the happy, pleasant life I feel it in myself to make and would but for him . . .
>
> I have too much at stake and am too rich a person to live as a martyr . . . I want a clean break, so I can breathe and laugh and enjoy myself again.[4]

Less than two months from the end, she still clung to her optimism; in the letters of 14 December and 21 December, she again insisted that she had "never been so happy in [her] life."

The tragic myth of her poetry and the doggedly optimistic success-myth of the journals and letters have in common a violent oscillation between extremes, a sense that the alternatives are unalloyed happiness and bottomless misery, with nothing between. Indeed, one can understand the tragic myth as a response to the impossibility of the complete success demanded by the other myth. Already, when she was laboring over the manuscript of *The Colossus*, she was apparently unable to conceive of literary progress as anything less than a "clean break," or as catapulting herself from the old to the new.

Some critics have found in Plath's work a preoccupation with spiritual rebirth, while others read it as the testament of suicidal despair.[5] But these parties have aligned themselves on opposite sides of a conflict within Plath herself, although the poems reveal the conflict without quite defining its nature. What one finds in Plath is a desire for self-transformation so extreme that it is closely akin to a desire for self-destruction, since the old self must be completely denied in the making of the new. The study of Plath's career can suggest a damning indictment of the entire confessional project: What if the stripping away of false masks is only a way of flaying oneself alive, uncovering no jewel of authenticity deep in the forehead, but only more bleeding layers of fallen, compromised selfhood?

The essential plot of the myth created in the poems is that of fall and reunification. With the death of her father when she was still a child, the speaker of the poems has been thrown into an unbearable state of separation. All other relationships seem insufficiently pure; what she really desires is a reunion with her father beyond death. The themes of uncontaminated authenticity, death, and the recovery of fullness are thus closely related. The repeated presentation of the poet as moon goddess, especially in the demonic aspect of Hecate, traced by Kroll through the poetry, expresses all of these at once. The moon is chaste and distant, uninvolved with this world; deathly and cold, associated with magic. Plath again and again uses the tidal pull of the moon as the source of a metaphor in which the sea appears as a masculine figure; the figure emerges with full clarity for the first time in "Moonrise" (1958):

> Lucina, bony mother, laboring
> Among the socketed white stars, your face
> Of candor pares white flesh to the white bone,
>
> Who drag our ancient father at the heel,
> White-bearded, weary.

I shall have more to say of this metaphor when we come to "The Moon and the Yew Tree," the most richly suggestive of the thirteen poems in which it appears. For the moment, it suffices that the moon, whose frightening truthfulness ("face / of candor") is hostile to all vanities of the "white flesh"), retains, in her barrenness, a fatal bond to the "ancient father," and she has power over him as she drags him "at the heel"—a phrase that evokes someone trying to train a recalcitrant dog.

The poet, as character in her poems, has the coldness—the refusal of what, in "The Moon and the Yew Tree," she calls "tenderness"—that she associates with the moon; at times it amounts to a hatred of life itself. And yet, through the metaphor of the tidal bond to the sea, she suggests that it is through this refusal of worldly attachment that she retains the bond to the father. In his absence, the world is empty, her relations to others within it inauthentic. Only through the recovery of a radical purity can she go back to the prior state of fullness, to the childhood happiness that preceded his death. Several of her most memorable endings equate death with a recovery of childhood innocence. In "A Birthday Present," for instance, if the present "were death,"

There would be a nobility then, there would be a birthday.
And the knife not carve, but enter

Pure and clean as the cry of a baby,
And the universe slide from my side.

One might also cite the endings of "Getting There," "Fever 103°," and "Ariel." Happiness, in this way of imagining her own life, was something lost with the death of her father, and recoverable, if at all, only by a radical self-repudiation and self-transformation. As her career advanced, the only sufficiently radical self-transformation came, increasingly, to be the repudiation of life itself. The inward state that Plath expressed with ever increasing clarity did not permit significant change; the kind of change that was possible gave her no hope. The same desperation shows in her attitude toward her work as a poet.

"What a trash / To annihilate each decade," says the speaker of "Lady Lazarus." For Plath, all her previous poems were but trash to be annihilated by the next. She demanded of her poetry an endless series of breakthroughs, each one of them a reproach to everything that had come before, which became, in retrospect, empty, inauthentic, fraudulent. Hughes's account of her struggles with the first book, in his introduction to the *Collected Poems*, shows the pattern very clearly. Proposing, on 10 February 1958, to use "The Earthenware Head" as the title poem of her first collection, Plath wrote in her journal: "Somehow this new title spells for me the release from the old crystal-brittle and sugar-faceted voice of *Circus in Three Rings* and *Two Lovers and a Beachcomber* [titles she had previously considered]." "A fortnight later," Hughes recalls, "the title had become *Full Fathom Five*." "The Earthenware Head," so recently hailed as a source of deliverance, was suddenly odious: "once, in England, my 'best poem'; too fancy, glassy, patchy, and rigid—it embarrasses me now. . . ." By the time she had sent the book off under its eventual title, *The Colossus*, she had experienced yet another literary conversion in "Poem for a Birthday" (November 1959) and declared, "The manuscript of my old book seems dead to me." As Hughes observes, "Her evolution as a poet went rapidly through successive moults of style";[6] she continually needed, as she put it in "Ariel," to "unpeel / Dead hands, dead stringencies." Or at least she needed to believe that she was doing so.

Without denying the obvious difference between the late poems and those of *The Colossus*, one may wonder whether critics who find a startling metamorphosis in the course of Plath's brief career have not been listening too credulously to the rhetoric of the poems themselves, which constantly protest that they are breaking out of one prison or another. As Kroll points out, Plath's poems all seem bent on expressing "the structure of her state of being," and as the architectural figure of "structure" and the etymological relation of "state" to "stasis" implies, they are all, in that respect, different versions of the same poem. Plath's conception of her inner condition as an absolute, inalterable ground of all experience accounts in part for the extraordinary immediacy of her imagery, in which "details often have the force of hallucination." But it also tells us

why there is no real temporal development in the late poems; for since the objects in these poems function as 'releasers' of a pre-determined meaning, there is no real openness to possibilities (though there is sometimes an apparent temporal development, as in "Kindness" or "The Bee Meeting," for the sake of drama). The object encountered by the persona does not have the potential for determining an outcome, and therefore a certain tension between object and subject is lacking. The tension in Plath's poetry is located instead in the pre-existing oppositions constituting the state of being which is 'released' by certain objects and situations through their inherent relevance to it, in a reenactment of her timeless myth.[7]

Here, Kroll has described what I take to be the most serious limitation of Plath's work. The growth from the early poems to the late consists in the discovery of increasingly adequate language for a condition of soul which, however complex and intense, remains impervious to change, closed to all becoming. She has been praised, in the rhetoric that Lowell brought into fashion, for her increasing openness to experience, for her movement away from her early, technique-obsessed manner, and yet her progress was almost entirely technical. Her conception of herself and of her relation to the world around her changes very little; what changes is rather her ability to express that conception in the style and form of her poems.

Plath conceives of herself as in need of radical transformation, but ironically, this theme of transformation is constant and generates a constellation of recurring motifs that can be traced through the whole body of her work, early and late. And already in her earliest mature work, we find the conviction that significant change requires a repudiation of all that one has been up to that point. The repudiation of all one has been is, of course, closely akin to suicide, which would be self-repudiation without the hope of a self-renewal to follow. Already in "Tale of a Tub" (1956), she finds that "each day demands we create our whole world over, / disguising the constant horror in a coat / of many fictions" (*SP*, 25). If one hears the apprentice poet imitating *Four*

Quartets in these lines, one also notes her characteristic revision of Eliot's desire, in "Burnt Norton," for

> both a new world
> And the old made explicit, understood
> In the completion of its partial ecstasy,
> The resolution of its partial horror.[8]

For Plath, the horror is "constant," not "partial," and it can be neither understood nor resolved, only concealed beneath "fictions" invented to evade the unbearable truth. In "Tale of a Tub," making the whole world over means covering it with fictive clothing; elsewhere, more characteristically, it means the reverse, the stripping away of inauthentic coverings and the refusal of evasion. But Plath almost always portrays the human condition as unremittingly desperate. Even moments of epiphanic beauty come, in her poetry, as a violence breaking into a state of acedic lassitude. "I only know," she says in "Black Rook in Rainy Weather" (1956),

> that a rook
> Ordering its black feathers can so shine
> As to seize my senses, haul
> My eyelids up, and grant
>
> A brief respite from fear
> Of total neutrality.

(SP, 57)

Like John Donne, she cries "Batter my heart"; she must be seized and hauled against her own will. Unlike Donne, she asks the world, not God, to do the hauling, and she hopes not for salvation, but only for "brief respite," until it is time, as Lady Lazarus would say, to do it again. The word "haul" returns in "Ariel," where it describes a similar kind of release: "Something else / Hauls me through air" (SP, 239). Only when thus overpowered can Plath be dragged from her old identity.

One may derive from these considerations a few cautionary warnings against confessional clichés. Plath's poetry shows how the pursuit of authenticity can erect barriers to change, by concentrating on the truth of one's inner being to the neglect of the interaction between self and world, which can gradually re-shape that being. And the harshness with which she turned on her past work with each advance, real or imagined, toward the "real" self shows the extent to which authenticity can become a tyrant. In their concern with liberation of the repressed self, advocates of confessional poetry do not heed Freud's warning that the superego is also unconscious and behaves much like the id. Plath's self-flagellation in her journals, in which she berates herself for being insufficiently spontaneous and insufficiently in touch with the dark gods of the blood, is much like Victorian self-reproaches for insufficient control of the very impulses that she would like to liberate. Hers is a Victorian superego in id's clothing.

Finally, there is the problem that poets such as Lowell and Plath herself raised quite deliberately: the conflict between the claims of immediacy and the claims of detachment. Clearly, the confessional poets reacted against what they considered an excessively tame, reserved, and aloof poetry. But one can see in Plath's work that giving all to the claims of immediacy renders moral self-knowledge extremely difficult. As articulate expressions of extreme inner states, her poems are justly celebrated. But as quests for self-knowledge, they are far less impressive. Plath was not very good at uncovering the relations between her inward state of being and her outward vicissitudes. The argument advanced by Alvarez and Rosenthal, that the confessional poet discovers in personal suffering a symbol of cultural crisis, applies much less convincingly to Plath than to Lowell; and, as I have argued, it is not always a satisfactory way of talking about Lowell's poetry either.

One can see Plath's strengths and characteristic weaknesses in two of her best-known poems, "Daddy" and "Lady Lazarus." The vacillation of tone and of point of view that mars Lowell's "Skunk Hour" becomes, in Plath, more like a violent oscillation. The extremes of passionate lyrical outcry and ironic self-deprecation are more sharply drawn, the transitions between them more abrupt.

"Daddy" is one of Plath's most detailed autobiographical poems, and perhaps for that reason, it occasionally takes the shared resonance of private references too much for granted. When Plath describes her father as a "Ghastly statue with one gray toe / Big as a Frisco seal," the reader may shrug and mutter, "Oh, well, a harmless touch of surrealism." If one reads Butscher's biography and learns that Otto Plath's fatal illness began when "he developed a sore on his toe in the middle of 1940 and neglected it completely until he required hospitalization,"[9] the literal significance of this otherwise arbitrary detail becomes clear. But one can read not only "Daddy," but all of the other poems as well, without finding the literal fact required to remove the lines about the "gray toe" from the opacity of private symbolism. One might also ask the motive for the portentousness surrounding the ages ten, twenty, and thirty (which requires Otto Plath to die when his daughter is ten rather than eight). Finally, the association of the father with Nazis becomes somewhat more comprehensible when we realize that Otto Plath died in 1940. The Plaths, as German Americans, were appalled by Hitler and followed the news from Europe closely. One can see how, to a child, the death of her father, roughly coinciding with a terrible threat emanating from the father's country of origin, might suggest fantasies of Hitler as her father's ghost, striking back from the grave. But all of this is guesswork based on information withheld from the poem—and withheld, it seems likely, from Plath's conscious recognition also. To interpret the poem thus is not merely to use biography as a way of understanding context, but to use it as a counter-text, correcting that of the poem. Such interpretations may be useful in reconstructing biographical truth, but they will not do for reading poems.

"Daddy" always makes a powerful and simple effect when read aloud. One hears the gradual release of suppressed anger, building to the triumphant dismissal: "Daddy, Daddy, you bastard, I'm through." The simplicity immediately evaporates when one begins to ask what attitude the poem encourages us to take toward its speaker. To what extent does this voice have the poet's endorsement? One finds, once the initial impact has worn off, many of the ironic disclaimers associated with dramatic monologue. By calling the poem "Daddy" rather than, say, "Father," Plath lets us know that she recognizes the outburst to follow as childish, truer to the child's fantasy of domination and abandonment than to the adult's reconstruction of the facts. The diction of the poem keeps reminding us of that childishness: "Achoo" as a verb, "gobbledy-goo," "pretty red heart." The obsessive repetition, not only of certain words but of the rhyme-sound *oo*, evokes the doggerel of playground chants or, more to the point, the stubborn reiterations of a temper tantrum. The poet shows her awareness that her rage *is* partly a tantrum by allowing the savagery to be touched with humor:

> There's a stake in your fat black heart
> And the villagers never liked you.
> They are dancing and stamping on you.
> They always *knew* it was you.

> (*SP,* 224)

But of course they couldn't know "it was you," since "daddy" is a vampire only in the privacy of the speaker's fantasy. The joke turns—although one may laugh at it without quite realizing this—on the brazen ratification of private nightmare as communal good sense.

There is some warrant, then, for claiming that the speaker of "Daddy" does not have the full endorsement of the poet, who knew

very well how excessive the speaker's outburst is and wrote that knowledge into the poem. On these grounds too, one might defend the
poem against Irving Howe's charge that "there is something monstrous,
utterly disproportionate, when tangled emotions about one's father are
deliberately compared with the historical fate of the European Jews." [10]
If we argue that the poet encloses the speaker's point of view within a
more mature authorial judgment, we can claim that the disproportion
is deliberate and ironic. The grotesque inflation of private suffering to
the scale of the holocaust would then illustrate the workings of the unconscious, in which such distortions occur as a matter of course, and
would not represent the poet's rational assessment of her condition. It
was not Plath or any other confessional poet, but W. H. Auden who
wrote:

> Accurate scholarship can
> Unearth the whole offense
> From Luther until now
> That has driven a culture mad,
> Find what occurred at Linz,
> What huge imago made
> A psychopathic god. . . . [11]

If, as Auden's lines would have it, the "psychopathic god" whom the
Nazis worshipped as their *Führer* was an externalization of typical
German fantasies about typical German fathers, why should we fault
Plath for looking through the other end of the telescope, finding in her
own fantasies about "daddy" the stuff of which psychopathic gods are
made?

Having made this defense, however, I find that the poem as a whole
will not sustain it. Sometimes, as in the simpering cuteness of "bit my
pretty red heart in two" or the impotently furious tautology of "the
brute, brute heart / Of a brute like you," Plath seems intent on making
her speaker sound foolish. But there is no mistaking the dead-serious
rage that generates the poem's hypnotic reiterations. The ironic self-
deflation fades in and out without warning:

> But the name of the town is common
> My Polack friend
>
> Says there are a dozen or two.
> So I never could tell where you
> But your foot, your root,
> I never could talk to you.
> The tongue stuck in my jaw.

It stuck in a barb wire snare.
Ich, ich, ich, ich,
I could hardly speak.
I thought every German was you.
And the language obscene

An engine, an engine
Chuffing me off like a Jew,
A Jew to Dachau, Auschwitz, Belsen.
I began to talk like a Jew.
I think I may well be a Jew.

(SP, 222–23)

One can get dizzy trying to follow the tonal shifts of this passage. The first lines are casual: the speaker can use the pejorative "Polack," since the friend knows it's a joke. "There are a dozen or two"—the precise number is of no great concern. "The name of the town is common," after all. One would never guess, from these three lines alone, the breathless intensity that prevails elsewhere in the poem. From their perspective, the story of Otto Plath is but one of many like it—many immigrants came to America from towns like his. But with the next lines, we are back inside the speaker's haunted psyche: the location of the town becomes a dark secret withheld, another proof that "I never could talk to you." With the return of the *oo* rhyme, the obsessive, angry voice that began the poem returns also. The speaker's comparison of herself to a Jew hauled off "to Dachau, Auschwitz, Belsen" is chilling, but the last two lines of the passage are again ironic, even incongruously funny.

Not only does the tone of "Daddy" veer precipitously between the luridly sinister and the self-deprecatingly clever, there are places where Plath's technical competence simply deserts her. Poems that ironically bracket the consciousness of the speaker within that of the poet must give assurances that the poet sees through the language of the speaker, and recognizes, as the speaker does not, its evasions and failures. Many lines, even whole stanzas, resist enclosure in an ironic discourse:

I have always been scared of *you,*
With your Luftwaffe, your gobbledygoo.
And your neat mustache
And your Aryan eye, bright blue.
Panzer-man, panzer-man, O you—

(SP, 223)

"Scared of *you*"—this is the speech of childhood, but in earnest. "Gobbledygoo" is also the language of childhood, but it is applied to the father, not the daughter, and seems to be chosen for reasons of sound, not sense. Why is "gobbledygoo" parallel to "Luftwaffe," as if it were an equally dreaded alternative? The rhythm of the last line, moreover, is extremely awkward. The sing-songy lilt of iambs and anapests suddenly reverses accent in a line of two dactyls followed by an iamb. (I assume demoted stress on the last syllable of "panzer-man," because otherwise there is total metrical chaos.) The exclamation "O you," since it cannot raise the already feverish emotional temperature any further, appears, like "gobbledygoo," to result from carelessness. My point is not just that the stanza is badly written, although it is, but that it sounds full of conviction, rather than ironically aware of its own badness. One cannot feel that the poet sees through the speaker's obsession and presents it to the reader for judgment.

My reservations about "Daddy" are similar to those expressed earlier about "Skunk Hour." Both poems memorably evoke intense and painful inward states but vacillate in their implicit interpretation of the experience they present. In both, the language fluctuates between lyrical endorsement and ironic critique of the speaker's despair. Such vacillation, of course, occurs in the experience of those who struggle against despair or madness, but if form is not to be mere imitative form, poetry about this kind of experience must clarify the motives of that vacillation rather than simply reproducing it.

"Lady Lazarus," another anthology-piece, reveals that this vacillation has, in addition to its misplaced mimetic function, a rhetorical function as well. This poem, much more overtly than "Daddy," anticipates and manipulates the responses of the reader. The speaker alternately solicits our sympathy and rebukes us for meddling.[12] "Do I terrify?" she asks; she certainly hopes so. By comparing her recovery from a suicide attempt to the resurrection of Lazarus, she imagines herself as the center of a spectacle—we envision Christ performing a miracle before the astonished populace of Bethany. But unlike the beneficiary of the biblical miracle, Plath's "lady Lazarus" accomplishes her own resurrection and acknowledges no power greater than herself. "Herr God; Herr Lucifer, / Beware / Beware," she warns. Her self-aggrandizing gestures invite attention, and yet we are to be ashamed of ourselves if we accept the invitation:

The peanut-crunching crowd
Shoves in to see

Them unwrap me hand and foot—
The big strip-tease.

(*SP*, 245)

The crowd is aggressive ("shoves"), its interest lascivious; it seeks an illicit titillation, if not from the speaker's naked body, then from her naked psyche.

Again, one might argue that the divided tone of "Lady Lazarus" is a legitimately mimetic representation of the psychology of suicide. A suicide attempt is partly motivated by the wish to get attention and exact revenge on those who have withheld attention in the past by making them feel responsible for one's death. Those who attempt suicide in a manner unlikely to succeed—and Plath's attempts, including the successful one, seem to have been intended to fail[13]—are torn between the desire "to last it out and not come back at all" and the hope that someone will care enough to intervene. Moreover, a suicide attempt is itself a confession, a public admission of inward desperation. Recovering from such an attempt, one would have to contend with the curiosity aroused in other people. One might indeed feel stripped naked, sorry to have called so much attention to oneself, and yet suddenly powerful in commanding so much attention.

Plath's analogy of the strip-tease or the sideshow conveys, with force and precision, the ambivalence of suicidal despair. Had she extended that metaphor through the entire poem, holding its complexities in balance, "Lady Lazarus" might have achieved the stability of tone and judgment lacking in "Daddy." But unfortunately, Plath succumbed to the urge to whip up further lurid excitement with the analogy of the concentration camp, introduced in stanzas two and three but dormant thereafter until it returns at the end of stanza twenty-one. It reenters stealthily:

There is a charge
For the eyeing of my scars, there is a charge
For the hearing of my heart.
It really goes.
And there is a charge, a very large charge,
For a word or a touch
Or a bit of blood
Or a piece of my hair or my clothes.

(*SP*, 246)

The first five lines of this passage, which continue the metaphor of strip-tease or freak show, are witty and self-possessed in their bitterness. "Large charge" is, of course, slang for "big thrill" and so glances at the titillation the audience receives as well as the price of admission. But with "a bit of blood / Or a piece of my hair or my clothes," we suddenly recall the "Nazi lampshade" of stanza two. The speaker's "enemy," whether it be Herr God, Herr Lucifer, or the peanut-crunching crowd, would kill her and dismember the body for commodities (or, in the context of biblical miracle, relics; in either case she is martyred). Interestingly, as the irony becomes less controlled, more phantasmagorical and unhinged, the rhythm begins to fall into anapests, and the rhyme on "goes" and "clothes" is one of the most insistent in the poem. The sound of the poetry, reminiscent of light verse, combines strangely with its macabre sense, rather like certain passages in "The Raven" where one feels that Poe has been demonically possessed by W. S. Gilbert ("For we cannot help agreeing that no living human being / Ever yet was blessed with seeing bird above his chamber door").

In the last twenty lines of "Lady Lazarus," irony vanishes, its last glimmer coming ten lines from the end in "Do not think I underestimate your great concern." By this point, the speaker has turned from the crowd to address a single threatening figure:

So, so, Herr Doktor
So, Herr Enemy.

I am your opus,
I am your valuable
The pure gold baby. . . .

(*SP,* 246)

The enemy, hitherto unspecified, turns out to be a German male authority figure, perhaps a scholar like Otto Plath ("Herr Doktor"), who thinks of the speaker as his "pure gold baby." An inward confrontation with this father imago replaces the confrontation with the intrusive crowd. The poem enters a realm of pure fantasy as the "Herr Doktor" rapidly assumes the cosmic proportions of "Herr God, Herr Lucifer." There is also a shift in the figurative language, corresponding to the shift in tone and implied audience. The clammy imagery of "the grave cave" and "worms . . . like sticky pearls" gives way to an imagery of death by fire. The resurrection of Lazarus becomes the birth of the Phoenix, and the extended metaphor of a public spectacle abruptly disappears. The threat of the final line, "And I eat men like air" (*SP,* 247), has little connection with anything in the first twenty-one stanzas.

As with "Daddy," one may try to save consistency by declaring the speaker a "persona." The poem, by this reckoning, reveals a woman gradually caught up in her anger and carried by it toward a recognition of its true object: not the crowd of insensitive onlookers, but the father and husband who have driven her to attempt suicide. The end of the poem, thus understood, breaks free of defensive irony to release cathartic rage. But it is hard to see why this rage is cathartic, since it no sooner locates its "real" object than it begins to convert reality back into fantasy again, in a grandiose and finally evasive fashion. Was it that Plath unconsciously doubted her right to be angry and therefore had to convict her father and her husband of Hitlerian monstrosities in order to justify the anger she nonetheless felt? Or did she fear that the experiential grounds of her emotions were too personal for art unless mounted on the stilts of myth or psycho-historical analogy? On such questions one can only speculate, and the answers, even if they were obtainable, could illuminate the poems only as biographical evidence, not as poems.

There are, in addition to the overtly confessional poems that have attracted the widest attention, some poems in Plath's later manner that glance at autobiography only indirectly. They have the same emphasis on painful and extreme emotions that one finds in the confessional work, and it may be that without the confessional poems, these others could not have been written. The best example of the kind of poem I have in mind is "The Moon and the Yew Tree," which, as a phenomenological description of "the structure of her state of being," is more revealing, I would argue, than "Daddy" or "Lady Lazarus." It explores, in a more closely argued way, Plath's underlying sense of tragic futility, her conviction, as she wrote in "Words," that "From the bottom of the pool, fixed stars / Govern a life" (*SP*, 270). Hughes recalls that the poem seemed to him and to Plath herself "a statement from the powers in control of our life."[14] Just as "For the Union Dead" shows Lowell using the possibilities of style and subject matter discovered in his confessional poems for nonconfessional purposes, "The Moon and the Yew Tree" has the emotional directness of a confessional poem without the impulse toward literal narrative. Written in October 1961, it comes just before Plath's first ventures into the confessional mode, unless one counts such incipiently confessional poems as "Tulips."

Kroll considers "The Moon and the Yew Tree" to be the first of Plath's late poems, for in it the poet identifies herself for the first time with the sinister moon goddess who was already a prominent figure in her imagination.[15] Although it has much in common with the later, more explicitly autobiographical poetry, it relies less than those later poems on the knowledge of events in the poet's life; it is a meditative distillation of emotions that she elsewhere ascribes to causes—her father's death, her husband's betrayal. That approach to autobiography clashes, as I have tried to show in discussing "Daddy" and "Lady Lazarus," with her tendency to regard her inward perception of father and husband as absolutely valid, unaccountable to any inquiry into what actually happened; as a result, outward events such as her father's death lose their power to clarify or explain the inward perception, since they are present only as distorted in fantasy. This is a more skeptical way of stating Kroll's thesis that Plath turned autobiography into myth. In "Daddy" and to a lesser extent in "Lady Lazarus" also, Plath undertakes to explain the emotions she presents; in "The Moon and the Yew Tree," there is presentation without the claim to understand. The more modest claim allows a fuller realization.

"The Moon and the Yew Tree," as I shall try to show by close reading, hangs together more successfully than the more explanatory poems. It is not distracted by attempts to manipulate the reader's sympathy and judgment of the emotion it reveals. The speakers of "Daddy" and "Lady Lazarus" are acutely conscious of an audience, but "The Moon and the Yew Tree" is intimate speech overheard. It opens not with a cry of refusal ("You do not do") or an ambiguous boast ("I have done it again"), but with a tentative groping for definition: "This is the light of the mind, cold and planetary. / The trees of the mind are black. The light is blue" (*SP*, 172).

In a sense, these opening lines show the poet constructing an objective correlative, Eliot-fashion. "This," as the first word of the poem, can only refer back to the landscape evoked by the title: the black-and-blue landscape outside the window is also the landscape of the mind, with its inward bruises. Typically, however, Plath feels threatened as well as expressively enabled by the impingement of the world on her own consciousness: "The grasses unload their griefs on my feet as if I were God, / Prickling my ankles. . . ." By post-romantic convention, poets are the gods of their own creations, but Plath would refuse that role. The griefs of the grasses (and by synecdoche, of the rest of the landscape) only burden and irritate her. She lacks God's power to console or heal, and indeed she has griefs of her own that she would unburden, if she could only "believe in tenderness."

"This place"—the place where the yew tree and church stand in the moonlight, but also, by the equation stated in the opening lines, the psychological landscape that the speaker inhabits—is "Separated from [her] house by a row of headstones." The phrasing makes the place seem very close (as if *only* the headstones lay between it and the house), but it also makes the headstones seem closer still, as if the graveyard reached to the front steps. Death is literally at the speaker's door, and beyond it lies a landscape that offers nothing, as we soon discover, but further symbols of death and of a faith that the speaker cannot possibly affirm. Hence, she "simply cannot see where there is to get to." That statement might stand as an epigraph to Plath's collected poems, since in the world as she portrays it there is never any point in getting anywhere, except perhaps through complete self-transformation.

The description of the moon at the beginning of the second stanza is one of the most memorable passages in Plath's work:

> The moon is no door. It is a face in its own right,
> White as a knuckle and terribly upset.
> It drags the sea after it like a dark crime; it is quiet
> With the O-gape of complete despair.

(SP, 173)

This figure of moon and sea, as noted earlier, occurs repeatedly in Plath's work, but it releases its full implications for the first time here. It is the power of these particular words, in this particular order, that eludes Kroll's mythographic approach and accounts for the distinctiveness of these lines.

"The moon is no door." But no one has said that it is; indeed, this is the first mention of the moon within the poem. So the idea that the moon *is* a door must be taken as an oblique allusion to a *topos*, to some conventional idea that Plath wishes to negate. In medieval cosmography, the moon marked the boundary between the immutable heavens and the mutable world; it was in that sense a "door" from the perishable to the transcendent. In post-romantic literary symbolism (and especially in the work of Yeats, whom Plath admired and in whose house she was to die), the moon also serves as an emblem of an elusive transcendence. If the moon *were* such a door, there would be somewhere "to get to" after all. But the speaker sees the moon instead as "a face in its own right." Taken, as it were, at face value, this correction means that the moon will not lend itself to our symbol-making. It has its own aspect, not the one our imaginations would lend it. But on second thought, one recalls that the "face" we construe from the markings on the moon is an anthropomorphic projection, derived from the barest suggestion in appearances. Looking for a "door" out of our own condition, we do not find it; nor do we find, as it seems at first, an otherness that refuses our projections. Rather, we meet ourselves. So we are not surprised that the moon, like the speaker, is "terribly upset." It is "white as a knuckle"—more precisely, the knuckle of a "terribly upset" person, since the knuckles become white only when the fist is clenched in tension. The moon, in short, is sub-lunary, as vulnerable and distraught as the woman who observes it. And as guilty: "It drags the sea after it like a dark crime."

The tidal pull of the moon upon the sea is the most constant motif in Plath's recurring lunar imagery. Most interesting on this occasion is the way the moon becomes burdened by the sea. Using other poems as context, one could translate this sense of burden into autobiography. The sea is usually associated with Plath's father, and so the "dark crime" would be parricide, since Plath, like any eight-year-old child, must have blamed herself for her father's death. Or perhaps, since the moon is not the speaker but the speaker's mother, the blame has been shifted to Aurelia Plath.

Nonetheless, I have been claiming preeminence for "The Moon and the Yew Tree" precisely because it does not require autobiographical decoding to hold our interest. Instead of trotting out the private mythology, therefore, we might do better to glance back at line three: "The grasses unload their griefs on my feet as if I were God." Like the moon, the speaker feels burdened by her own power; the grasses turn to her for comfort when she herself feels weak and "upset." When she herself looks to the moon for a "door," or for the protection of a mother or goddess, she finds only the projection of her own condition. The "O-gape of complete despair" replaces the anticipated door: instead of an opened doorway, a mouth opened as if to speak, but "quiet," silenced by despair. To go through this doorway is to be swallowed rather than rescued.

"I live here," the speaker abruptly declares, after her description of the moon. Literally, "here" refers forward, to the place where the church bells ring twice each Sunday, but it seems at first to refer back to the moon or to the spiritual condition the moon represents. The ambiguity is in this case enriching rather than self-canceling. The three lines about the church bells recapitulate the movement of the poem through the first two stanzas. At first, Plath describes the bells with a heaven-storming magniloquence reminiscent of Dylan Thomas or Hart Crane; they are "Eight great tongues affirming the Resurrection." Here again is the promise of rebirth or transcendence, in a language sonorous enough to carry conviction. But "At the end, they soberly bong out their names." Tolled abruptly back to their sole selves, they can affirm nothing beyond their own bell-nature. Like the moon, they offer a "door" that only leads back to where one started. The remainder of the poem moves by oscillation; one might criticize its lack of development, since it merely repeats the pattern of hope and negation established in the first two stanzas. But unlike the shifts of tone in

"Daddy" and "Lady Lazarus," these oscillations are motivated by the progression of thought; they are not arbitrary tricks of perspective.

The last two stanzas, moreover, are not completely static. In addition to the thematic complication introduced by the religious motifs associated with the church, there is a remission of the sinister Gothic rhetoric, which only reasserts itself in the last two lines. The most luridly sinister effects in Plath's late poetry have been taken as the most sincere, proving that she had looked unblinkingly into the most fearful recesses of the unconscious. And yet such brilliantly disturbing writing as the lunar passage in stanza two only gains its full effect when juxtaposed with the simple, almost childlike voice heard in stanza three: "How I would like to believe in tenderness." This simpler voice implicitly questions the grandiose fatalism urged at the beginning and the end of the poem.

The beginning of the third stanza contributes strongly to the sense of futile oscillation:

> The yew tree points up. It has a Gothic shape.
> The eyes lift after it and find the moon.
>
> (*SP*, 173)

But of course the eyes have already found the moon in the previous stanza, only to be directed, as we have seen, back to the earth. Surveying the earthly prospect, the speaker finds the yew tree, which directs her gaze back to the moon once more. "The eyes" act on their own, as if their possessor had no choice but to obey the yew tree. And yet the poem begins, in an understated way, to question the yew tree's message. "The moon is my mother. She is not sweet like Mary." This is the voice of a child disappointed in a parent: I wish Mary had been my mother (if only the grasses had been right in taking me for "God," she would have been!). Instead, my mother is the moon. Both are virginal, and both wear the color blue. It was easy to get them confused, until mother began to "unloose small bats and owls."

Unlike the defiant lady Lazarus, the speaker of "The Moon and the Yew Tree" regrets being chosen by fate for the role of Sibyl, Hecate, or Medea:

> How I would like to believe in tenderness—
> The face of the effigy, gentled by candles,
> Bending, on me in particular, its mild eyes.
>
> (*SP*, 173)

The "effigy" (presumably of Mary) represents a desire not so much for religious consolation as for the kind mother displaced by the moon. By representing her as an "effigy," Plath reminds us again that the desire is futile—an effigy cannot bend its head, and its eyes see no one. But even the balked desire for tenderness, for a personal affection addressed to someone "in particular," is rare in Plath's work, which usually presents the self as isolated amidst impersonal forces. In the context of such prevailing harshness, the desire for tenderness is all the more fragile and touching. Moreover, it gives us something against which to measure the surrounding despair, which becomes comprehensible as the loss of a capacity—still experienced in brief flashes— for affection and hope. Otherwise, one might suppose that despair, for Plath, was simply inherent in the nature of things. But upon recognizing her own disbelief in "tenderness," the speaker declares that she has "fallen a long way."

With the flicker of gentleness once more extinguished, the poem modulates back to the color symbolism of its opening lines:

> Clouds are flowering
> Blue and mystical over the face of the stars.
> Inside the church, the saints will be all blue,
> Floating on their delicate feet over the cold pews,
> Their hands and faces stiff with holiness.
>
> (*SP*, 173)

The image of the clouds "flowering" may seem at first more beautiful than threatening, but the warm candlelight that "gentled" the "face of the effigy" has reverted to the blue "light of the mind," and the responsive face, "Bending, on me in particular, its mild eyes" becomes the remote "face of the stars," veiled in "mystical" clouds. Just as the moon proved *not* to be "a face in its own right" so much as a projection of the speaker's condition, the "face of the stars" is obscured by clouds that sympathize, in their color, with "the light of the mind." Once again we have been led to a door—this time, the door of the church—only to be turned away. When the speaker says that "the saints will be all blue," the word "will" appears to convey the intention of going in to see them; the tone is childlike as in stanza three, suggesting an anticipated return to a favorite sight. But the word also conveys the idea that she has already been in the church, knows very well what she would see if she did go in, and expects nothing new from that quarter. The saints, frozen "stiff with holiness," lit with the same blue light as the night sky and the despairing mind, will not bend to her "in particular" but will stare fixedly over her head as they float "over the cold pews." And so, still unable to "see where there is to get to," the speaker returns to her mother the moon, who "sees nothing of all this"; the yew tree has the last word with its "message" of "blackness and silence."

"The Moon and the Yew Tree" may be less immediately overpowering than "Lady Lazarus" or "Daddy," but it has at least two things worth having that these poems lack. First of all, it has a clear psychological progression leading from each part toward the next, providing the speaker's emotional intensity with a plausible motivation. It is not a very complex progression, since its movement is essentially that of Sisyphus making a few trips uphill with his stone. But it is sufficient to endow the characteristic Plathian despair with some credibility as an account of someone's experience rather than an all-purpose judgment about Life. Less autobiographical than the other two poems we have examined, "The Moon and the Yew Tree" is nonetheless more intimate, more personal in that respect. Second, "The Moon and the Yew Tree" reconciles its intensity with traditional and, I believe, still valid standards of poetic form. Its metaphors are mutually reinforcing, mutually allusive, mutually illuminating. There is little, if any, striking but arbitrary figuration like the "toe / big as a Frisco seal" in "Daddy" or the "pure gold baby" in "Lady Lazarus."

Doubtless "The Moon and the Yew Tree" gains something from the context of the more explicitly autobiographical poems, which provide a sense of the particular events from which the emotions more purely crystallized in "The Moon and the Yew Tree" arose. But the poems in which Plath goes into particulars are not, as a rule, the best ones. Her myth-mongering prevents her from understanding her life as a story that takes place in mundane historical time, like the stories of other people's lives, and so the emotions fail to become convincing as responses to the events. Most of the best poems, such as "Berck-Plage," "Ariel," "Poppies in October," "Nick and the Candlestick," "The Night Dances," and "Totem," require relatively little autobiographical decoding. It helps to know that "Nick" is the poet's infant son Nicholas, or that "Ariel" refers to a horse rather than (or perhaps in addition to) the ethereal being in *The Tempest*, but such contextual clues are of another order entirely than knowledge of the poet's suicide attempts, early loss of her father, or anger against her husband.

The contribution of confessionalism to recent poetry appears, in retrospect, to have had more to do with the breaking of taboos against passionate language, literal observation, and novelistic detail than with the psycho-historical claims initially made for it by Alvarez and Rosenthal. Sometimes the revelation of public crises in private woes is more apparent than real—to read "Daddy" as in some way "about" the holocaust [16] is to render it indefensibly presumptuous; only by taking the holocaust as the manifest content in a private nightmare can one absolve the poem of outrageous moral confusion. And often, when the poet really does seem intent on such analogies, they are flimsy or confused. Poems such "The Moon and the Yew Tree" represent moments of balance in which the access to direct experience, or to private pain, has not tempted the poet to depend on the reader's knowledge of that experience or sympathy for that pain.

6

Deep Images, Shallow Psychologies: The Unconscious as Pastoral Retreat

Confessional poetry enjoyed immense critical esteem in the sixties, but in the seventies its prestige began to wane.[1] As confessional poetry began to go out of fashion, an alternative mode, which had also come into existence at the end of the 1950s but had attracted less attention, began to emerge as a widely shared and widely admired group style. Paul Zweig called it "the new surrealism,"[2] but its other name, "deep image," conveys a more accurate sense of its implicit intentions, as well as suggesting why a poet such as Gary Snyder, who is not a surrealist at all, belongs in some respects within the definition, while such accredited surrealists as Philip Lamantia and Michael Benedikt belong outside it. (I do not mean to suggest that they are better, only that they are different.) The best-known poets whose work shares, to a significant extent, the tendencies of this style are W. S. Merwin, Robert Bly, James Wright, Galway Kinnell, Mark Strand, James Tate, and Charles Simic. In addition to Tate and Simic, younger poets influenced by this style include Peter Everwine, William Matthews, Gregory Orr, Richard Schramm, Greg Kuzma, to name only a few.

It is clear, from the way that critics have praised poetry of the deep image, that it is supposed to be terribly mysterious and profound. Richard Howard says that Charles Simic's poems "come to us . . . from an enormous otherness, a distance beyond words, wrought out of remote elements of the imagination of the hinterlands." "Crunk," the pseudonymous reviewer of Robert Bly's magazine, *The Sixties*, assures us that James Wright "goes long distances when he starts, and gives the impression of someone obeying ancient instincts, like some animal who spends all summer with his herd, and then migrates alone, travelling all night, drinking from old buffalo wallows." Mark Strand says that "the perils of the present, the terrifying compromises we make with the moment, the whole provisional nature of being when the self is mistrusted or simply not there, are what James Tate's work is about."[3] These remarks have in common their insistence that the poetry comes from an ahistorical and mysterious source outside the ego ("when the self is mistrusted or simply not there"), from a primitive "hinterlands" unlike our waking selves, or from a deeply buried animal instinct beneath the socialized self, which emerges in nocturnal solitude ("migrates alone, travelling all night"). This poetry comes from a source beyond the socialized self, far away from the prosaic doings of our daylit lives among others.

This is a rather different language than that used to praise confessional poetry. Admirers of confessional poetry speak of a confrontation with the self and with the ways in which the self has been twisted by its social determinants; admirers of the deep image speak of encountering an otherness beyond or beneath the historically entangled "I." The symbolism of confessional poetry, as we have seen, tends to be derived from context: things from one part of the poem are connected with those in another. Confessional poetry is praised for honesty, for stripping away the veil, not for taking us into regions of mystery. Conversely, when confessional poetry has been attacked, it has been attacked for literalism—for subordinating poetic form and language to reportorial detail or for egotistically invoking private symbols not shared with the reader—the father's "toe / Big as a Frisco seal" in "Daddy," or the numerous allusions in Lowell's *Notebook* sonnets or Berryman's *Dream Songs* to events and persons only a friend of the poet could fairly be expected to identify.

One encounters, in deep-image poetry, a different kind of obscurity than that which one meets with in confessional poetry or even, for that matter, in modern symbolist poems. One finds neither the sustained meditation on a single natural symbol that can be found in the lyrics of Frost, Hart Crane, or Yeats, nor the elaborately interconnecting allusions that run through such longer poems as *The Waste Land, The Cantos, The Bridge,* or even *Paterson.* A critic well versed in the reading of earlier modernist poetry in English is not necessarily prepared by that experience to encounter the newer idiom. Here, for instance, is W. S. Merwin's "The Night of the Shirts," from *The Carrier of Ladders* (1970):

Oh pile of white shirts who is coming
to breathe in your shapes to carry your numbers
to appear
what hearts

are moving toward their garments here
their days
what troubles beating between arms

you look upward through
each other saying nothing has happened
and it has gone away and is sleeping
having told the same story
and we exist from within
eyes of the gods

you lie on your backs
and the wounds are not made
the blood has not heard
the boat has not turned to stone
and the dark wires to the bulb
are full of the voices of the unborn.[4]

And here is James Atlas, now a well-known critic of modern and contemporary literature, trying in an early essay to make sense of this poem:

What is the purpose of asking all these questions? Is the line "to appear" essential, or just a repetition of the previous line? What motivates the metonymous "hearts"? Where is "here"? What is "the same story"? How does it happen that "we exist from within / eyes of the gods"? What are "the wounds," what "the blood"? Where does "the boat" enter in, to what does it refer? What suggests that it should have "turned to stone"? The poem has no meaning, not even a style; it sounds like a poor translation."[5]

Although I cannot answer all of Atlas's questions, I can answer most of them. But I can do so largely because, years after his essay was written, one can recognize the language of "The Night of the Shirts" as belonging to a shared rhetoric that seems, in retrospect, almost like a fixed code. Deep-image poetry is hermetic, in that it asks, not merely occasionally but continually, that we attribute an inherent significance to a recurring symbolic vocabulary, quite apart from the uses to which that vocabulary is put in any particular poem. Learning to read it is largely a matter of initiation into that vocabulary. Paradoxically, the initial strangeness of deep-image writing rests on an extremely formulaic approach not only to diction, but also, as we shall see, to syntax and content. It is as conventional, in its way, as eighteenth-century neoclassicism, even as it implicitly claims to rebel against conventionality.

In answering Atlas's questions about "The Night of the Shirts," one must begin by getting one's bearings: "Where is "here"? It is a mistake to imagine the poet in a literal situation—at the laundry, for instance, picking up his shirts and looking at all the other shirts awaiting their owners' return. "Here" is an interior place, and the poem refers to shirts in the mind's eye, not shirts on the hanger. We are inside the psyche, in some mysterious place where recurring images like "the boat" appear and undergo strange transformations—as, for example, into stone. This interior space is magical, sacred, and so it is that "we exist from within / eyes of the gods." These gods are the sacred presences within the self, and what truly exists in us comes from them; we are most truly alive when we live in the inner self. The poem is about the descent from the quotidian into the depths of the psyche. The "it" that has gone away is the "nothing" of the previous line; the nothing that has happened disappears and becomes less than nothing. In a world where nothing happens we are left with "the same story," the descent into the self, as the only possible event.

But Merwin's poetry, unlike that of the more optimistic Bly, Wright, and Simic, is a poetry of tantalizing, failed transcendence. If we could really get far enough down into the psyche, the blood would hear and the boat would turn to stone; but the journey fails, and the poet is doomed to repeat it again and again, as indeed he has done. The shirts (apostrophized throughout the poem) represent the external life, the socialized self. They lie on their backs, but cannot fall deeply enough asleep, are not filled with the flesh and blood of the inner, unconscious life; the external world fails to become the dream. Merwin's poem becomes more intelligible, though not necessarily better, when one understands its convention of poetry as a voyage inward, a quest for union with the unconscious. That convention is the single most important rule in deep image poetics, and from it the smaller rules are generated.

Sometimes poems in this manner offer fairly explicit portraits of the inner depths, and the composite iconography that emerges is rather consistent. Journeys inward and downward do not end in a dense tangle of repressed memories, forbidden desires, and multiple associations, as Freudian theory might lead us to expect, but in the encounter with a mysterious presence, sacred and impersonal, inhabiting an interior space. Consider, for example, James Wright's well-known short poem, "The Jewel":

There is this cave
In the air behind my body
That nobody is going to touch:
A cloister, a silence

Closing around a blossom of fire.
When I stand upright in the wind,
My bones turn to dark emeralds.[6]

Clearly, this poem describes a sacred space within the self. The vocabulary insists on enclosure and interiority, sharp demarcation from the external world. The word "cloister," of course, points to a religious content, but equally decisive is the language of synesthesia and paradox, which invites and then frustrates visualization and leaves us at last with the contemplation of a mystery. One cannot envision "silence / Closing around a blossom of fire." The blossom of fire, like the fire and the rose in T. S. Eliot's "Little Gidding," is an image of mystical reconciliation between living form and inchoate energy. The title, "The Jewel," applies to the sacred mental space but also to the emerald bones of the last line. This interior sacredness extends to the body as well as to the mind, transforming even the bones. Conspicuously absent from Wright's poem is any evocation of a struggle to arrive at or establish this sacred space, or any hint of its relation to the ordinary reality outside it. The imagery is completely divorced from any profane content, or any reference to time and change. (The transformation of the bones is a partial exception, but it is recurrent—"*When* I stand upright in the wind," the change occurs.) In this separation it parts company with "Little Gidding," and its complete isolation from the external life—guarded, as it were, by the chip-on-shoulder third line—gives it a disturbingly defensive, solipsistic quality. The transcendence does not overcome any resistance and therefore arouses a suspicion of its authenticity.

Other portraits of the inner mystery have a similar ambience. Here, for example, is a passage from Charles Simic's "Knife":

We go down
An inner staircase.
We walk under the earth.
The knife lights the way.

Through bones of animals,
Water, beard of a wild boar—
We go through stones, embers,
We are after a scent.[7]

As with Wright, we are once again inside a cave. The stones, bones, and embers suggest that it was once inhabited by primitive man; by going "through" the bones of animals, we reenter a state more primitive still, early in our evolution. The revelations of the "inner staircase" are impersonal and archeological, connecting the psyche to some mysterious ancient presence that is tangible but vague, like a "scent."

Much the same atmosphere informs Robert Bly's poem "Moving Inward at Last":

> The dying bull is bleeding on the mountain!
> But inside the mountain, untouched
> By the blood,
> There are antlers, bits of oak bark,
> Fire, herbs are thrown down.
>
> When the smoke touches the roof of the cave,
> The green leaves burst into flame,
> The air of night changes to dark water,
> The mountains alter and become the sea.[8]

Again, the poet imagines the psyche as a cave in which man has built his fires; and again this place is sacred, impersonal, and primitive. In this case it is magical as well, changing air to water and mountains to sea.

These poems have nothing to do with the Freudian unconscious but a great deal to do with the collective, theogonic unconscious proposed by Jung, who broke with Freud over the question of whether the unconscious was the abode of banished desires or the wellspring of religious revelation. Even the dream that led Jung to postulate a collective unconscious has a symbolic vocabulary startlingly similar to that of the poetry quoted above. In that dream, recounted in *Memories, Dreams, Reflections,* Jung descends from the second story of a house to the ground floor and then into the basement. As he proceeds downward, the furnishings become progressively older. Beneath the basement lies the oldest and deepest region of all:

> I looked more closely at the floor. It was of stone slabs, and in one of these I discovered a ring. When I pulled it, the stone slab lifted, and again I saw a stairway of narrow stone steps leading down into the depths. These, too, I descended, and entered a low cave cut into the rock. Thick dust lay on the floor, and in the dust were scattered bones and broken pottery, like remains of a primitive culture. I discovered two human skulls, obviously very old and half disintegrated. Then I woke up.[9]

For Jung, the psyche is like the house in the dream, and its deepest recesses are the cave beneath the basement. The unconscious of Freud, which contains repressed wishes and memories of early traumatic events, is but an upper story; beneath it lies a collective, impersonal unconscious, which preserves, under the modern rational personality, an "archaic" self. In the collective unconscious, religion, magic, and myth continue to live for us as they do for primitive peoples, through the production of archetypal images in dreams, fantasies, and works of art.

The status of a symbol is not the same for Jung as it is for Freud, and the difference is important in understanding the essentially Jungian symbolism of deep-image poetry. Freud believed that even a dream, the most nearly direct expression of the unconscious, was "a thought like any other" that had been repressed. The strangeness of dreams comes not from the unconscious idea—which, once inferred, is readily intelligible—but from the elaborate disguises the unconscious idea must assume in order to escape the censorship of the ego. The unconscious thought cannot emerge directly, since it "has no access to consciousness *except via the preconscious* [Freud's emphasis], in passing through which its excitatory process is obliged to submit to modifications." Therefore, "an unconscious idea is as such quite incapable of entering the preconscious and . . . it can only exercise any effect there by establishing a connection with an idea which already belongs to the preconscious, by transferring its intensity on to it and getting itself 'covered' by it." [10] To arrive at the meaning of a dream, one must work backward through a chain of substitutions. A word or image in the manifest dream will call others to mind until, gradually, a common theme emerges from the associations, and this common theme is the clue to the unconscious meaning.

In the *Introductory Lectures on Psychoanalysis*, Freud warned his auditors to suspect even an apparently coherent dream, for "even if it has an apparently sensible exterior, we know that this has only come about through dream-distortion and can have as little organic relation to the internal content of the dream as the façade of an Italian church has to its structure and plan." [11] Jung conceded the metaphor but drew other conclusions: "The so-called façade of most houses is by no means a fake or deceptive distortion; on the contrary, it follows the plan of the building and often betrays the interior arrangement. The 'manifest' dream-picture is the dream itself, and contains the whole meaning of the dream." [12]

Proceeding from his conviction that the dream is an autonomous structure rather than an oblique commentary on the experience of the dreamer, Jung constructed a set of fixed categories, or archetypes, to explain the meaning of symbols in dream, myth, and art. Such a system pays little attention to the historical context in which these symbols have been produced, since it attributes their origin to a universally inherited predisposition to imagine certain categories of symbols, rather than to any culturally or historically specific situation. In Freudian interpretation, we recover part of our self-knowledge, part of our response to the external world, which we had disowned and feared; in Jungian interpretation, we must give ourselves over to the unconscious as to a god whose scripture is the dream. Jung, to his credit, was aware of the danger of solipsism in his own psychology and warned that a process of "individuation," connecting the collective unconscious to one's own particular situation, was necessary to prevent the unconscious from engulfing the entire self.[13] But this part of the theory seems to have got lost in popularization and has little counterpart in deep-image poetics.

Although Robert Bly has made explicit use of Jungian archetypes in his poems and in his essays on poetry, the connection to Jung is not always as direct as that. Indeed, one could not infer from their poems that all or even most of the poets in question are avowed Jungians. But one can immediately see, in the examples already quoted, a curious self-referentiality of symbolism. When Bly opens his poem with "The dying bull is bleeding on the mountain," he raises questions like the ones Atlas puts to Merwin: who or what has wounded the bull; where is the mountain; why has the bull gone up on the mountain to die? But the poem, instead of allowing us to infer the answers, immediately moves away from this image and makes no further reference to it, although the mountain returns, now plural, in the last line just in time to be changed into the sea. It seems that merely by uttering the words "bull," bleeding," and "mountain," the poet expects to awaken powerful resonances in us. These words suggest masculine power, violence, and grandeur, but the rest of the poem does not press this vague suggestiveness toward sharper definition; it simply goes on to something else.

Certain words, as Marvin Bell and Robert Pinsky noticed in the late seventies,[14] come up in deep-image poetry over and over again, carrying a heavy burden of portentousness in each instance. By editing their lists and adding a few candidates of my own, I come up with the following central lexicon: wings, jewels, stones, silence, breath, snow, blood, eats, water, light, bones, roots, glass, absence, sleep, and darkness. Pinsky calls this vocabulary a "poetic diction,"[15] and he is right, but the issue goes further than the calcification of conventions into clichés. The nouns on this list have roughly the same status in discourse as Jungian archetypes: their significance is innate and prior to context. The point is not only the predictability of the diction, but also the way in which the key words are used, as if they came to the individual poem already charged with significance.

The diction, if not quite reducible to formula, is predictable enough. One could easily present scores of examples containing two or more of the overfamiliar words listed above. Here is one from Robert Bly's "Unrest":

> now the darkness is falling
> in which we sleep and awake—a darkness in which
> Thieves shudder, and the insane have a hunger for snow,
> In which bankers dream of being buried by black stones. . . .[16]

And here is the beginning of "She Who Was Gone," an example obtained by a "*Sortes Merwinianae*" in *The Moving Target*:

> Passage of lights without hands
> Passage of hands without lights
> This water between
>
> I take in my arms
>
> My love whose names I cannot say
> Not knowing them and having a tongue
> Of dust
>
> My love with light flowing on her like tears. . . .[17]

Even this poem, chosen at random, does not fail us: here are "water" and "light," and the fifth through seventh lines are a sort of cadential trill on the concept of silence. Or consider these lines, from Charles Simic's poem "Sleep":

> My blood runs
> Past dark inner cities on fire.
> I climb into deep wells,
> Rock bottoms and bone bottoms. . . .[18]

Here are two passages, the first from Mark Strand's "The Stone" and the second from Gregory Orr's "A Final Aubade," which might almost be taken for parts of the same poem:

> The stone lives on.
> The followers of the man with the glass face
> walk around it
> with their glass legs
> and their glass arms.[19]

>   [Strand]

Behind it [the "deeper darkness"] a river flows over stones
shaped like hands. The dead with their glass legs
walk by the river. The river
seems to pass through them.[20]

[Orr]

Or there is Galway Kinnell, in *The Book of Nightmares*, asking us

to touch
the almost imaginary bones
under the face, to hear under the laughter
the wind crying across the black stones.[21]

But enough. Any reader even casually familiar with contemporary poetry will have seen many further examples of this vocabulary of stones, bones, and silence.

Reading poetry that depends so much on a revealed symbolism, rather than a symbolism created by the arrangement of the poem or the exploration of a recognizable subject, one may begin to wonder what consequences, if any, this interior revelation may have for life as a whole. To judge from the nature of the key words, we are being asked to dismiss the quotidian world and take refuge in the collective unconscious. Some of these words—darkness, silence, absence—tell us how inscrutable, how inaccessible to sight or hearing, the inner mystery is. The more concrete nouns seldom combine to form an exact image of something in the world, but remain, in Pinsky's phrase, the names of "blank, simple substances."[22] The diction is impersonal, animistic, primitive: all things finally come down to bone and blood, water and stone. Above these elemental realities, history and culture weave their fraudulent patterns, unregarded by the enlightened poet. What motive lies behind this extreme antihumanism and this extreme preoccupation with the unconscious?

If we can withdraw our rapt gaze from the vast otherness and the old buffalo wallows to look at the historical context in which deepimage poetics took shape, the motive becomes fairly obvious. Even more than confessional poetry, deep-image poetry responds to the central fear expressed by the organization critics and the emerging New Left: that the very consciousness of the individual has been poisoned by a repressive or "one-dimensional" society. The confessional poets, at least as Rosenthal and Alvarez understood them, responded by exhibiting the poisoned self as a representative instance of a shared predicament. The poets of the deep-image sought a fastness within the self to which the corruptions of society had not reached.

It is rather late for moralizing about the New Left. But one need not be a neoconservative New-Left-basher to recognize that for its predominantly white, middle-class constituency, the movement represented not only a genuinely political opposition to the war in Vietnam and to racism at home, but also a welcome escape from cultural guilt. As we have seen in our initial sketch of the New Left's emergence from postwar social thought, the emphasis on the cure of consciousness made it tempting to confuse political activism with therapy. Just possibly, activism could change the world; quite certainly, it could provide a certificate of exculpation. The sentimental reasoning that bridged the gulf between revolution and therapy went something like this: White Americans and western Europeans, from whom I am descended, have imposed their will on other peoples in terrible ways. What they have done to others is analogous to what they have done to their own instincts, justifying such oppression and repression by appeals to reason and law. It is the ego that has done this; away with it, therefore, and with reason and law, which are its instruments. If I side with the instincts and the unconscious, I declass myself, and my guilt falls away. In such a view, all culture, all social and political institutions, and all attempts to govern human affairs according to reason are nothing but shams, designed to aid the despotic ego in its work of repression.

The confessional poets also made use of psycho-political thinking like that of the New Left, sometimes before there was a clearly defined American New Left to influence them; in their case, one can only argue a simultaneous emergence of similar attitudes, a view made plausible by the anticipation of the new attitudes in much of the most well-known social criticism of the previous decade. The correlation between the deep-image style and political radicalism, however, is quite clearly evident. Not all of the poets of the deep image have announced their political convictions as loudly as Robert Bly, but Merwin, Kinnell, Wright, Strand, and Snyder were all quite active in the antiwar movement and have written explicitly about politics, in poetry, in prose, or in both. The correlation is stronger, and the appropriation of radical psycho-politics is less wary.

As I have already argued, the confessional poets sometimes used psycho-political ideas in a sentimental way, but at least, in most of the work of Ginsberg, Plath, and Lowell, the self remains aware that consciousness is not everything. Except in Plath's most solipsistic flights, the poetry has a way of acknowledging the limiting pressures of a social and material world. Its psychology is essentially Freudian—that is to say, contextual, secular, and historical. Poets of the deep image have a much stronger tendency to reduce all things to psychology. Kinnell,

Wright, and Snyder (who is only a half-way adherent anyway) resist that tendency enough to transcend it at times, but it remains a problem in their work.

It is not a coincidence, I believe, that the ascendancy of deep-image poetics to something like an orthodoxy occurred at the end of the sixties and during the early seventies, just as the New Left was falling apart and its adherents were settling into a mood of exhausted quiescence. The withdrawal into the "vast otherness" represents a giving up on the outside world, a retreat from psycho-politics to a solipsistic religion of the unconscious.

The desire to recover innocence and faith at any cost, even the abolition of social reality and the conscious self, explains the ubiquity of the most popular key word in the deep imagist's vocabulary: stone. Galway Kinnell, early in *The Book of Nightmares*, writes:

I sit a moment
by the fire, in the rain, speak
a few words into its warmth—
stone saint smooth stone. . . .[23]

Simic's devotions to Saint Stone include a book title, *Somewhere Among Us a Stone Is Taking Notes*, and a poem called "Stone," beginning "Go inside a stone / That would be my way. . . . I am happy to be a stone." Orr has a sequence titled "The Adventures of the Stone"; Wright begins a poem with the line "Hiding in the church of an abandoned stone . . ."; Merwin uses the word dozens of times per volume; I have already quoted from Mark Strand's "The Stone." And there are large outcroppings elsewhere, even among poets only tangentially related to the style—like Tom Clark, who wants to be "open to the stones / really open to them." James Richardson trumped everybody with a long poem in sixty-odd sections called "The Encyclopedia of the Stones: A Pastoral," speculating on the mental and social life of stones.[24] By calling his lithic encyclopedia a "pastoral," Richardson gives a clue to the talismanic appeal of stone imagery. The stones have such pastoral charm because they are the furthest things from the human—the least conscious, the simplest, the most innocent. They have never discriminated against blacks or destroyed Vietnamese villages, never deceived themselves with a clever argument or capitulated to social convention. In their modest way, stones are perfect. But there is a positive, mystical implication behind the obsession with stones as well as a merely negative desire to be rid of cultural guilt. For this meaning we may turn again to Jung, who found, in the turbulence of his youth, that it was strangely reassuring and calming to sit on my stone. Somehow it would free me of all my doubts. Whenever I thought that I was the stone, the conflict ceased. "The stone has no uncertainties, no urge to communicate, and is eternally the same for thousands of years," I would think, "while I am only a passing phenomenon which bursts into all kinds of emotions, like a flame that flares up quickly and then goes out." I was but the sum of my emotions, and the Other in me was the timeless, imperishable stone.[25]

Galway Kinnell expresses much the same idea in an interview:

If you could go even deeper, you'd not be a person, you'd be an animal; and if you went deeper still, you'd be a blade of grass, eventually a stone. If a stone could speak, your poem would be its words.[26]

Stone, then, is the sacred Other within—the collective, impersonal unconscious. It is our immortal part, but its immortality, like that of the lovers on the Grecian urn, is purchased at the cost of being dead: if you are not alive in the first place, you cannot die, and so become "immortal." If Keats's urn is a "cold pastoral," then the stone is the pastoral of absolute zero.

But perhaps one can go further still. In their darker moods, Merwin, Strand, Tate, and Kinnell suspect that the authentic self is not even a stone but an absence; indeed, Tate calls one of his books *Absences*. Mark Strand begins his poem "Keeping Things Whole" by saying:

In a field
I am the absence of field.
This is always the case.
Wherever I am,
I am what is missing.[27]

And yet the concept of absence takes on a religious meaning; it means purity, abandonment of the false strivings of the ego. As James Tate puts it,

I who have no home have no destination either,
one bone against the other,
I carve what I carve
to be rid of myself by morning
by deep dreams disintegrated.[28]

Merwin, in a tentative statement of faith sharply hedged by the opening "Maybe," shows us how nearly interchangeable with presence" this religious absence can become:

Maybe he does not even have to exist
to exist in departures
then the first darkness falls
even there a shining is flowing from all the stones
though the eye is not yet made that can see it
saying Blessèd
are ye[29]

Here the absence of the divinity is hypostatized into a more rarefied form of presence; the "departures" somehow become a guarantee of the existence.

What all of these formulations have in common is their location of the sacred or the authentic in some extremely "deep" layer of consciousness that lies at the other extreme from language, culture, and conscious thought, at the point where we are connected to unconscious animal nature or even to inanimate nature. Robert Bly, in his essay "The Live World and the Dead World," makes a sharp contrast between human nature considered in itself and considered as part of nature as a whole. Bly objects to a literary "landscape dominated by Robert Lowell, Arthur Miller, [and] Saul Bellow," because these writers, while they "bring us news of the human mind," have omitted "microbes, gods, oceans—what is missing is the universe." For Bly, this is a moral as well as artistic omission:

Suppose a country's literature . . . insists, like Snodgrass in *Heart's Needle*, or Lowell in *Life Studies*, on studying the exclusively human over and over? Suppose also that the human being is not studied in relation to non-human lives, or lives in other countries, but simply in relation to itself. One can predict first of all that such a nation will bomb foreign populations very easily, since it has no sense of anything real beyond its own ego.[30]

The outrageous coarseness of this libel against Lowell and Snodgrass obscures the useful criticism of the confessional mode offered in Bly's main argument. Unfortunately, however, the melodramatic hyperbole of this passage is typical not only of Bly's polemical style, but of the response in deep-image poetics to the tension between nature and culture. Because cultural anthropology has deprived the term "human nature" of most of its fixed content, the deep image poets, in trying to reaffirm a human nature beneath the corruptions of culture, are tempted to abandon the modifier "human" and assert their identity with animals (Wright "is like some animal . . . who migrates alone") or even with inanimate objects.

Rather than seeing human life within culture as enclosed in a larger, natural context, these poets too often dismiss human life within culture as a trivial phenomenon of the surface. The collective unconscious becomes, for them, important as the repository of a racial memory of the archaic, of an existence prior to civilization and even to the later stages of our evolution. The unconscious is nature surviving within us. Gary Snyder, in making this point, begins with the same idea that Rosenthal and Alvarez attribute to the confessional poets: the self is society internalized. But instead of dramatizing the plight of the socialized self, he points to a way out of it: "Class-structured society is a kind of mass ego. To transcend the ego is to go beyond society as well. 'Beyond' there lies, inwardly, the unconscious. Outwardly, the equivalent of the unconscious is the wilderness: both of these terms meet, one step even farther on, as *one*."[31]

Snyder becomes intolerably sentimental at times in his faith that false consciousness can simply be washed away. "The practice of meditation, for which one needs only 'the ground beneath one's feet' wipes out mountains of junk being pumped into the mind by the mass media and supermarket universities. The belief in a serene and generous fulfillment of natural loving desires destroys ideologies which blind, maim, and repress," he claims, in "Buddhism and the Coming Revolution."[32] Would that it were so. If the temptation of the confessional poet is self-aggrandizement or self-pity, that of the deep-image poet is sentimentality, the belief that one can simply walk out of the ego, and thus out of history, into the benign pastoral of the collective unconscious.

We have already seen how the drive to archetypal simplification affects the vocabulary of the deep-image poem. It also affects rhythm and syntax, the modes by which words combine into lines, and lines into poems. As Alan Williamson has remarked, with the hostility toward the ego in deep-image poetics "comes a special and in some ways hostile attitude toward language itself."[33] In the passages already quoted in this chapter, the reader will perhaps have noticed the prevalence of short, declarative sentences, and the absence of tension between the line breaks and the divisions of syntax. Merwin heightens the effect by abolishing punctuation, so that even the unavoidable distinctions of syntax are emphasized as little as possible. Elaborate syntax, like complex formal structures, would suggest too obviously the contrivance of the ego. If the poet aspires to speak as a stone would speak, then even the plainest utterance is inevitably too florid. Like the ritualization of archetypal vocabulary, the stripping-down of syntax, however striking it may seem when first encountered, limits the possible range of rhythm and tone; most deep-image poetry sounds solemn and flat, as if intoned in a trance.[34]

One can see the consequences of these simplifications—of vocabulary, of syntax, and of moral attitude—even in a relatively well-written piece such as James Wright's poem on Eisenhower and Franco, which is quite powerful on first reading but does not wear very well:

Eisenhower's Visit to Franco, 1959

> . . . we die of cold, and not of darkness.
> —Unamuno

The American hero must triumph over
The forces of darkness.
He has flown through the very light of heaven
And come down in the slow dusk
Of Spain.
Franco stands in a shining circle of police.
His arms open in welcome.
He promises all dark things
Will be hunted down.

State police yawn in the prisons.
Antonio Machado follows the moon
Down a road of white dust
To a cave of silent children
Under the Pyrenees.
Wine darkens in stone jars in villages.
Wine sleeps in the mouths of old men, it is a dark red color.

Smiles glitter in Madrid.
Eisenhower has touched hands with Franco, embracing
In a glare of photographers.
Clean new bombers from America muffle their engines
And glide down now.
Their wings shine in the searchlights
Of bare fields
In Spain.[35]

One notices immediately the inversion of the traditional moral symbolism of light and dark—the villains are wearing the light images, and the good guys are wearing the dark. Light keeps its traditional associations of reason, power, and avowed opposition to "The forces of darkness," but since reason and the attempt to repress the "forces of darkness" in the psyche have been discredited, the sinister "heroes" are really imperialist oppressors. The poem insists on a stark division into "heroes" like Eisenhower and Franco (one need not admire

Eisenhower very much to protest that there *is* a difference) and their victims, such as the poor in the villages of Spain, the "cave of silent children / Under the Pyrenees," and the "old men" with the "dark red" wine "sleeping" in their mouths. (The wine is stored—where else?—in *stone* jars.) The defenseless children and the enfeebled old men, the poor and the weak, are in touch with darkness, silence, and the unconscious—just like poets, just like Antonio Machado, who is invoked as their witness. The poem tacitly assumes the helplessness of the poor and the poet's identification with them. Both assumptions are sentimental and, taken together, self-exculpating: the poor are helpless victims, like poets; I'm a poet, so don't blame me. The clipped, simple sentences in which the poet speaks through most of the poem assure the reader that he has disowned the repressive complexities of the ego for the innocence of the dark unconscious.

When deep-image poetry becomes explicitly moralistic or political, it seldom avoids altogether the tinge of self-righteousness that mars "Eisenhower's Visit to Franco," and usually, it indulges that self-righteousness less subtly. In Robert Bly's "Romans Angry About the Inner World," for instance, political struggle has been reduced to psychic melodrama. Life is a mental war between "the executives," who know nothing of the lives of children or of floating "joyfully on the dark places," and the representatives of "the other world," which

> is like a thorn
> In the ear of a tiny beast!
> The fingers of the executives are too thick
> To pull it out!
> It is like a jagged stone
> Flying toward them out of the darkness.[36]

Here, once more, is the stone, come to take its notes and judge the quick and the dead.

Deep-image poetics, at its passionate worst, is a desperate attempt to cure the discontents of civilization by radical surgery. By removing the part of the psyche that has been tainted with the arrogance, guilt, and skepticism of the culture we live in, we may regain our innocence and our capacity for belief. But could the psyche survive such an operation, even if it were possible? And would civilization really be any better for it? The offending part is nothing less than the entire ego, which is by definition the part of the psyche that has dealings with the outer world.[37] Without the mediation of the ego, the unconscious has no access to people and things outside the self, except, in the Jungian revision, through the shadow-community of the archetypes. One can say of deep-image poetics what Philip Rieff, in *The Triumph of the Therapeutic*, said of Jungian psychology:

Inside his private myth, the individual can safely claim his discharge of catholic obligations. In the ritual of dream and fantasy he gains membership in the invisible church of common meanings. A socially and politically inconsequential universe is thus constituted.[38]

But even Jung knew better than the Jungian poets when he wrote:

If anyone should set out to replace his conscious outlook by the dictates of the unconscious . . . he would only succeed in repressing the former, and it would appear as an unconscious compensation. The unconscious would thus have changed its face and completely reversed its position. It would have become timidly reasonable, in striking contrast to its former tone.[39]

Jung's prophecy has come to pass. The unconscious has become so timidly reasonable that it consents to communicate through a thoroughly predictable literary diction, in the syntax of a grade-school primer.

The following two chapters offer a closer look at poets of considerable talent hindered, to a large extent, by the assumptions we have been examining here. W. S. Merwin, from *The Moving Target* (1963) through *Writings to an Unfinished Accompaniment* (1977), wrote a musical, hauntingly suggestive, but astonishingly self-repetitive poetry. How he came to work in such a narrow idiom, and how, recently, he has attempted to work his way back out of it, makes for a piece of representative stylistic biography. James Wright, a close friend of Robert Bly who obviously shared many assumptions about poetry, was nonetheless a poet of broader range than any other who might be fairly numbered among the pursuers of the "deep image." Wright's strong regionalist fascination with the life and landscape of industrial Ohio exerted a strong pull outward, balancing the tendency toward solipsism in the archetypal style of his later years. Although, as I shall argue, Wright had a great deal of difficulty integrating his regionalism with his mystical pursuit of the deep image, the attempt, and its occasional success, make him a more interesting, if less graceful, poet than Merwin.

7

To the Interior and Back: W. S. Merwin

Among the first generation of poets who have pursued the "deep image," none has followed it to such remote recesses as W. S. Merwin.
Despite their frequent overreliance on archetypal or "primitive" language to confer resonance and unity on their poetry, Bly, Wright, and
Kinnell seldom erase all vestiges of the historical world from their
poems, and often they preserve at least an attenuated sense of an occasion to which the poem responds. Indeed, Wright is as much a regionalist as a deep-image seeker, and Snyder, whom Williamson groups
with these others, has an interest in random quotidian detail that one
associates more with the tradition extending from Pound through
Williams, Olson, and the projectivist school. But in most of his poems
from *The Moving Target* (1963) through *Writings to an Unfinished Accompaniment* (1973), Merwin has tried to work in a voluntary blindness, without any of the usual windows that lyric poetry opens from
the inwardness of feeling to its historical sources in the external world.
More recently, beginning with the poems in the third and fourth sections of *The Compass Flower* (1977) and continuing with the prose
memoirs of *Unframed Originals* (1982) and the most recent collection
of poems, *Opening the Hand* (1983), he seems to have sought a passage
back to a more historical, intersubjective sense of reality.

This journey and return, aside from what they may imply about
Merwin's shifting intentions, also can reveal much about the continuity
between the poetics of the 1950s and the interiorized, archetypal style
of deep-image poetics. The recent work reveals much about the difficulties of accommodating that style, which would give all to myth and
archetype, to the claims of history and particularity.

The relation between poetic and political radicalism is less straightforward for Merwin than it is for Bly, Kinnell, or Snyder. Merwin has
long been a political activist. His participation in the peace movement
dates back before the rise of the New Left to protests against nuclear
testing such as the voyage of the *Everyman* in 1962, which he sympathetically chronicled for *The Nation*. [1] When he received the Pulitzer

Prize in 1971, he wrote a letter to the *New York Review of Books*, explaining that

after years of the news from Southeast Asia, and the commentary from Washington, I am too conscious of being an American to accept public congratulation with good grace, or to welcome it except as an occasion for expressing openly a shame which many Americans feel, day after day, helplessly and in silence.[2]

He gave half of the prize money to the Draft Resistance and half to a painter on Telegraph Avenue in Berkeley who had been "blinded by a police weapon . . . while he was watching American events from a roof, at a distance."[2]

Despite his political activism, however, few of Merwin's poems make any explicit reference to political matters, even in a fairly general, non-topical way. In "To Name the Wrong," an essay of 1962 on the sufferings of the black Angolan poet Agostinho Nito under the Portuguese dictator, Salazar, he wrote of the dangers involved when a poet begins to "feel himself obligated to try to speak for those who are in circumstances resembling his own, but who are less capable of bearing witness to them." Among these is "the danger that his gift itself, necessarily one of the private and integral things he lives for, may be deformed into a mere loud-speaker, losing the singularity which made it irreplaceable, the candor which made it unteachable and unpredictable."[3] Although Merwin admires Nito's poetry as well as his courage, the essay reveals his skepticism about political poetry in general: one is driven to write political poetry in evil times, despite the risk to one's artistic integrity.

The same skeptical note can be heard eight years later when, pondering the relation of his poetry to "the anecdotal, localised American scene," Merwin told Frank MacShane:

As for political poems—I believe that one can write poems from whatever touches off their true source, and I don't see why public events shouldn't do that. It's just that I think they probably do it rather seldom, in comparison with the number of times that they touch off the *intention* to write poetry or anything else, which of course isn't remotely the same thing. No, I've no principle against political poems. I just wish, sometimes desperately, that mine or anyone else's turned out more often to be poetry. There are after all several political poems toward the end of *The Lice*. But in the main I think poetry itself remains political, and will do so more and more, by remaining the expression of the authentic, which is of course necessarily individual, in an age that is the enemy of anything of the kind.[4]

In this last sentence, Merwin's relation to the commonplaces of cultural radicalism becomes visible—poetry represents the individual and authentic in political opposition to the collective and inauthentic.

With the sense of poetry as the preserve of individual consciousness comes the sense of language as something to be rescued from public debasement, even wrested from its undeniably public status as something culturally shared. "The vernacular of the imagination," wrote Merwin in 1966, "conveys something of the unsoundable quality of experience and the hearing of it is a private matter, in an age in which the person and his senses are being lost in the consumer, who does not know what he sees, hears, wants, or is afraid of, until the voice of the institution has told him."[5] The deeply private "attempt to give utterance to the unutterable experience of being alive, and consciously mortal, and human, in any time" is the work of the poet. To utter the unutterable, one must divest language of its public quality. Speaking of his change of style in *The Moving Target* in an interview for *Road Apple Review*, Merwin said that he "wanted to make language itself almost something you cannot catch hold of." "Public convention," he added, "began holding me down."[6]

If the political implications of Merwin's poetry are as a rule oblique, they have nonetheless seemed evident and important to some of his readers, late and early. Cary Nelson argues, in *Our Last First Poets*, that "the revolution in Merwin's style" was "highly responsive to the general political environment."[7] Robert Hass, reviewing *The Lice* for *The Nation*, praised such poems as "Unfinished Book of Kings," "I Live Up Here," and "Caesar" for "describing from the inside the irrationality of the political world and the way in which authority has become a form of internal coercion." He took *The Lice* to be a collection of "American poems of fear, timidity, and helplessness in the face of violence and death," written "from a peculiar depth." And, he concluded, "in a few of them, one has the strange sense that Merwin with a new freedom has begun to write about the concentration camps of the free world."[8] (This peroration, incidentally, is another vintage specimen of overheated New Left rhetoric to set beside Levertov's denunciation of "antilife and oppression.")

Whatever the relation of Merwin's middle style to contemporaneous events, it also has, despite its obvious strangeness, an equally clear relatedness to earlier modernist poetry in English, as well as to the European and Latin American influences commonly associated with deep-image poetics. The influence of T. S. Eliot on Merwin has often been noticed,[9] and it was Eliot who famously defined the process of writing poetry as "a series of raids on the inarticulate," a formulation that

closely resembles Merwin's "attempt to give utterance to the unutterable experience of being alive, and consciously mortal, and human."
The evolution of Merwin's style from *A Mask For Janus* (1952) through
The Moving Target reveals a continuity between modernist extensions
of the symbolist tradition and the experiments of Merwin's middle
style, affinities between imagists and deep imagists. Moreover, one
recognizes how much of the oblique political implication Hass found in
Merwin's middle style is also there in earlier modernist styles associated with vastly different political outlooks. One is thus forced to ask
how much determinate political content can be attributed to such poetry, and whether its content is not rather something prior to politics, a
way of "naming the wrong," in Merwin's words, that is compatible with
widely varying notions of appropriate redress. The poetry, one might
argue instead, offers an intimate description of emotional or spiritual
desolation without having much to say about the sources of that condition and is, if anything, profoundly apolitical in treating that desolation
as a deeply ingrained fact of existence rather than a response to social
circumstances of any determinate kind. It is possible that Hass and
others have read Merwin's middle poetry as political largely because, in
the years when that work appeared, one was prepared to find the political everywhere, especially in a poet who, outside the poems, had
made his political convictions evident.

In examining the early style, one must pose several questions at
once. To begin with, in just what sense is the early work more "formal"
than the later, and how successful is it granted its own premises? How
deep is the split between the early and the middle style, and what continuities persist beneath the difference? Is it fair to take the earlier
poems as evidence of a superficial rationalism while crediting the
middle style with an exploration of the more irrational, "deeper" part
of consciousness? Are the poems of the second four books (*The Moving
Target, The Lice, The Carrier of Ladders,* and *Writings to an Unfinished Accompaniment*) unequivocally better than anything in the
first four, which have been reissued in a single volume and thus implicitly consigned to the same category of "early" work?

The early work is not entirely uniform. Merwin's fourth book, *The
Drunk in the Furnace* (1960), has usually been regarded as transitional,[10] but the change that becomes obvious in that volume really begins in the third collection, *Green with Beasts* (1956). The first two volumes, *A Mask for Janus* (1952) and *The Dancing Bears* (1954), are very
much alike. As Richard Howard has observed, the first four books can
be further divided into two pairs.[11]

One must make allowances for the fact that *A Mask for Janus* and

The Dancing Bears represent the work of a poet in his mid-twenties. Nonetheless, it must be said that, compared with Richard Wilbur and Howard Nemerov, who were formal poets in the fifties and remained so afterwards, or compared with Robert Lowell, Adrienne Rich, and James Wright, who in varying degrees repudiated their early formalism in mid-career, Merwin seems narrow from the beginning, less worldly in temperament and more obsessed with pursuit of elusive hints of the absolute. Moreover, a close look at the first two books shows that what is stiflingly formal in them has less to do with prosodic constraints, such as accentual-syllabic meter or elaborate rhyme schemes, than with tics of the period style in matters of syntax and diction: defiantly unidiomatic inversions of word-order, convoluted torturing of ill-defined similes into still vaguer conceits (a result, perhaps, of trying to combine symbolist suggestiveness with Metaphysical wit), and a weakness for impenetrable pronouncements about some shadowy collectivity named "we." And there is, from the outset, a thinness of external incident, a lack of a strong sense of occasion, that leaves the utterance of the poems without discernible motivation in the speaker's experience. The formal artifice, therefore, often seems to exist for its own sake, rather than to express or give shape to any compelling expressive impulse.

Despite the presence of a sonnet ("Epitaph on Certain Schismatics") and two examples of the sestina, a form that was universally fashionable (and almost universally deadly) in the fifties, Merwin's most characteristic forms in the first two books are ballad-like stanzas, often with refrains, with a surprisingly loose accentual meter, sliding, in many instances, back and forth between two and three accents per line, with no set pattern of alternation. The rhythmic texture seems often an homage to Old English and Middle English verse or to folk ballads rather than the more high-hat imitation of Donne and Dante encouraged by the prestige of Eliot. "Rime of the Palmers," though formal in its four-line stanzas and its *abab* pattern of slant rhymes, resembles a good many other poems in the first two books in its deliberately unstable accentual meter:

Where, and in the morning,
Palmers, do you pass?
The sudden birds sing
In the poplar trees.

(*FFBP,* 10)[12]

The first line contains two strong stresses, with the hint of a third secondary stress on "in." The second could plausibly be read as containing either two stresses or three, depending on how much emphasis one placed on "do." Both lines hover indecisively between dimeter and trimeter. The third line clearly has three stresses, but the line falls into the familiar sequence of iamb and anapest, so that despite the accentual context one must resist the impulse to denote stress on "birds" and hear it as two feet. As the poem continues, one finds some lines unequivocally heard as two ("We seek the still . . . ," "And into absence . . . "), others unequivocally heard as three ("Staff and shadow break," "Bone and vein are full"), and a great many suspended uncertainly between the alternatives. In poems such as "Carol of the Three Kings," where there are no stanza divisions and rhyme is intermittent and very faintly heard, this meter sometimes sounds like free verse:

> We have been blindness
> Between sun and moon
> Coaxing the time
> For a doubtful star.

(FFBP, 51)

"Ode: The Medusa Face" (*FFBP,* 36) *is* free verse, by some definitions, although it is *vers libéré* rather than *vers libre,*[13] divisible for the most part into feet but with irregularly shifting line lengths and attenuated, intermittent rhyme. "Over the Bier of the Worldling" is similarly irregular, though its rhymes are more frequent and assertive.

The point of this digression into Merwin's prosody, in a discussion otherwise addressed to the implicit philosophical underpinnings of contemporary styles, is that before assimilating Merwin to the going clichés about the revolt against formalism, we must be clear about the nature and degree of his formalism in the first place. In its neo-medievalizing angularity, in its frequent use of accentual rather than accentual-syllabic meters (and unstable accentual meters at that), and in its preference for short lines (a remarkable number of poems are in dimeter, trimeter, or a free oscillation between the two), Merwin's early formal poetry is atypical of the period; it is not representative in its prosody of fifties baroque in the way that the poetry of Wilbur, Nemerov, or Merrill, written in the same years, undeniably is. In poems of the kind I have analyzed, the continual uncertainty of stress creates an irresolute flatness remarkably similar in its effect, though not in its literal rhythmic contour, to the benumbed, unpunctuated free verse of *The Moving Target* and subsequent volumes.

The ornate syntax, with its long sentences and frequent inversion of word order, is, it must be granted, quintessential fifties baroque. So too is much of the diction, although many of the obsessively repeated words of the later style are already prominent in the early work: stone, mirrors, silence, and darkness. But within the busy whir of syntax surrounding them, they do not stand out so sharply. There are even a few passages that would fit, with only slight alteration, seamlessly into the middle style: "I became the man who fell / After the lightning long ago / At his own window" ("Herons," *FFBP*, 44–45). (The need to provide a rational account of the metamorphosis—"I became the man who"—is the main sign of the early mode. Ten years later, Merwin would probably have written: "I fell / After the lightning / Long ago / At my own window.")

In the early poems, the dominant emotional affect of Merwin's middle style—what Howard calls "a phenomenology of darkness, . . . of loss, absence, and removal"[14]—is already in place, even if it does not yet "govern the imagery" as programmatically as in the later style. The very first poem, "Anabasis (I)," opens with a burst of negation:

> Then we poised, in time's fullness brought
> As to a new country, the senses
> In the mutations of a sallow light,
> A season signs and speechless;
>
> Thought momently on nothing, knew
> No oratory, no welcome:
> Silence about our silence grew;
> Beached by the familiar stream.
>
> (*FFBP*, 3)

The first line and a half seem to promise a New World. We have been "brought" somewhere "As to a new country." But only "as," only "as if." Already with "sallow" in line three, the suggestion of "fullness" has been undermined. The discovered realm, however "new" it may be in the sense of being unfamiliar, is a land of stasis, where even the leaves are "Exhausted." The discovery provokes no excitement; the new landscape merely stuns the onlookers with its incomprehensible strangeness, leaving them "speechless," and, later in the poem, "disbodied," "Estranged almost beyond response." Throughout the first two volumes, the poet is haunted by intimations of an elusive spiritual presence, occasionally glimpsed but forever receding into mysterious distances: "we became / The eyes of sleep that chased receding fires / Through the bodiless exile of a dream" ("Anabasis (II)," *FFBP*, 9).

The pursuit of elusive transcendence is, of course, a familiar motif in post-romantic tradition. This aspect of Merwin's early style is quite traditional, even conventional—and, since it remains an important aspect of the middle style, it should remind us how much of what Hass understood as contemporary spiritual devastation can also be understood as a late, atonal variation on themes by Baudelaire and Mallarmé. But Merwin, even early on, diverges from that heritage by his resigned futility, his sense that no alchemical feat of imagination can even begin to wrest the unnameable into the realm of the articulate. The poetry is less the testimony of a struggle to apprehend the elusive absolute than a commentary on the hopelessness of that struggle.

In *Green with Beasts,* and still more in *The Drunk in the Furnace,* Merwin seems ready to turn aside from the defeated symbolist quest and accept more mediated forms of confrontation with the inarticulate intimations that haunt him. Through these books, one can trace a growing interest in the depiction of particular landscapes, persons, and situations, rather than failed raids on the inarticulate. The settings that most interest him—seascapes with shipwrecks or the bleak altitudes of "The Mountain" and "The Station"—confront us with the hostile and the unknown in nature, remote from the habitual comforts of settled life. They provide natural symbols for the inarticulate, anchoring Merwin's ethereally visionary imagination in a physical world. In "Saint Sebastian" and "The Annunciation," the speakers try to understand their inarticulate experience of divine presence. Because they are figures in stories known to the reader, however, and because the poems follow the conventions of dramatic monologue, in which the title immediately identifies the speaker as someone in history or myth, and not the poet, the approach to the mystery is more indirect and at the same time more focused. Mary's experience of the Annunciation and Saint Sebastian's experience of his martyrdom are both religious experiences, and both resist adequate description, but they are distinct forms of religious experience. Moreover, the speaker's identity in the story gets, at least to some degree, into the poems. Merwin's Virgin Mary, though she often sounds as if she has read *Four Quartets,* is also a very young woman, to whom the idea of a husband is almost as mysterious as the idea of God, and the first perplexity becomes a lower analogue for the second.

At times one is not sure where the status of particulars as symbols for the pervasive mystery leaves off and their irreducible importance in their own right begins. In the context of the other poems in *Green with Beasts,* "The Station" would seem to concern, like the earlier pair of "Anabasis" poems, a figurative rather than a literal journey, a quest for a mysterious realm of the spirit:

From that point already so remote that we
Continually caught ourselves talking in whispers
No path went on but only the still country

Unfolding as far as we could see
In the luminous dusk its land that had not been lived on
Ever, or not within living memory.

(*FFBP,* 161)

But the opening description of the shelter from which this prospect is seen insists on verisimilitude. The first details seem intended to signal the conventions of realism: "Two boards with a token roof, backed / Against the shelving hill, and a curtain / Of frayed sacking. . . ." The description of the travelers, too, has the texture of the literal; it reminds one of newsreel footage from some disaster in an "under-developed" nation:

Some as they arrived appeared to be carrying
Whole households strapped onto their shoulders,
Often with their tired children asleep
Among the upper baskets, and even
A sore dog limping behind them.

(*FFBP,* 161)

Are these avatars of alienated Modern Man, or are they flesh-and-blood displaced persons, trying to find "a sheltered valley / Along a slow river, where even the clumsiest farmer / Would grow fat on the land's three crops a year" (*FFBP,* 162)? Finally the poem coheres only if taken as primarily figurative, but the pull toward a more literal reading is quite strong in many passages.

The Drunk in the Furnace continues several lines of development from the earlier books: in "One-Eye" and perhaps "Burning Mountain," the parable or folktale; in the group at the beginning of the volume, the seafaring motif—treated, in "The Portland Going Out" and "Sailor Ashore," with greater concision and imagination than previously. But Merwin departs strikingly from his earlier work in the group of poems about his family and the milieu of his childhood. There is nothing like these in his earlier work and, aside from a few poems at the beginning of *The Moving Target,* there is nothing like them in the work to follow until *Opening the Hand* (1983). They are not, it must be conceded, the most accomplished work in the volume, although they seem to promise most for the expansion of the poet's range. The verse is sometimes wooden, the syntax lacking in patterns of tension and release. The kind of poetry Merwin had been writing hardly gave him much technical practice in anecdote, description, or the rhythms of idiomatic, casual speech. Nonetheless, in such passages as the ending

of "Grandmother Dying," one can see Merwin's possibilities as a poet of
the quotidian life:

> Outside,
> The crooked river flowed easy, knowing
> All along; the tracks smiled and rang away;
> Help would come from the hills. One knotted hand
> Of hers would hang up in the air above
> Her head for hours, propped on its elbow, waving
> In that direction. And when she heaved up
> Her last breath, to shake it like a fist,
> As out of habit so old as to be
> Nearly absent, at the dirty river
> Sliding away there the same as ever,
> Bid says you could not hear her because there
> Came a black engine that had been waiting
> Up the tracks there for ninety-four years, and
> Snatched it out from her lips, and roared off
> With it hooting downriver, making the tracks
> Straighten out in front of it like a whip,
> While the windows rattled loud to break, the things
> On the shelves shook, the folds of her face jarred
> And shivered; and when it was gone, for a long
> Time the goosed laundry still leaped and jiggled
> In the smutty wind outside, and her chair went on
> Rocking all by itself with nothing alive
> Inside it to explain it, nothing, nothing.

(FFBP, 250–51)

Richard Howard, who justly remarks that Merwin's "autobiographical American studies" have "an ungainliness and an intimacy one would
have thought inaccessible not only to the singer of all those carols and
cansos, but even to the connoisseur of numinous landscapes and emblematic weathers," is nonetheless only loosely right in claiming that
these poems "turn from the example of Robert Graves . . . to that of
Robert Lowell." [15] There is in Lowell's autobiographical poetry of the
same period very little of the attempt, so evident in this passage, to
imagine how parents and grandparents experienced their own being;
Lowell is concerned with the way his relatives appeared to him when
he was a child and with their place in the chain of causation leading to
his adult crises. A closer likeness would be the poetry of James Wright
with its similar compassion for stunted lives, its drab Ohio industrial

towns corresponding to Merwin's Scranton and Union City further east. Wright's poetry also resembles the autobiographical poems of *The Drunk in the Furnace* in its juxtaposition of almost reportorially "objective" description with the language of myth or dream, as when the train that has been "waiting / Up the tracks there for ninety-four years" carries away the grandmother's last breath. The poems at the end of *The Drunk in the Furnace* suggest a road not taken.

Vain though it may be to speculate on what might have happened, I sense an emerging richness in these poems that was sacrificed to a narrower intensity in *The Moving Target*. Moreover, their idiom might have provided a more direct way of integrating the Merwin who contributed political journalism to *The Nation* in the early sixties with Merwin the poet. In their awareness of physical suffering and the impact of social class structure on individual lives (e.g., "The Native," *FFBP*, 252–53), they are in some respects more politically suggestive than the poems at the end of *The Lice*.

In *The Moving Target*, Merwin returns to his central "attempt to give utterance to the unutterable experience of being alive, and consciously mortal, and human, in any time." Once again, he writes about the one rather than the many, about Being rather than particular beings. But he returns to the old theme with a new, radically stripped down style. One can see the new style forming in a few poems near the beginning of the volume. There are several gnomic poems, some of them very sharply focused, even "rational"; here, for instance, is "By Day and by Night":

Shadow, index of the sun,
Who knows him as you know him,
Who have never turned to look at him since the beginning?

In the court of his brilliance
You set up his absence like a camp.
And his fire only confirms you. And his death is your freedom.

(*MT*, 9)

The theme of this poem may be mystical—the intimacy of apparent opposites, the mutual dependence implicit in their enmity—and even antirational in its questioning of the validity of distinctions. But it is tightly argued, and its intellectual cleverness is part of its appeal. "Index" retains its root meaning of pointing, like an index finger; once we recall this meaning, it seems just the right word for a shadow in strong sunlight. Although shadow has "never turned to look at the sun," no one knows the sun better, since wherever the sun is present, shadow is present also. The stronger the sunlight, the deeper the shadow: "his fire only confirms you." With the setting of the sun, shadow is freed from the determinate shapes cast during the day and becomes the darkness of the night: "And his death is your freedom."

But the next poem, "In the Gorge," is different:

Lord of the bow,
Our jagged hands
Like the ends of a broken bridge
Grope for each other in silence
Over the loose water.
Have you left us nothing but your blindness?

(*MT*, 9)

It is, to begin with, unclear who the "Lord of the bow" is: a figure from Western myth, Apollo perhaps, or a less determinate figure, a master archer out of, say, the ancient Chinese *Book of Songs?* Why is he blind? Nor is there an obvious connection between the figure of the bow and that of the "broken bridge," although one can imagine hands that "grope for each other" as being like the "ends" of such a bridge. The connections between the parts are more tenuous. Some of the word choices are hard to explain, whether or not they strike one intuitively as "right." Why is the water "loose"? The ends of a broken bridge are "jagged," but what do "jagged hands" look like? Merwin has begun to abandon the close determination of poetic argument for a less determinate, associative movement from one line to the next. There is less pressure from what has come before on what is to follow, which allows greater surprise and freedom but also courts the arbitrary.

Early in the book, one comes upon a poem called "Finally" that shows the degree to which Merwin conceived his new style as an exploration of the depths of the self and a turning away from the phenomena of the surface, including the kind of socially detailed observation that had appeared briefly in *The Drunk in the Furnace*. The concern with consistency in the extension of a metaphor, still evident in "By Day and by Night," as well as the construction of intricate stanzas, already on the way out in *Green with Beasts* and *The Drunk in the Furnace*, had also come to seem formalistic, obstructing rather than giving shape to the most essential kinds of imaginative experience. "Finally" announces Merwin's quest for the inward and the authentic. The elusive transcendence that had fled now approaches, is indeed the "self" returning from its projection outward:

My dread, my ignorance, my
Self, it is time. Your imminence
Prowls the palms of my hands like sweat.
Do not now, if I rise to welcome you,
Make off like roads into the deep night.
The dogs are dead at last, the locks toothless,
The habits out of reach.
I will not be false to you tonight.

Come, no longer unthinkable. Let us share
Understanding like a family name. Bring
Integrity as a gift, something
Which I had lost, which you found on the way.
I will lay it beside us, the old knife,
While we reach our conclusions.

Come. As a man who hears a sound at the gate
Opens the window and puts out the light
The better to see out into the dark,
Look, I put it out.

(MT, 22)

The poem welcomes the unconscious and the irrational; one puts out the light and peers into the darkness. "The habits are out of reach"— presumably, that includes literary habits of the sort that still linger in the sentence, "Your imminence / Prowls the palms of my hands like sweat," with its aggressive alliteration and slightly overwrought figurative verb. The ego's defenses—dogs and locks—will no longer drive away the authentic self. There is a faint tinge of social implication in this poem, since the defenses of the socially habituated self are linked with the defense of property, as if to say that self-possession and possession are forms of mean-spirited suspicion, even repressiveness. The last four lines are especially interesting; they begin as if about to launch into a Homeric simile and end by obliterating the distinction between tenor and vehicle: I put out the light like a man who puts out the light. Simile, traditionally used for intellectually exact analogies, is one of the lights by which poets illuminate the inarticulate intuitions of the imagination; even as he declares "Look, I put it out," Merwin extinguishes it.

But in this poem, as in the handful of others in Merwin's middle style that wear well, not all the lights are out, and not all the habits are out of reach. Only by setting up a familiar rhetorical pattern—and rhythm—can he close "Finally" with such power, collapsing his simile upon itself. Nor does this poem suffer from the fault, already noticeable in *The Moving Target* and compulsively dominant in the next three books, of returning constantly to a few totemic words to invest the language with the hushed mystery of archetype. For the most part, the words belong where they are for reasons apparent to a careful reader. Even the "knife," elsewhere used as a formulaic image, has a particular appropriateness here. Merwin asks the approaching true self to "bring integrity as a gift" and then says, "I will lay it beside us, the old knife, / While we reach our conclusions." Integrity can cut like a knife; as the old cliché has it, the truth hurts. It is also a lost, valued possession about to be returned—an *old* knife, perhaps a family heirloom ("Let us share / Understanding like a family name"). And while the "I" of the poem negotiates his reunification with the deeper self, he sets this knife beside them, as if to indicate that he is ready to use it if necessary but would rather be spared the most lacerating, violent forms of self-unmasking implied in the choice of this symbol.

In general, the best poems are those that retain the vestiges either of extended metaphor in the manner of "By Day and By Night" or of a plot or a determinate occasion. As examples, one might consider "Their Week," from *Writings to an Unfinished Accompaniment* and "The Hydra," from *The Lice.* "Their Week" offers a sketchy account of the rituals and religion of some unspecified culture:

The loneliness of Sundays grows
tall there as the light
and from it they weave
bells of different sizes

(WUA, 22)

Unlike Christian church bells, these bells toll a reminder not of communion but of "loneliness" and division, and they hang everywhere, "from branches," "in barns" (places associated with abundance), and "in each room like lamps." Then Merwin describes the creation myth of this culture of ritualized loneliness:

they believe it was on a Sunday
that the animals were divided
so that the flood could happen
and on a Sunday that we were severed
from the animals
with a wound that never heals
but is still the gate where the nameless
cries out.

(WUA, 22)

This is, I think, the most memorable expression of Merwin's abiding obsession with the inarticulate mystery of being. To be "severed / from the animals" by our human consciousness leaves us cut off from the instinctual and unconscious life, unable to enter "the gate where the nameless / cries out." In this passage, Merwin is able to write articulately *about* the inarticulate and nameless rather than presenting us with an opaque language of mystification that remains itself inarticulate. The poem closes with a sort of recessional, returning to the motif of the bells:

> they believe that everything
> that is divided
> was divided on a Sunday
> and they weave the bells
> whose echoes
> are all the days in the week.

(WUA, 22)

The middle section about the division of the animals and our severance from them reveals the meaning of the ceremonial bells. Just as the other six days are broken fragments of the primal unity of Sunday, the bells are reminders of that primal unity. Their presence reminds the people of that unity within the dividedness of the other days, on which the wholeness and contemplative repose of Sunday is "divided" into the varied activities of work and domestic life.

"The Hydra" is a less transparent poem than "Their Week," but the passage that provides it with a center and brings its other associations into relation contains a ghostly narrative:

> A long time ago the lightning was practising
> Something I thought was easy
>
> I was young and the dead were in other
> Ages
> As the grass had its own language
> Now I forget where the difference falls

(L, 5)

The simple distinction between "a long time ago" and "now" reveals change—the poem describes a passage from innocence to experience, and the speaker has not always thought of "the dead" in the way that he "now" does. When he was young the dead "were in other / Ages," as remote from his own condition as the grass with "its own language." But "Now I forget where the difference falls"—it is easier, as one grows older, to imagine the living, including oneself, passing into the realm of the dead. The dead are no longer unimaginably remote, but near at hand, terrifyingly near at hand. One could slide into their midst unawares, uncertain of the boundary between the realms. The Hydra that "calls" to oneself and to "Everybody" waits on the other side, and although "sometimes a piece of us / Can stop dying for a moment," sooner or later we go, with the dead, "into those names." The Hydra, a single monster with many heads, is like the collective abstraction "the dead": many dead persons, each with his or her own name, collapsed into a single noun and a single condition.

Even these poems push to the edge of the inarticulate; they try to compress sprawling mysteries into brief parables with just enough exactness to limit their vague suggestiveness or, in the metaphor of "By Day and By Night," to give the shadow a definite shape. But in most of the poems of the middle style, the death of even the most oblique forms of rational connection gives the Merwinian shadow its "freedom." For every poem with the sharpened meditative focus of "Their Week" or "The Hydra," one encounters two dozen like "The Night of the Shirts" which are parades of characteristic vocabulary and attitudes rather than fully written poems. I choose "The Search" (*WUA*, 106) as a representative case, but many other choices would have done as well:

When I look for you everything falls silent
A crowd seeing a ghost
it is true

yet I keep on trying to come toward you
looking for you
roads have been paved but many paths have gone
footprint by footprint
that led home to you
when roads already led nowhere

still I go on hoping
as I look for you
one heart walking in long dry grass
on a hill

around me birds vanish into the air
shadows flow into the ground

before me stones begin to go out like candles
guiding me

Short, parable-like poems can ill afford to dither for six lines decorating what is essentially a cliché: the road back to "you" is hard to find. To visualize "one heart walking in long dry grass / on a hill" is to find one-self suddenly astray in an animated cartoon. And the last four lines end the poem in a shower of stock Merwin words for lonely contemplation of mystery: birds, shadows, stones, candles. Most important, the poem lacks a passage like the middle portion of "Their Week" or the contrast between "A long time ago" and "Now" in "The Hydra"—something that provides a core of relatively determinate meaning around which the free-floating associations of the poem can cohere. As Helen Vend-ler remarked in a review of *The Carrier of Ladders* and *The Miner's Pale Children* (which she discusses as prose-poetry), "Merwin's abstraction cloaks the human cause of these poems," and, in the absence of such a cause, "one feels that these poems were written not so much from sentiments requiring expression as from obsessive counters de-manding manipulation."[16]

Such a poetry, even in its most successful moments, is too disem-bodied to support the kinds of claims that Nelson or Hass make for it as political discourse, unless one sees the habitual grain of consciousness itself as an inevitably political matter. There are times, however, when Merwin juxtaposes his language of psychological depth with emblems representing, though in an allegorized way, the socialized realm of the surface. In "The Asians Dying," one of those political poems near the end of *The Lice*, the language is very similar to that of Merwin's poems of more generalized desolation, but the title asks us to refer this lan-guage specifically to the war in Vietnam. In the closing lines, we iden-tify the "possessors" as the American forces, who

> move everywhere under Death their star
> Like columns of smoke they advance into the shadows
> Like thin flames with no light
> They with no past
> And fire their only future
>
> (L, 63)

Having made this identification, one can then take "They with no past" as a comment on the American indifference to history and the "fire" as a reference to the military destruction unleashed on the Asians. The problem, however, with "The Asians Dying" as a political poem is that its connection to its topical focus is provided mainly by the title and by a few scattered words and phrases: "The ghosts of the villages trail in the sky / Making a new twilight" can mean that the smoke created when the villages burn makes a darkness like that of the forests of the first line; "When the forests have been destroyed their darkness remains" as the darkness of the smoke. But the poem offers this kind of cleanly defined connection to a differentiated external world only at a few scattered points of contact. Not only "everywhere" in Asia, but everywhere in Merwin's poetic universe, shadowy forces advance "under Death their star." Lines such as "The nights disappear like bruises but nothing is healed," or "Rain falls into the open eyes of the dead," or "Like columns of smoke they advance into the shadows" could be dropped intact into any number of other poems that have nothing to do with Asians dying or with any comparably definite subject. Even in "The Asians Dying," which is about as occasional as Merwin gets in this phase of his career, the connection between style and occasion, between utterance and motive, is extremely tenuous, flickering on and off as the poem progresses. Encountering this poem in the context of others in the same style, one feels that what is happening to the Asians is only what always happens in a Merwin poem. One could take this similitude—as Hass apparently did—to imply the Marcusean point that in one-dimensional society, all the world's a concentration camp. But one might argue that on the contrary, Merwin has trivialized the horrors of the war, rather than bringing home to us the horrors of our own situation, by finding the same language for both.

Probably the best of the political poems in the middle style, "The Last One," is not topical at all; rather, it is a psycho-political parable of Western acquisitiveness and rationalism.[17] "They," who are never identified but would seem to be ourselves, "made up their minds to be everywhere because why not. / Everywhere was theirs because they thought so." And then "they cut everything because why not." When at last "they cut the last one" (presumably the last tree, but deliberately left inclusive and vague), its shadow remains "on the water," and this they cannot destroy. But they make the attempt: "They shone lights on it the shadow got blacker and clearer"; "They started to scrape the shadow with machines. / When it touched the machines it stayed on them." Neither the light of reason nor the power of technology is effective against it. All the while, the shadow keeps growing, and finally it takes its revenge:

They began to stomp on the edge it got their feet.
And when it got their feet they fell down.
It got into eyes the eyes went blind.

The ones that fell down it grew over and they vanished.
The ones that went blind and walked into it vanished.
The ones that could see and stood still
It swallowed their shadows.

Then it swallowed them too and they vanished.
Well the others ran.
The ones that were left went away to live if it would let them.
They went as far as they could.
The lucky ones with their shadows.

                                                      (*L*, 11–12)

The shadow is the uncontrollable and irrational within the world, whatever in it does not submit to our dominion. "The shadow" is also the name Jung gave to the uncontrollable within the self. Those who deny the shadow cause it to increase, and they project it outward on everything they encounter; eventually, denial of the shadow leads to crisis, to the collapse of the self. "The Last One" is rather prolix (it does not seem to need all of its sixty-five lines), but it has a pointedness lacking in "The Asians Dying." Its implied critique of Faustian greed and will to dominate is hardly original, but the fable by which the critique is expressed has memorable force and clarity. Unfortunately, "The Last One" is in that respect quite atypical.

Beginning with some of the poems in *The Compass Flower* (1977), there is another important turn in Merwin's development, confirmed in the autobiographical prose of *Unframed Originals* (1982) and the poems of *Opening the Hand* (1983). These writings show Merwin returning from the extreme interiority of his work from 1963 through 1973 and developing an interest in particulars of place and incident. *The Compass Flower*, whether its arrangement follows chronology or a deliberately chosen pattern, seems to progress toward a more extroverted style. One first becomes aware of a new realism in "City," "Line," and "St. Vincent's" in the second section, and several poems scattered through the third confirm the impression of emerging change. In the fourth and concluding section, almost all of the poems are written in the new mode. Despite Merwin's continued refusal to punctuate, the syntax has changed to meet the demands of an increased concern with particular happenings in this place or that time. One can see the difference immediately in the opening of "The Coin":

I have been to a fair alone
and across the river from the tented marketplace
and the church
were the green sagging balconies from which
during the occupation
the bodies of many
of the men of the town

hung for days in full view
of the women who had been their wives

(CF, 75)

"During the occupation" places the poem in France. The balconies, made particular by the adjectives "green sagging" and by their location "across the river" from the marketplace and church, are the very ones "from which"—a locution that would not occur in the middle style—the bodies once hung. The place as it is now carries the historical memory of the same place then, as it could not have done in the poems of 1963 to 1973. The language is heavily freighted with modifiers and with words that express temporal or spatial relation: "across," "from," "during," "of," "in."

Even here, however, in one of the volume's most tightly written passages, one notices the awkward prepositional logjam in "the bodies of many / of the men of the town," underscored by the fourth "of" at the beginning of line nine. It is almost as if the graceful management of syntax has atrophied from lack of practice—in the previous style, Merwin never had to worry about setting up a chain of modifiers expressing the relation among several things at once, since his nouns floated in a purely psychological space, untroubled by history or by a determinate location in a physical world. In *Opening the Hand,* one finds surprisingly clumsy narrative pacing. The casual "and" for instance, may be an effective way of suggesting artless immediacy, but Merwin frequently overdoes it:

and since it is a day without precedents the son
hears himself asking the father whether he may
please see what is down the wagon track and he surprises
himself hearing the father say yes but don't go far
and be very careful and come right back
so the son turns to his right and steps over
a smoky fire on the flat sloping rock
and after a few steps the branches close overhead
he walks in the green day in the smell of thawed earth
and a while further on he comes to a turn to the right
and the open light of cleared ground falling away

("The Houses," OH, 11–12)

The lack of punctuation, however effective it may have been in conveying the oneiric dislocation of the middle style, becomes an obstruction in narrative, continually forcing the reader to slow down and piece together the grammatical relations; in the example at hand, one is likely to stumble for a moment before recognizing "in the smell of thawed earth" as an appositive. The grammatical ambiguity opens on no depths; it is only a pointless annoyance.

The poems of *The Compass Flower* and *Opening the Hand*, one hopes, will turn out to have been transitional, first steps toward a more resonant and syntactically muscular language. Already, one can begin to see, especially with the help of the prose recollections of *Unframed Originals*, the "human cause" that Vendler had missed in *The Carrier of Ladders* and *The Miner's Pale Children*. One can understand why the son of a stern Presbyterian minister, continually warned by his father not to touch anything, would be haunted, as he tells us in "Apparitions," by the image of his father's hands "that always appeared   to be different from my own" (*OH*, 15; spacing *sic*). Having read about Merwin's secretive family, especially his grandmother who "tended, as a matter of habit, to turn aside questions that were put to her, and to suspect the motives of anyone who questioned her,"[18] one begins to supply a context for his obsession with mystery and absence—the history of his family, the events that created the ambience in which he grew up, were withheld from him, exiled to the realm of the unnameable. One understands why, in "Finally," "my dread" and "my ignorance" are other names for "my self." But in the poems so far, the reimagining of this central experience in historical rather than mystical terms has not been completed.

It remains to be seen whether Merwin's recent attempt to remake his style will succeed, but the very fact that he has made the attempt forces us to revise the teleological interpretation of his career in which the first four books become mere preparation for the liberating turn inward of *The Moving Target*. It would seem that in his last two collections of poetry, Merwin has tried to pick up where he left off at the end of *The Drunk in the Furnace*. In doing so, he tacitly acknowledges the limits of his middle style. To see a poet of his fame and long experience struggling with the most basic problems of narration and description is to realize how much his middle style excludes.

8

Ohio and the Collective Unconscious: The Dilemma of James Wright

Anyone seeking to refute the assertion that deep image poetics, by its own implicit logic, excludes representation of social reality could reply, "What about James Wright?" Unlike the rather ethereal Merwin, Wright from the outset tried to include in his poetry a "spirit of place." He began as an admirer of Frost, Hardy, and Robinson, all of whom were haunted by that spirit, and to the end he counted himself among those for whom "poetry of place" represents "an important way of participating in the life around them." Unlike his three early masters, however, Wright grew up in a heavily industrialized setting. His problem, as a child, "was to get out"; as a mature poet, he struggled to believe that "anything can be the location of a poem as long as the poet is willing to approach that location with the appropriate reverence. Even very ugly places."[1]

Wright's Ohio landscapes, more often than not, are neither the rural havens celebrated in poems such as "A Blessing" or "Two Horses Playing in an Orchard" (both of which are set in Minnesota) nor urban prospects in which the human has completely displaced the natural, as in Lowell's "For the Union Dead." The characteristic Ohio setting of Wright's poetry includes nature, but finds nature everywhere disfigured by factories, strip mining, and pollution. In his "Ohioan Pastoral," a creek, a sumac, and some "wild grimed trees" persist in a landscape spoiled by "oil cans," "A buried gas main," and a "lost / Bathtub" (*TJ*, 46).[2] Although the industrialized towns of southern Ohio take on sinister iconographic significance in many of the poems, they are small enough to permit an intimate relationship between the poet and his fellow townspeople. Wright had none of Frost's gift for bringing the voices of others into his poems and little of his gift for storytelling. Nonetheless, anyone familiar with all of Wright's work can easily generate a fairly extensive list of characters. The notorious George Doty comes first to mind, perhaps, but there are also, to name a few, the poet's uncle Willie Lyons, "a craftsman of hammers and wood"; Charlie, the drunk whose kidneys finally killed him; the "defeated savior" who failed to pull a drowning boy from the Ohio River; Mr. Bluehart, from whose orchard the neighborhood boys stole apples; Homer Rhode-heaver, the itinerant preacher "wanted in Pittsburgh on a paternity charge"; and Ralph Neal, the scoutmaster, who "loved us . . . because he knew damned well what would become of most of us."[3]

Critics have, for the most part, understood Wright's poetic matura-tion as one of the many Surprising Conversions at the end of the fifties: like Lowell, Plath, Merwin, Berryman, and Rich, he is said to have discarded an exhausted academic formalism for a more daring style closer to the truth of experience.[4] But we have already seen that this cliché obscures continuities in the work of Lowell, Plath, and Merwin; once again, the conversion theory oversimplifies. Although Wright said, in his *Paris Review* interview of 1971, that after finishing *Saint Judas* (1959), he felt he had come "to something like a dead end," he also said on the same occasion that of all his books, *Saint Judas* was his favorite. He repeatedly affirmed the underlying continuity of his po-etry. "There wasn't a truly radical change taking place between the books *Saint Judas* and *The Branch Will Not Break* [1963]" he main-tained in an interview for *Southern Humanities Review* the following year. And in an interview for *Unmuzzled Ox*, he advised Michael An-dré not to look for "development" in his poetry. "I think I knew pretty well what I was going to do from the beginning. I was just trying to find out ways to do it."[5]

Not only did Wright warn against overestimating the degree of "de-velopment" in his style, he insisted with almost perverse vehemence that he was no stylistic innovator. He considered the influence of sur-realism "dangerous" and protested that when his poems "sound sur-realistic, all that means is that my attempt to be clear has failed." He repeatedly claimed that his work was "Horatian and classical," in-formed, early and late, by his attempt "to subordinate . . . language to one single effect, every time."[6] If he could make the usual complaint that in the fifties "people who were teaching in universities . . . were generally trying to write . . . 'the square poem,'" he could also turn around and defend a 'square' poet:

Ransom is in slightly bad odor right now, partly because he writes the so-called "square" poem. . . . Furthermore, Ransom plainly shows in his poems that he is willing to let his conscious intelligence operate in the poems and this is very much out of fashion. It's ridiculous that it should be out of fashion. It is part of the terribly self-flattering, self-indulging anarchic spirit of our times, the spirit of confusion.

In praising the work of Richard Wilbur, he observed that

For a while during the fifties most writers were tending to write in too facile, too glib a way in regular meters and rhyme. Some of us turned away to free verse. Since then I think that whenever one opens a magazine nearly all the poems one sees will be in free verse. More and more they strike me as being just as facile and automatic in their way as the earlier poems had been in other ways. That is, it isn't a solution to one's artistic problems just to stop rhyming.[7]

All through the last decade of his life, Wright insisted in his public statements that he was a conservative, a classicist, and a defender of the intellectual dimension in poetry.

If few critics have accepted Wright's Horatian self-portrait as accurate, that may be partly due to his close association with Robert Bly, whose thoroughgoing distrust of rhyme, meter, and the display of conscious intelligence is well-known. The influence of Bly on Wright's work is undeniably significant, but one can occasionally detect Wright's need to insist on his independence. William Heyen asked him, in the *Southern Humanities Review* interview, whether he considered himself "a rebel like, say, Robert Bly? I think of Bly," Heyen added, "because we once talked about aspects of formalism and Bly was saying, 'Let's face it. Rhyme is boring. Rhyme is dead. No one wants to hear rhyme any more, today.'" To which Wright replied, "That depends on who the rhymer is."[8]

Wright must have thought that someone wanted to hear rhyme, because despite the predominance of free verse in his later books, none is without at least one or two metrical, rhyming poems. His posthumous collection, *This Journey*, even contains a Petrarchan sonnet, "May Morning"—disguised, for some reason, as unlineated prose!

But even after one has acknowledged the complexity of Wright's attitude toward traditional forms, one remains suspicious of his Horatian pose; his neoclassic aspirations represent one side of an internal conflict that remained unresolved throughout his poetry. On one side is the Horatian neoclassicist, the former student of John Crowe Ransom, the admirer of Hardy, Robinson, and Frost. This is the Wright who wishes to remain grounded in shared experience, in a commonly shared language, and in Anglo-American literary tradition. When he writes from this side of his divided poetic self, Wright gives us the spirit of place, mean though that spirit may sometimes be; his language, whether in rhymed or free verse, is spare and understated. On the other side of the dichotomy is the Wright who informs us that

A cop's palm
Is a roach dangling down the scorched fangs
Of a light bulb.
The soul of a cop's eyes
Is an eternity of Sunday daybreak in the suburbs
Of Juárez, Mexico.

(JW, 140)

These lines come from "The Minneapolis Poem," in *Shall We Gather at the River* (1968), but the same sense of metaphor run amok, egregiously *not* subordinated "to one single effect," already informs these as well, from "The Quail" in *The Green Wall* (1956):

The blue dusk bore feathers beyond our eyes,
Dissolved all wings as you, your hair dissolved,
Your frame of bone blown hollow as a house
Beside the path, were borne away from me
Farther than birds, for whom I did not care,
Commingled with the dark complaining air.

(JW, 32)

If the early example may be understood as a representative example of fifties baroque, in which quasi-metaphysical conceits were beaten to the airiest (and windiest) thinness possible, it nonetheless has affinities with the surrealism of the later passage also. Both make the hermetic poet's assumption that the truth of perception is by its nature inaccessible to language, private and strange rather than shared and familiar.

Wright understood that the allure of radically unfamiliar language sometimes led him to wretched excess: "I have a tendency to get too lush with sounds," he confessed, "and I have a tendency to get lost in the confusion of certain figures of speech."[9] But these "tendencies" cannot be explained as deficiencies of craftsmanship or judgment, though lapses of craftsmanship and judgment sometimes result from them. Within Wright's imagination, opposed to the spirit of place, was a contrary yearning to be done with places altogether, to escape into some dark and secret recess of the self.

In his essay on Wright, Robert Hass acutely remarks that the poetry sometimes irritates by its "familiar celebration of whatever is not mind, of everything unformed, unconscious, and suffused, therefore, with yearning."[10] His example, a passage about the "grown man" in "Many

of Our Waters: Variations on a Poem by a Black Child," catches Wright
at his most wretchedly excessive:

> The long body of his dream is the beginning of a dark
> Hair under an illiterate
> Girl's ear.

(JW, 208)

Hass's most telling criticism occurs in his discussion of "On Minding
One's Own Business" (*Saint Judas*), in which the speaker and his companion, out rowing on a lake, steer clear of an abandoned shack on the
shore, because someone may be hiding within it:

> From prudes and muddying fools,
> Kind Aphrodite, spare
> All hunted criminals,
> Hoboes, and whip-poor-wills,
> And girls with rumpled hair,
> All, all of whom might hide
> Within that darkening shack.
> Lovers may live, and abide.

(JW, 59)

Of this stanza, Hass says:

> Maybe the worst thing about American puritanism is the position it
> forces its opponents into. If the puritan can't distinguish a hobo from a
> hunted criminal, a little nighthawk from a girl who does the sorts of things
> that rumple hair, the poet won't. Hunted criminal, in fact, equals hobo
> equals bird equals girl. The puritan can't tell one from another and knows
> they are all bad; the poet can't tell either, only he knows they belong to the
> dark and are good. When he agrees to disagree with the puritan on his own
> terms, he gives away will, force, power, weight because they are bad Ameri-
> can qualities and he settles for passivity and darkness.[11]

This statement, interestingly, concedes without cross-examination the
truth of a highly doubtful assertion: that postwar American culture is
dominated by an attitude called "puritanism," and that to "the puritan," sex (the girl), nature (the whip-poor-will), social marginality
(the hobo), and crime are all aspects of one bad thing. As I have argued
in my opening chapter on postwar social thought, the notion that all of
American culture has been welded together into an all-enveloping repressive whole is a commonplace of our time. Hass, in his otherwise
penetrating critique, still takes this notion as axiomatic.

We have already seen, in Allen Ginsberg's poetry, one poetic response to the vision of a world divided between those who (in Wright's words) "pitch and moan all night / For fear of someone's joys, / Deploring the human face," and their dreamy, socially marginal victims. What gives Wright's own response its own characteristic stamp is his language of interiority and exteriority, of place as both origin of self and violation of self.

By following Wright's treatment of light and darkness, motifs prominent in his diction from the outset, one can trace the emergence of his second style from the preoccupations of his first. As I have already remarked in my chapter on deep-image poetics, there is a reversal of the traditional moral symbolism of light and darkness in Bly, Wright, Merwin, and Kinnell. Darkness becomes a sign of wise humility, of turning inward from the illusions of a corrupt culture toward the mysteries of being. Wright's political poem, "Eisenhower's Visit to Franco, 1959" (*The Branch Will Not Break*), has already been discussed as an example of this reversal.

If we look back to Wright's first book, *The Green Wall*, we find that "dark" usually carried for him, at first, the conventional associations with death, privation, and grief. In "To a Hostess Saying Good Night," the speaker, touched by the woman's beauty, says: "O dark come never down to you" (*JW*, 25); he wishes she could be spared everything that "dark" represents. The vision of innocence in "A Little Girl on Her Way to School" begins "When the dark dawn humped off to die," leaving an idyllic morning in which "clearly the country bells / Rang in the light." At the end of the poem, the child follows "the white swan through the hedge" (*JW*, 45). Again, dark and light have their conventional sense here. The "dark" again seems a merely destructive force in "Poem for Kathleen Ferrier": "The sounds go on, and on, / In spite of what the morning / Or evening dark has done" (*JW*, 22); here "the morning / Or evening dark" is the quotidian routine that slowly carries us toward death. Even in "A Poem about George Doty in the Death House," which in many ways anticipates Wright's poetry of the 1960s, "dark" represents the despair (but not yet the sacred inwardness) of the criminal and the outcast; the "bums" outside the jail were "Bred to the dark," and Doty was driven to his crime when "Sick of the dark, he rose / For love" (*JW*, 26).

Already in the first book, however, one can find some poems in which the treatment of light and darkness is more complex. In "Eleutheria," the speaker is fatally attracted to a woman portrayed in imagery of darkness:

The dark began to climb the empty hill.
If dark Eleutheria turned and lay
Forever beside me, who would care for years?

(JW, 27)

The language of this passage hints that Eleutheria may be a destructive presence, luring him to a *Liebestod;* the closing metaphor of the poem suggests more unambiguously that their love must be secret, illicit:

She will return some evening to discover
The tree uplifted to the very root,
The leaves shouldered away, with lichen grown
Among the interlacings of the stone,
October blowing dust, and summer gone
Into a dark barn, like a hiding lover.

(JW, 28)

Here, darkness becomes associated with secrecy and with protection for vulnerable passions threatened by an intolerant world. If the "hiding lover" remains, like the bums and criminals of "A Poem about George Doty . . .," an outcast, the fate of being cast out into darkness begins to seem less a negation of one's being than a way of taking sanctuary. One finds a similar implication in "The Quail" ("A quail implored the hollow for a home, / A covey of dark to lie in under stars" [JW, 32]) and in "Morning Hymn to a Dark Girl" ("Pity the rising dead who fear the dark. / Soft Betty, locked from snickers in a dark / Brothel, dream on" [JW, 31]). In these various poems, Wright has assembled the symbols of persecuted vulnerability that converge on the abandoned shack in "Minding One's Own Business."

To complement his increasingly benign imagery of "darkness," which comes to stand for a secret realm of safety and regeneration within the self, Wright developed a sinister imagery of light, which appears unmistakably for the first time in "American Twilights." This poem concerns the execution of Caryl Chessman (protests against which, according to Michael Rossman, marked the beginning of the American New Left).[12] Chessman, like Judas and like the Ohio rapist and murderer, George Doty, becomes in Wright's imagination a scapegoat. Chessman must take upon himself the existential despair of the human condition, which "American Puritanism" disavows: "Lo now, the desolation man / Has tossed away like a gnawed bone / Will hunt him." In the opening section of the poem, Chessman's captors appear in images of light, while they heap the burden of darkness upon their prisoners:

The buckles glitter, billies lean
Supple and cold as men on walls.
The trusties' faces, yawning green,
Summon up heart, as someone calls
For light, for light! and evening falls.

Checking the cells, the warden piles
Shadow on shadow where he goes. . . .

(JW, 79)

The locks of the cells are "clean," making an antiseptic seal between
the righteous keepers and their contaminated prisoners. Wright used
this word again, with a similar irony, in "Eisenhower's Visit . . .":
"Clean new bombers from America muffle their engines / And glide
down now" (JW, 122).

If "American Twilights" points most clearly, among the early poems,
toward the characteristic diction of Wright's second style, "At the Executed Murderer's Grave" points most clearly to a characteristic moral
dilemma. In taking up, once more, the fate of George Doty, this poem
to some extent disowns the poet's earlier treatment of the subject. So
one might interpret Wright's self-contempt near the end of the opening
section:

I walked here once. I made my loud display,
Leaning for language on a dead man's voice.
Now sick of lies, I turn to face the past.

(JW, 82)

On the first encounter, Wright could see Doty only as victim, as a
"poor, stupid animal" doomed to defeat when "Sick of the dark, he
rose / For love," and went, rejected, "Back to the broken ground."
This time, instead of a pitiable animal, Wright sees a "revolting" one:

Idiot, he demanded love from girls,
And murdered one. Also, he was a thief.
He left two women, and a ghost with child.
The hair, foul as a dog's upon his head,
Made such revolting Ohio animals
Fitter for vomit than a kind man's grief.

(JW, 83)

Not only does he withdraw his sympathy from Doty, he insists that "no
love's lost" between himself and "the crying / Drunks of Belaire, Ohio,
where police / Kick at their kidneys till they die of drink" (JW, 83).
The sadistic treatment these men receive at the hands of the police

makes us see them as victims, yet somehow Wright cannot deny sympathy to Doty without witholding it from them also. Doty, the drunks, and presumably all the other outcasts and failures mourned elsewhere in Wright's poetry "Can do without my widely printed sighing / Over their pains with paid sincerity" (*JW*, 83). Here, the contempt shifts back once more from Doty and the drunks to the poet himself, for his sentimental use of them in his art. Wright's language insists repeatedly on a self-conscious toughness, as if to spare no illusions: "Nature lovers are gone. To hell with them" (*JW*, 83).

And yet, the poet's sense of identification with the criminal and the outcast persists, as Wright compares his own sense of guilt to that of a criminal facing execution:

> Doty, if I confess I do not love you,
> Will you let me alone? I burn for my own lies.
> The nights electrocute my fugitive,
> My mind.
>
> (*JW*, 82–83)

He implicitly acknowledges the irrationality of this guilt when he next compares himself to the "bewildered mad," who are "Pleased to be playing guilty after dark." Whether guilty or merely playing guilty, Wright understands himself to be so much like a hunted criminal that his sympathy for Doty is really a displaced form of self-pity: "I pity myself, because a man [Doty] is dead" (*JW*, 83).

Wright's difficulty in coming to terms with Doty was closely related to his difficulty in coming to terms with what Ohio stood for in his own life. The first lines of "At the Executed Murderer's Grave" concern the poet and his father, not George Doty:

> My name is James A. Wright, and I was born
> Twenty-five miles from this infected grave,
> In Martins Ferry, Ohio, where one slave
> To Hazel-Atlas glass became my father.
>
> (*JW*, 82)

Wright presents his father as a victim of Hazel-Atlas glass; the factories of Ohio appear consistently, in the later poetry, as destroyers of the landscape and of the men who work in them. Ohio is "a dead place," and when Wright says that "Ohio caught George Doty," he does not mean simply that the state successfully prosecuted Doty for rape and murder; he means that the spiritual death called "Ohio" overcame Doty and drove him to his desperate actions. Wright portrays himself as one who has escaped Ohio, and returns "Only in memory now,

aloof, unhurried." Presumably, those caught by "Ohio" can either resign themselves to industrial slavery, like the poet's father, or lash out
in some nihilistic form of protest, like Doty; the only other alternative
is, as Wright himself put it, to "get out." In his kind father, as well as in
the brutal Doty, Wright sees a thwarting of possibility from which he
has narrowly escaped. He is torn between asserting the bond of origin
that ties him to these two men and the fierce need to deny it. The
poem builds toward an affirmation of universal brotherhood, opening
into a vision of the Last Judgment, "When all are caught with what
they had to do / In fear of love" (JW, 83). On that day, "God's unpitying
stars" will no longer

> mark my face
> From any murderer's, buried in this place.
> Why should they? We are nothing but a man.
>
> (JW, 84)

The last line of the poem both confirms and qualifies this assertion of
all-encompassing sympathy; Wright calls Doty not "flesh of my flesh"
but "Dirt of my flesh" (JW, 84).

"At the Executed Murderer's Grave" powerfully registers, but
scarcely begins to clarify, Wright's unsettled attitudes toward both his
native place and its ill-starred son, George Doty. Wright can either
sneer at those who were so weak as to be "caught by Ohio," or he can
pity them; in either case, he sees people as essentially passive, unable
to resist the forces that dehumanize them. Ohio becomes a regional
incarnation of Ginsberg's Moloch, and Doty is Ohio's victim. The
toughness of the first four sections registers Wright's awareness that, of
course, Doty was also a victimizer, responsible to some degree for his
violent crime, but the repudiation of Doty in the third section rings
false; the solicitude of "A Poem About George Doty . . .," however excessive, is truer to Wright's fatalistic sense of the world.

In the place that most deeply informs his own identity, Wright finds
almost nothing but symbols of spiritual impoverishment and death.
The closing lines of "In Response to a Rumor that the Oldest Whorehouse in Wheeling, West Virginia, Has Been Condemned" sum up his
antagonism memorably:

> For the river at Wheeling, West Virginia,
> Has only two shores:
> The one in hell, the other
> In Bridgeport, Ohio.

And nobody would commit suicide, only
To find beyond death
Bridgeport, Ohio.

(JW, 166)

Between hell and Bridgeport, apparently, there is little to choose. Wright's discovery of deep-image poetics gave him an affirmative counterforce to oppose to "dead Ohio," but at the cost of turning the inward life into the sole sanctuary of value; the second style depends on a continual juxtaposition of imagery from within (exotic, beautiful, dark) with the demonic surrounding world. The exceptions occur primarily in poems such as "A Blessing" or "Lying in a Hammock at William Duffy's Farm in Pine Island, Minnesota," which abandon industrial Ohio for more pastoral settings. Later on, Wright would find in Europe, and especially in the Italian countryside, an external antidote for Ohio. Like W. S. Merwin in *Opening the Hand*, he began, in his last two volumes, to evolve a third style in which the external and the literal become less hostile to the inward domain of the imagination. But for Wright's poetry from *The Branch Will Not Break* through the selection of new work in *Collected Poems*, the first section of "Two Hangovers" may stand as representative: within, the poet is "dreaming / Of green butterflies searching for diamonds / In coal seams" (JW, 124–25). Outside, there are coal seams aplenty, but no diamonds and butterflies; even the sparrows sing "of the Hanna Coal Co." (JW, 125). The bluejay who appears in the second part of the poem and abandons himself "To entire delight" (JW, 125) is a welcome but atypical visitor in Wright's Ohio poetry; he seems to have flown down from the woods in Minnesota.

Early in *The Branch Will Not Break*, one happens on two adjacent poems that, taken together, establish the symbolic geography of Wright's imagination. Since Wright paid close attention to the order in which poems appeared in each of his collections,[13] the juxtaposition may have been intentional. These two poems, "Autumn Begins in Martins Ferry, Ohio" (JW, 113) and "Lying in a Hammock at William Duffy's Farm in Pine Island, Minnesota" (JW, 114) have been widely acknowledged as among Wright's best.

In "Autumn Begins . . .," the poet has returned to his birthplace; as he revisits "the Shreve High football stadium," he thinks

of Polacks nursing long beers in Tiltonsville,
And gray faces of Negroes in the blast furnace at Benwood,

And the ruptured night watchman of Wheeling Steel,
Dreaming of heroes.

The poet speaks as someone intimate with the place, who can speak of "Polacks" without giving offense. (In "Youth," he again strikes the same tone, describing his father at the Hazel-Atlas factory, "Caught among girders that smash the kneecaps / Of dumb honyaks" [*JW*, 154]. He imagines himself as trapped along with the "Polacks" and "honyaks.") The language suggests a life deprived of all vitality: the night watchman is ruptured, and the faces of the Negroes turn to a dreary "gray" in the glare of the blast furnace; even "nursing" recalls its other associations with hospitals and old people's homes. In the hard lives of these steelworkers, nursing a beer and dreaming of heroes provides the only respite from boredom and exhausting labor. It is not yet clear who the "heroes" might be.

The next three lines move from the workplace to the bedroom:

All the proud fathers are ashamed to go home.
Their women cluck like starved pullets,
Dying for love.

It is easy to see why the fathers are ashamed; what they are proud of, like the identify of the "heroes," remains unclear. The women are emotionally and sexually "starved"; they are "dying" both to obtain love and for the sake of it, enduring their frustrating marriages out of loyalty to their husbands. By this point in the poem, one senses a connection between the workplace and the bedroom: grinding, ill-rewarded, and undignified work breaks the spirit of the men, thus ruining their relations with their wives. The notion that conditions of work in industrial America repress sexuality is again commonplace in the radical social criticism of the late fifties and early sixties, especially in the work of Marcuse.[14] One can detect the guidance of the *Zeitgeist* in the juxtapositions by which Wright defines the sorrows of Martins Ferry.

In the last four lines, the poem makes a startling turn:

Therefore,
Their sons grow suicidally beautiful
At the beginning of October,
And gallop terribly against each other's bodies.

"Therefore," standing alone as a line in itself, is the only explanatory word in the poem, but with it, the remaining connections fall into place. From frustration in the workplace grows frustration in the bedroom, and from frustration in the bedroom issues the ritualized vio-

lence of football (a sport with deeper cultural significance in Ohio, perhaps, than anywhere else in the nation).[15] The idea that violence
originates in sexual frustration completes the psycho-political argument implicit in the poem, but Wright's poem complicates and revises
the familiar cliché. When the sons "gallop terribly against each other's
bodies," they express a desperate desire for contact as well as a licensed release of violence. The meeting of their bodies is a displacement of the thwarted sexual energy of the starved women and their
shamed husbands. And in Ohio (more than in most parts of the country, perhaps) football is an ethic as well as a sport, and the cooperation
of the team represents an old-fashioned ideal of community that the
sport supposedly fosters in the young.

The heroes, then, are football heroes, of the kind that the ruptured
watchman, beer-nursing Polacks, and gray-faced Negroes dreamed of
being, or perhaps actually were, briefly, in their youth. The fathers are
"proud" of their "suicidally beautiful" sons. In the deeds of their sons
on the field, the broken fathers see their former hopes revived, their
lost strength recovered. But the beauty of the sons is "suicidal" not
only because they court injury "galloping against each other's bodies,"
but because it is only a matter of time before Wheeling Steel and the
blast furnace at Benwood will grind it away, until they too are "proud
fathers ashamed to go home." The cyclical return of autumn evoked by
the title becomes an emblem of the cyclical futility of life in Martins
Ferry and places like it. The sons have their moment of glory, perhaps,
but Ohio catches them in the end.

"Autumn Begins in Martins Ferry, Ohio" finds Wright preoccupied
with time as destroyer, and with the bond of community. But community, in this poem, becomes common entrapment in an exhausting and
isolating society that delivers its children up to time the destroyer pre-
maturely, with all their desires unrealized outside the narrow bounda-
ries of the football field. "Lying in a Hammock at William Duffy's Farm
in Pine Island, Minnesota," by contrast, is a poem of solitude, and of
release from the oppressive fear of time and mortality. For Wright,
community on any scale larger than friendship is almost inconceivable
except as common bondage; freedom is loneliness, but a loneliness
transformed almost beyond recognition. He says of the two ponies in
"A Blessing" (JW, 135) that "There is no loneliness like theirs"—it is
different from the familiar loneliness of Wright's outcasts and victims.
It is a self-sufficient conviction of well-being that requires no one else
to confirm it. The two ponies are glad to have the company of the poet
and his friend. "They can hardly contain their happiness / That we
have come"—but this is a new happiness added to a happiness that is

inherently theirs. For people, the solitary conviction of well-being is not as easy to sustain as it is for horses. "Lying in a Hammock . . ." is the utterance of a man briefly granted such a conviction; at the end of the poem, he has already become self-conscious enough to reflect upon it, as he could not do unless the conviction had already begun to fade.

In "Autumn Begins . . .," the poet revisits the football stadium, the communal gathering-place of Martins Ferry; in "Lying in a Hammock . . .," he is alone. There is a house, but it is "empty"—the inhabitants, presumably, are out somewhere communing with nature, as the poet is. The only other presences are animals, and even some of these are present only indirectly. And yet the world around the solitary poet takes on a plenitude that it lacks in "Autumn Begins. . . ."

In Martins Ferry, Wright sees no colors, aside from "gray" which is in effect a negation of color. But in Pine Island, no sooner does he look up from his hammock than he sees

> the bronze butterfly,
> Asleep on the black trunk,
> Blowing like a leaf in green shadow.

This image immediately implies analogies to the speaker's own state of mind. The butterfly, a frail creature, is "bronze"; the word not only describes its color but also endows it with substance and weight. Though it is "Blowing like a leaf in green shadow," it will not blow away, any more than its bronze likeness would—or than a leaf itself would, attached as it is to the branch. "Asleep on the black trunk," the butterfly participates in the mood of secure, self-sufficient repose that informs the entire poem.

The middle part of the poem describes an environment in which natural processes go quietly on without need of human assistance:

> Down the ravine behind the empty house,
> The cowbells follow one another
> Into the distances of the afternoon.
> To my right,
> In a field of sunlight between two pines,
> The droppings of last year's horses
> Blaze up into golden stones.

"The cowbells follow one another" in orderly procession, and the cows move off, somewhere, "Into the distances of the afternoon," passing into and back out of the speaker's awareness. The horse droppings are changed from dung to "golden stones" by the natural alchemy of sunlight, much as the butterfly turned to "bronze." The mention of "Last year's horses" gently disturbs the illusion of temporal suspension, but time remains a benign force; it has taken away the odor of the horse droppings, cleansing them of their rankness and preparing them for their transformation into "golden stones."

It is the last line of "Lying in a Hammock . . ." that everyone re-members,[16] but a close look at the two lines preceding it reveals that Wright very skillfully turns the poem toward its ending; the last line has a subtle but convincing connection with them:

I lean back, as the evening darkens and comes on.
A chicken hawk floats over, looking for home.
I have wasted my life.

As if prompted by the reminder of time in the words "last year's horses," the poet notices that the day approaches its end. He is finished looking about and leans back, passively waiting for the evening, which quite actively "darkens and comes on." With the arrival of the chicken hawk, "looking for home," the poet realizes that he too must go home; it is time to rise from the hammock and return to the "empty house." It is this impending return that prompts him to compare reality as seen from the hammock with the quotidian reality awaiting him in the house. After his experience of solitary plenitude, his usual pursuits seem a waste of time; the hammock seems more truly "home" than the house does.

As my discussion of them has sought to show, these are wonderful poems, and yet they define the limits as well as the capabilities of Wright's imagination. In order to arrive at plenitude and well-being, one must retreat into nature and solitude; within the fallen world of Martins Ferry, there is only deprivation of the spirit. The only avail-able poetic response, apart from the depiction of Ohio as a hell by the shore of a river, is to internalize Pine Island, to create a pastoral inner space within the self. In the representation of this inner realm, the poetics of the deep image enters Wright's style.

"Lying in a Hammock . . ." is followed by "The Jewel," which, as I have already remarked, strongly conveys Wright's sense of an inward, sacred space that must be defended against desecration from without. In "Lying in a Hammock . . .," the poet is secure in his solitude, but now he must make sure that "nobody is going to touch" the "silence" that he has found there. He can no longer lie in his hammock but must "stand upright in the wind," assertively proclaiming his inwardness against a hostile world. His "bones turn to dark emeralds"—here the language turns to surrealism to render the strangeness (imagine a transparent green skeleton), spiritual value (emeralds are precious stones), and mystery ("*dark* emeralds) of the inward realm.

If *The Branch Will Not Break* makes fully articulate, for the first time, the opposition between Ohio and the collective unconscious, *Shall We Gather at the River* is the book in which Wright most frequently portrays the underground existence of the inward mystery within the spiritual desolation of the Ohio steel towns, or of Minneapolis where men "labor dawn after dawn / To sell me my death" (*JW*, 141). In poems such as "Before a Cashier's Window in a Department Store" and "Willy Lyons," Wright extended his range; in others such as "The Minneapolis Poem," he attempted to extend his range with more equivocal results. *Shall We Gather at the River* is more ambitious and sombre than *The Branch Will Not Break*, continually testing the inward sources of joy that Wright discovered in "A Blessing" and "Lying in a Hammock . . ." against outward conditions that make such joy seem solipsistic and untenable. If that confrontation sometimes strengthens the poetry, it also tempts Wright into defensive rhetoric and posturing. In the years immediately following *Shall We Gather at the River*, Wright published his weakest poetry—the selection of new work in the *Collected Poems* of 1971, and *Two Citizens* (1973), which Wright himself dismissed as "just a bust." [17] The characteristic problems of that poetry begin to emerge in *Shall We Gather at the River*.

One might as well begin with the accomplishments. Such poems as "Inscription for the Tank," "In Terror of Hospital Bills," and "Before a Cashier's Window in a Department Store" depict sub-middle-class existence not as a convenient symbol of victimization in general, but as something to be experienced first-hand rather than pitied at a distance. Asked by Michael André whether these poems were "taken from life," Wright replied,

The one in the drunk tank and "In Terror of Hospital Bills," yes, that's right. I didn't have enough money to pay a hospital bill, and it's very frightening. And the one about not being able to pay my bill at, what the Hell's the name of that department store in Minneapolis? Of course, I got out of that very easily, but I realized after their fish eye that there were a lot of people who weren't going to go back as a professor at a university. . . . There are plenty of people who can't do that, and I just got a flash of that, in the moment. And it's no goddamn joke, to have people look at you like that. [18]

"Before a Cashier's Window . . ." is the best-written of the group, and in it, Wright's characteristic opposition of dark inwardness and glittering oppression becomes uncharacteristically informed with a sense of class conflict.

In this poem, darkness is not entirely an inward mystery; it is a socially defined category to which middle-class courtesy does not extend. The speaker, unable to pay his bill, becomes a nonperson, entitled to no dignity or consideration:

> The beautiful cashier's white face has risen once more
> Behind a young manager's shoulder.
> They whisper together, and stare
> Straight into my face.
>
> (JW, 148)

They would never stare so intrusively into the face of a paying customer. The "beautiful cashier" is implicitly likened to the moon, a comparison resumed in the third section of the poem: "she sails there, alone, looming in the heaven of the beautiful." The heaven of whiteness and beauty belongs to those who can pay their bills; those who cannot must hide in a "cellar" or "Under a stone bridge," waiting until "the troops pass." The cashier's stare is cold, like moonlight, and like moonlight, it pries into the secrets of the night:

> Beneath her terrible blaze, my skeleton
> Glitters out. I am the dark. I am the dark
> Bone I was born to be.
>
> (JW, 148)

One thinks immediately of "The Jewel": when the poet assertively stands "upright in the wind," his "bones turn to dark emeralds." Here, the "skeleton / Glitters out" in the unbearable glare of the cashier's gaze. It is as if she has stripped away not only the debtor's humanity but his very flesh, burning him up with shame. But the skeleton not only glitters, it "Glitters *out*" with a defiantly assertive energy. It represents the irreducible core of identity that cannot be stripped away; it is, the poet twice affirms, what "I am."

The closing sections move away from the anecdotal core of the poem. In the fourth, Wright moves without transition to the statement that

> Tu Fu woke shuddering on a battlefield
> Once, in the dead of night, and made out
> The mangled women, sorting

The haggard slant-eyes.
The moon was up.

(JW, 149)

The moon, which unsparingly reveals the carnage on the field, had metaphorically stood for the unpitying cashier in the first three sections. Its symbolic associations have shifted subtly; the moon no longer inflicts pain but cruelly reveals pain that is already present. Tu Fu's life was the harshest endured by any of the great Chinese poets. Not only did he suffer in the wars at the Northern border, he was so bitterly poor that one of his children died of starvation.[19] Wright obliquely claims Tu Fu as guardian spirit to help him through his own hard times. If this claim seems slightly too high-flown and self-pitying, the brief last section undercuts its pretensions with three flat statements:

I am hungry. In two more days
It will be spring. So this
Is what it feels like.

(JW, 149)

Never mind fantasies of dining with Tu Fu at journey's end: hunger is an irreducible fact. It will soon be spring, but the promise of renewal in the season grates ironically against the bleakness of one's own prospects. "This" (being hungry on the threshold of spring) is what "it" (real poverty, permanent exile from the material and spiritual comfort of the middle class) feels like.

In "Willy Lyons" (a poem that Wright himself did not especially like[20]), one finds a comparable subtlety of feeling and resistance—for the most part successful—to sentimentality.

It opens in a matter-of-fact tone similar to that of the closing lines in "Before a Cashier's Window:

My uncle, a craftsman of hammers and wood,
Is dead in Ohio.
And my mother cries she is angry.
Willy was buried with nothing except a jacket
Stitched on his shoulder bones.

(JW, 158)

Willy is not only dead, he is "dead in Ohio"—another victim of that "dead place," as Wright had called it in "At the Executed Murderer's Grave." We are not told why the poet's mother (Willy's sister) is angry rather than sorrowful, but one gathers, from the next lines, that Willy has worked hard with little to show for it; her anger probably arises from her recognition that Willy has been unjustly destroyed or thwarted, though she cannot say by whom or by what. At this point, Wright introduces, characteristically, "the other world" secretly abiding within or behind Ohio—but here, it is the world beyond death, the one evoked by the hymn tune that gives the book its title:

> She does not know how the roan horses, there,
> Dead for a century,
> Plod slowly.
> Maybe they believe Willy's brown coffin, tangled heavily in moss,
> Is a horse trough drifted to shore
> Along that river under the willows and grass.
>
> (JW, 159)

In "On Hearing a Rumor . . .," the Ohio River becomes the Styx, over which one might pass from Bridgeport to hell (or, what for Wright is even worse, from hell to Bridgeport); here, the river is Jordan, and the ghostly horses come to fetch Willy and preside over his passage.

"Let my mother weep on, she needs to, she knows of cold winds. / The box is empty" (JW, 159), the poem continues, and here Wright seems momentarily tempted by sentimentality. One can easily imagine a gaudily surreal ending in which the horses carry Willy across the river, just as a great white bird flies off with the "legless beggars" in "The Minneapolis Poem." But Wright, at this crucial moment, turns his poem back toward the harsher truth of its occasion. "The horses turn back toward the river"; their office accomplished, they leave Willy to work his own passage. Even in "the other world," he remains a craftsman of hammers and wood, building, as D. H. Lawrence would counsel, his ship of death:

> Willy planes limber trees by the waters,
> Fitting his boat together.
> We may as well let him go.
>
> (JW, 159)

Having imagined the passage to the other world in images that are at once mysteriously beautiful and uniquely appropriate to the soul of a carpenter, Wright closes by turning back to this world, taking his place beside the other mourners.

The balance of tenderness and restraint in a poem such as "Willy Lyons" makes the overwrought melodrama of lines such as these, which begin "The Poor Washed Up By Chicago Winter" (JW, 145), painfully obvious:

Well, I still have a train ticket valid.
I can get out.
The faces of unimaginably beautiful blind men
Glide among mountains.
What pinnacles should they gaze on
Except the moon?
Eight miles down in the secret canyons and ranges
Of six o'clock, the poor
Are mountainously blind and invisible.

Like "Willy Lyons," this poem begins with a tough, matter-of-fact tone but moves quickly toward some "other world"; unlike "Willy Lyons," however, it loses the relationship between that world and this. By treating "the poor" as icons of vulnerability, as guardians of the "secret canyons and ranges" of a submerged kingdom of transformed consciousness, Wright romanticizes them beyond recognition and cheapens the compassion that the poem would extend to them.

If the poor, in *Shall We Gather at the River*, are beautiful dwellers in the depths of the psyche, the police are easily available villains. Not only is "a cop's palm," to quote those dreadful lines once more, "a roach dangling down the scorched fangs / Of a lightbulb," a lost child is apt to be "dragged by a glad cop through a Chicago terminal" ("A Poem Written Under an Archway in a Discontinued Railroad Station, Fargo, North Dakota," *JW*, 152). In his terror of hospital bills, the poet fears he will have to "learn to scent the police"; in "Confession to J. Edgar Hoover," the FBI chief is addressed as "Our father," as if he were a wrathful god (*JW*, 163). No wonder that when Wright finally describes "a good cop" in "Speak" (*JW*, 149–50), he must add "Believe it, Lord, or not"—one would not have supposed that a good cop could possibly exist.

In *Shall We Gather at the River*, the self-consciously tough tone first encountered in "At the Executed Murderer's Grave" ("Christ may restore them whole, for all of me"; "To hell with them") begins to reappear. Wright's language in this mode has the same stripped-down syntax we have noted in his more hushed, mystical moments. But whereas in those passages, the bare syntax makes the 'I' of the poem "numb, neutral, universal,"[21] here it permits the bluntest possible assertion of the self. The poet steps forcefully into the poem and lets the reader know, in no uncertain terms, what attitude he takes toward what he has presented. Sometimes these intrusions convince us that they are motivated by passion too urgent to restrain, as in the unforgettable ending of "To the Muse":

I admit everything. But look at me.
How can I live without you?
Come up to me, love,
Out of the river, or I will
Come down to you.

(JW, 69)

The simple, exact phrasing of the last three lines persuades us that "How can I live without you," even if it is a cliché, is also the purest way of saying what it says. But in the previous stanza, the same bluntness betrays Wright into melodrama. It is as if he knows that his response is self-pitying but hopes to present it in such a 'sincere' manner as to disarm criticism:

Oh Jenny,
I wish to God I had made this world, this scurvy
And disastrous place. I
Didn't, I can't bear it
Either. . . .

(JW, 168–69)

Two Citizens opens with a tough-talking epigraph from Hemingway's "The Killers." With the "New Poems" included in the *Collected Poems* of 1971, *Two Citizens* marks Wright's most disastrous overestimation of the power of simple assertion. Instead of letting the modulation of his style imply an attitude he demands the reader's sympathy. In "Many of Our Waters: Variations on a Poem by a Black Child," he announces:

If you do not care one way or another about
The preceding lines,
Please do not go on listening
On any account of mine.
Please leave the poem.
Thank you.

(JW, 207)

"You are going to believe this," he insists in "The Young Good Man" (*TC*, 15); even the title, which makes the young man "good" by authorial fiat, is overbearing.

The defensive bluster of these poems, however, has a comprehensible motive. In *Two Citizens* especially, Wright begins to treat Ohio less as a demonic spirit of place and more as the setting of particular events. Many of the poems recount childhood experience in more detail than Wright had attempted earlier, and many of them are addressed to friends, or again to "Jenny." Wright seems embarrassed by the possibility that he is becoming too personal, touching on experience charged with resonance for himself and for a few intimate friends, but not for the reader. The narration is halting and unclear, as if the poet were reluctant to tell strangers more than he has to and could not decide how much is enough. However inept, *Two Citizens* anticipates the more interesting work of the last two volumes, *To a Blossoming Pear Tree* and *This Journey*. It begins to use European travel as a way of gaining perspective on Ohio; it begins Wright's implicit criticism, in his last years, of the Manichaean dichotomy of secret inwardness and an utterly loveless outer world that informs his Ohio and Minneapolis poems of the 1960s. "The middle of America" remains a "brutal and savage place," but one that Wright can nonetheless "love" ("Paul," *TC*, 24).

In *To a Blossoming Pear Tree*, Wright abandons the tough, anti-intellectual posturing that mars *Two Citizens* (though even in that anti-intellectual book, Wright continued to claim literary descent from Horace in "Prayer to the Good Poet," *TC*, 10–11). There are Latin epigraphs, an homage to W. H. Auden, and even, in "Written on a Big Cheap Postcard from Verona," a surprisingly professorial digression on the sources of plots in Shakespeare's plays. There are also three metrical poems, but the most interesting works, as a rule, are neither in meter nor in free verse, but in prose. We have already seen that Lowell, hoping to restore to poetry some of the particularity of incident that it had ceded to fiction, turned to prose in "91 Revere Street," and that Merwin was able, in the prose of *Unframed Originals*, to explore the motivations of his preoccupation with silence and absence, recovering the texture of everyday life in ways that have thus far eluded him in his poetry. Wright insisted that the unlineated pieces in his late work "are not poems. They are prose pieces." [22] (Be that as it may, one of them, "May Morning," would make a Petrarchan sonnet if broken into lines [*TJ*, 23], and another, "On Having my Pocket Picked at Rome" [*TJ*, 61], begins with cadences that would easily fall into five lines of iambic pentameter, suggesting that it may at first have been intended as a formal poem.)

Some of these prose meditations, such as "Two Moments in Rome" or its companion piece, "Two Moments in Venice," begin as if they were just entries in a traveler's journal, though even here, the imagination continues, at the slightest prompting, beyond what the eye records; glimpsing an old chimney-sweep in a square in Venice, Wright will half believe that he had just climbed up some of those odd stairs out of a nearby narrow canal. How can I know what he was doing under water? The very streets of the city are water; and what magnificent and unseemly things must sway underneath its roads; the perfect skeleton of a cat, his bone tail curled around his ribs and crusted with salt three centuries ago; even a chimney, swept free, till this hour passes, of all the webs they weave so stoutly down there, the dark green spiders under the water who have more than all the time they need.

(*BPT*, 47)

With the imagined underwater chimney, the progression of imagined images returns to its literal source. Although Wright's underwater man in Venice may remind us of the ghosts of the drowned in the Ohio River, this Italian fantasy is more benign; the canal is not like the Acherontic Ohio, but like the transforming waters in *The Tempest*, permitting the rich and strange.

Despite the satirical "Notes of a Pastoralist" in *This Journey*, the Italian landscapes of Wright's last two books are indeed pastoral. Although he is aware of "the gasworks at the edge of Mantua" ("The First Days," *BPT*, 52), one more typically finds him

sitting contented and alone in a little park near the Palazzo Scaligeri in Verona, glimpsing the mists of early autumn as they shift and fade among the pines and city battlements on the hills above the river Adige.

The river has recovered from this morning's rainfall. It is now restoring to its shapely body its own secret light, a color of faintly cloudy green and pearl.

("The Secret of Light," *BPT*, 38)

Solitary well-being, of the sort to be found at William Duffy's farm in Pine Island, is easily available; the "city battlements" blend harmoniously with the river and the pines. Unlike the befouled Ohio river, the Adige has the power to recover and restore itself and retains "its own secret light." A woman of "startling" beauty, with "hair . . . as black as the inmost secret of light," sits on a nearby park bench, then walks away. "I hope she brings some other man's secret face to light, as somebody brought mine," the poet says, and at the end: "I feel like the light of the river Adige. By this time, we are both an open secret." In Ohio, the response to beauty must be carried out in secret and goes counter to the spirit of the place; in Verona, the entire landscape cooperates with the the poet's response to the woman; it is a place of pure permission where secrets can become "open."

Those of the prose pieces that return to Ohio treat the place less purely as an emblem of death and ugliness and begin to populate it with people and their stories. The story of how Homer Rhodeheaver, Billy Sunday's assistant, gave the police the slip as they tried to bring him back to Pittsburgh "on a paternity charge" (*BPT*, 9–10) and the portrait of Ralph Neal, scoutmaster of Troop 62 (*BPT*, 14–16) convince one, for the first time, that Wright knew his small-town Ohio intimately, instead of simply hating it from a distance.

The piece on Ralph Neal ends with a familiar complaint, yet Wright has given it a new twist: "The very name of America often makes me sick, yet Ralph Neal was an American. The country is enough to drive you crazy." In context, the reason the country can "drive you crazy" is not simply, as in Ginsberg, Lowell, and earlier Wright, that the country itself is crazy; rather, it can drive you crazy because, just when you think you are fed up with it and ready to denounce it, you must account for the qualities of a man like Ralph Neal, which are also, in some defining sense, American.

My own favorite of these Ohioan prose sketches is "Honey" (*TJ*, 82). It begins:

My father died at the age of eighty. One of the last things he did in his life was to call his fifty-eight-year-old son-in-law "honey."

This decidedly un-macho expression of endearment turns out to have been an expression of reconciliation also; the poet remembers how, "one afternoon in the early 1930's," he heard his father

offer to murder his future son in law. . . . They weren't fighting about Paul's love for my sister. They were fighting with each other because one strong man, a factory worker, was laid off from his work and the other strong man, the driver of a coal truck, was laid off from his work. They were both determined to live their lives, and so they glared at each other and said they were going to live, come hell or high water. High water is not trite in southern Ohio. Nothing is trite along a river.

"Honey" returns to the theme of "Autumn Begins in Martins Ferry, Ohio": the transformation of frustration into violence. The earlier poem is more compressed and brilliant, whereas "Honey" is more prolix. But if "Autumn Begins . . ." offers more epigrammatic generalizing power, it is also shallower; compare the arrogant contempt of

All the proud fathers are afraid to go home.
Their women cluck like starved pullets
Dying for love

with the dignity of the passage from "Honey," in which one detects, alongside the Hemingwayesque deadpan of the last two sentences, the distant echo of the King James Bible ("one strong man, a factory worker, was laid off from his work and the other strong man, the driver of a coal truck, was laid off from his work").

One does not want to claim too much on behalf of Wright's last two books. In them, he is able to write well about a range of experience that had previously eluded him, and yet in order to admit that experience, he relaxes the demands of compression that one makes of poetry, and that at least a few of his poems in *The Branch Will Not Break* or *Shall We Gather at the River* manage to satisfy. Instead of remaking his technique to accommodate a new intention, he simply loosened the reins. Nonetheless, to the end of his life he was aware of his own limits and sought ways of expanding them, and he resisted the temptation to allow his own innovations to atrophy into mannerisms. Wright's work, though uneven and sadly denied its full course of development by his early death, is the best that has emerged from the generally unfortunate pursuit of the "deep image."

9

Black Mountain: A Critique
of the Curriculum

At the very beginning of the 1950s, before Lowell and Plath had made
their first confessions, before Merwin, Bly, and Wright had gone div-
ing for images, before Allen Ginsberg, even, had raised his howl,
Charles Olson was already calling—by manifesto and by the example
of his own poems—for a new poetics. Through his friendship with
Robert Creeley, and later through his activities as editor and teacher at
Black Mountain College, Olson influenced a group of other poets,
most notably Creeley, Robert Duncan, Edward Dorn, and Denise
Levertov. Though diverging from Olson and from each other, these
poets have acknowledged the importance of Olson's work in their development. Olson has become something of a cult figure. The "Black
Mountain" poets, whatever their differences as artists, tend to see each
other as the most important poets of their time; they do not, in their
writings or interviews about poetry, pay attention to Lowell, Berryman,
and Plath, or Bly, Wright, or Merwin. These poets, in turn, have been
indifferent to the Black Mountain group. A few have even been hostile.
Bly criticized Olson's projectivism as "a wrong turning in American poetry," and Creeley is the despised "Mr C" of Berryman's "In & Out":

> "Dear Mr. C, A reviewer in *The Times*
> considering 200 poems of yours
> produced over a period of fifteen years
> adjudged them 'crushingly dull'; my view too,
>
> though you won't suppose of course I read them all.
> Sir, you are trivial.
> Pray do not write to me again. Pitch defileth.
> Yours faithfully, Henry." [1]

Olson began, like the other poets we have considered, by reacting
against American poetry and culture in the years of Truman and Eisenhower. But he proposed a different kind of response, one which, at first

glance, seems a refreshing corrective to the excesses of the confessional autobiographers and the hierophants of the deep image. Although his program delivers much less than it promises, it warrants attention here, both because it has influenced other poets and because it claims to have political as well as poetic consequences.

I shall begin with a discussion of Olson's own poetics and practice. Olson, though very much a political poet, was not a topical one. Though he lived through the turbulence of the late 1960s and welcomed the counterculture as a sign of an emerging new consciousness,[2] he did not write directly about the events of those years; but Robert Duncan and Denise Levertov did confront the times directly. I shall conclude, therefore, with an assessment of their political poetry, giving special attention to the question of whether Olson's poetics still guides that work and, if so, whether the guidance helps or hinders.

The Poetics of Charles Olson

Like the poets of self-disclosure and of deep image, Olson rejected prevailing styles of poetry as too rational, ego-centered, and distanced from experience. But although he wanted to "get rid of the lyrical interference of the individual as ego" (SW, 24), his alternative to the ego was not migration to the individual or collective unconscious. Instead, Olson demanded a continual dissolution of selfhood in the continuous process of response to the world, of being into ceaseless becoming. His criticism invokes metaphors of surfaces rather than depths. It is true that he admired Jung from the outset and that the later portions of *The Maximus Poems*, especially, owe something to Jung in their use of mythology.[3] But he did not derive from Jung a notion of the collective unconscious as interior space, a dark silent vault in which the archetypal images shine by their own light. He uses figures of surface and of extension into external space, rather than of depth. Bly, when he wants to praise Robert Creeley, uses a metaphor of interiority: "he is living far back in the archaic part of his cave"; Olson, dedicating *The Maximus Poems* to Creeley, calls him "the figure of outward" (*MP I*, 3).[4] Olson places the poet not back in the cave, but close to the front door:

The meeting edge of man and the world is also his cutting edge. If man is active, it is exactly here where experience comes in that it is delivered back, and if he stays fresh at the coming in he will be fresh at his going out. If he does not, all that he does inside his house is stale, more and more stale as he is less and less acute at the door.

(SW, 62)

Bly derives from Jung a sense of stability, of an inviolably primal essence persisting within the psyche, beneath the ego. For Olson, change is, paradoxically, essence. "What does not change," as he put it in "The Kingfishers," "is the will to change" (*SW*, 167). Where he sees stillness, he expects to see stagnation also. As Paul Christensen points out, the psychology with which Olson has most affinity is not a depth psychology, whether Freudian or Jungian, but that of the Gestalt school, especially as expounded by Paul Goodman, a colleague of Olson's at Black Mountain. For Goodman as for Olson, the self is not an essence hidden beneath a surface appearance, describable in a metaphor of depth, but a constantly changing "system" built up through interchange with the environment:

The self is the system of contacts in the organism/environment field; and these contacts are the structured experience of the actual present situation . . . the existing field passing into the next moment is rich with potential novelty, and contact is the actualization. Invention is original; it is the organism growing, assimilating new matter and drawing on new sources of energy. The self does not know beforehand what it will invent, for knowledge is the form of what has already occurred. . . . The complex system of contacts necessary for adjustment in the difficult field, we call "self."[5]

Olson's poems may be said to look outward not only in their transactions with the world, but also in their relationship with the reader—or at least, despite their frequent obscurity, in their intended relationship with the reader. As Robert von Hallberg remarks, Olson often wrote "as though the offices of poetry and expository prose had not been separate for two hundred years." In a time of ironic equivocations between assertion and denial, he wrote a poetry "closed to compromises and unequivocal about what it knows."[6] Even more than Pound, Olson is at times willing to use verse simply to convey information or to state judgments, such as this one of Nathaniel Bowditch:

He represents, then, that movement of NE monies
away from primary production & trade
to the several cankers of profit-making
which have, like Agyasta, made America great.

Meantime, of course, swallowing up
the land and labor. And now,
the world.

("Letter 16," *MP I*, 72)

This passage strikes us by its bluntness. It simultaneously explains and condemns, and the condemnation is done in broad, even coarse strokes.

The easy irony of "made America great" and the half-dead metaphors of "cankers" and "swallowing up" convey an impatience with subtlety, as if subtlety might imply diffidence about the judgment itself.

If Olson wished to return poetry to a more active relation with the environment (both physical and social) and make it less equivocal about what it knows, how did he propose to do it, and what obstacles stood in his way? Not content with a criticism of his contemporaries, Olson rested his poetics on nothing less than his interpretation of Western history. If Eliot had posited a historical fall in the seventeenth century, when "a dissociation of sensibility set in," Olson went him one better by two millennia: for him, the decline of the West begins with Socrates, Plato and Aristotle, the figures traditionally venerated as the source of its greatest achievements. In "Human Universe" (1951), he blames Socrates' "readiness to generalize" for creating "a 'universe' out of discourse" (SW, 54) that is not accountable to the physical universe. Aristotle introduced "logic and classification," which "have so fastened themselves on habits of thought that action is interfered with. . . ." Plato too is responsible for our estrangement from the real, for "His world of Ideas, of forms as extricable from content," which "is as much and as dangerous an issue as logic and classification" (SW, 55). These Greek thinkers have taught us habits of language and thought that screen out full experience of reality:

> What makes most acts—of living and of writing—unsatisfactory, is that the person and/or the writer satisfy themselves that they can only make a form (what they say or do, or a story, a poem, whatever) by selecting from the full content some face of it, or plane, some part. And at just this point, by just this act, they fall back on the dodges of discourse, and immediately, they lose me, I am no longer engaged, this is not what I know is the going-on. . . . It comes out a demonstration, a separating out, an act of classification, and so, a stopping, and all that I know is, it is not there, it has turned false. For any of us, at any instant, are juxtaposed to any experience, even an overwhelming single one, on several more planes than the arbitrary and discursive which we inherit can declare.
>
> (SW, 55)

What Olson hopes to discover, in place of the discursive, is "a way which bears *in* instead of away, which meets head on what goes on each split second, a way which does not—in order to define—prevent, deter, distract, and so cease the act of, discovering" (SW, 56). Among peoples such as the Maya (whom Olson had been studying in Yucatan when he began the essay), logic and classification had not separated human consciousness from the physical world. Olson ends his essay by recounting, in breathless run-on sentences, a Mayan myth of the sun and moon, as if to say that mythmaking delivers more of experience than Aristotelian method ever can: "O, they were hot for the world they lived in, these Maya, hot to get it down the way it was—the way it is, my fellow citizens" (SW, 66). To restore a similar sense of immediacy, one must restore contact with the sensuous world.

Despite Olson's typical presentation of himself as the only sighted man addressing a blind audience, much of this argument was commonplace, even in 1951, when "Human Universe" was written. Not only is there an obvious debt to D. H. Lawrence, Ezra Pound, and W. C. Williams, Olson even shares a surprising amount of common ground with Ransom and Tate, poets about as formal and nonprojective as one could find. A brief comparison is useful because it disentangles what is distinctive in Olson's position from what is really uncontroversial, or even hackneyed.

Ransom and Tate couldn't have agreed more with Olson's dislike of abstraction in poetry, of language that selects "from the full content some face of it, some plane." For Ransom, poetry is the art that restores our sense of "things as they are, in their rich and contingent materiality." The prestige of science has led us, he argues, to overvalue abstractions from experience and neglect the texture of experience itself: "The image which is not remarkable in any particular property is remarkable in its assemblage of many properties, a manifold of properties, like a mine or a field [Olson's very word!], something to be explored for the properties; yet science can manage the image, which is infinite in properties, only by equating it to the one property with which the science is concerned. . . ." Like Olson, he thought the influence of Plato, in the arts at least, to be dangerous, and despite his admiration for Aristotle, considered him, like Plato, to be insufficiently interested in the uniquely particular: "Individuals are ultimate, Aristotle conceded, but the interest he took in them was cursory; he had a temperamental deficiency, and many moralists, scientists, and philosophers share it with him."[7] Tate considered "the pure scientific spirit" to be a form of "Platonism," by which we impose "practical abstractions upon . . . experience." But the "creative spirit" of the artist has a different "function": "the quality of experience, the total revelation— not explanation for the purpose of external control by the will."[8]

But even in these brief quotations, the obvious differences between Olson's conception of poetry and that which was to a great extent shared by Ransom and Tate begin to appear. To begin with, Tate's phrase "practical abstractions" reflects his belief that abstraction accompanies will or appetite, the desire to accomplish some practical purpose. To retrieve "the quality of experience" in its totality, therefore, one must restrain appetite and will. Hence the emphasis, in his poetics, on contemplation. Ransom, too, imagines poetic creation as a loving contemplation of the real and justifies the stylization of formal poetry as a restraint on the appetitive "natural man"; it "removes him to where he cannot hurt the object, nor disrespect it by taking his practical attitude towards it, exchanging his actual station, where he is too determined by proximity to the object, and contemporaneity with it, for the more ideal station furnished by the literary form."[9] For Olson, however, the relation of imagination to the real is one of *eros*, not of *agape:* "O, they were hot for the world they lived in, these Maya, hot to get it down the way it was." Ransom and Tate are fond of the word "object," which implies that the real is divisible into discrete entities that will hold still for observation; Ransom describes the "properties" of an object as infinite in number, but they are still discrete attributes, any one of which can be isolated for purposes of "abstraction." Olson envisions the real as indivisible process, "the going-on." For Ransom and Tate, creation is an act of seeing the object while restraining the urge to handle it; Olson often imagines artistic creation as tactile. Ransom and Tate want to slow the poet down, whereas Olson wants him to "get on with it, keep moving" ("Projective Verse," *SW*, 17).

Olson's quarrel with the kind of poetics offered by Ransom and Tate, then, is not a dispute between an embattled particularist and an orthodoxy of abstractionists. Both parties agree on the need for "a way which bears *in* instead of away." The disagreement concerns first of all the nature of that "way" and, second, the nature of the reality they wish to recover from estrangement. Olson, had he answered Ransom directly, would have claimed that appetitive immersion, rather than disinterested contemplation, was the true way back into reality. His poetics counters Ransom's Kantian idealism with a materialist insistence that "a man is himself an object, whatever he may take to be his advantages"; his figure of artistic creation is not the painter but the woodworker, in constant tactile interchange with his medium and producing, more often than not, an object that has practical as well as aesthetic value: "The work of art should "be as clean as wood is as it issues from the hand of nature, to be shaped as wood can be when a man has had his hand to it" ("Projective Verse," *SW*, 24). His didacticism follows from his pragmatism: poetry, too, may be of practical use without abdicating its aesthetic function.

If Olson would have disputed Ransom's version of the way to recover "things as they are, in their rich and contingent materiality," he also would have rejected Ransom's account of materiality itself. For Olson, the very notion of a world divisible into "objects" with "properties" was a distortion inherited from "discourse." In "Equal, That Is, to the Real Itself," he appealed to the authority of non-Euclidean mathematics and quantum physics to support his belief that the world cannot any longer be understood solely as a "discrete manifold." Beginning in the nineteenth century, mathematics and science began to discover that "Reality was without interruption, and we are still in the business of finding out how all action, and thought, have to be refounded" (*SW,* 48). Poetic conventions had to be "refounded" too: "What is measure when the universe flips and no part is discrete from another part except by the flow of creation itself, in and out, intensive where it seemed before qualitative? Rhythm, suddenly, which had been so long the captive of meter, no matter how good . . . was a pumping of the real so constant art had to invent measure anew" (*SW,* 48). Again, Olson's metaphor of "pumping" implies that "the real" is fluid rather than solid.

With Olson's rejection of a world of discrete objects for one of fluid process came a rejection of symbolism, allegory, and perhaps of mimesis altogether. This rejection is expressed in "Equal, That Is, to the Real Itself" by Olson's distinction between Euclidean and non-Euclidean definitions of "congruence." In Euclidean geometry, said Olson, "congruence" concerns "the measure of the space a solid fills in two of its positions" (*SW,* 49): the triangle that exists in the first position can be replicated in the second. Like symbol and allegory, such congruence implies concepts of "mirror and model": the second triangle is a mirror image of the first, or is modeled after it. But in topology, congruence becomes, as Olson rather inarticulately puts it, "a point-by-point mapping power of such flexibility that anything which stays the same, no matter where it goes and into whatever varying conditions (it can suffer deformation), it can be followed" (*SW,* 49). He is referring to the definition of congruence as the possibility of mapping each point of one figure onto another and, in particular, to the possibility of defining the self-identity of a figure through various transformations. If one can map the points of the figure at one stage of transformation onto the figure at another stage, then it remains "congruent" to itself. Thomas Merrill quotes the more articulate explanation of H. Graham Flegg:

Arbitrary deformations of curves, surfaces, and figures are allowed as long as connectivity is maintained. Therefore, distortion, bending, battering, etc., is allowed, but tearing, cutting, breaking, joining or sticking together, welding, cementing, disregarding of holes, etc., is forbidden. In this type of geometry square and circle, cuboid and sphere are equivalent.[10]

When Olson tells us that Melville "was essentially incapable of either allegory or symbol" because "mirror and model are each figures in Euclidean space, and they are *not* congruent" (*SW*, 51), he means that the symbol has not maintained "connectivity." It breaks the thing into two discontinuous parts, its "literal" existence and its representation in the symbol. No classification, no analogies, no imitative mirroring: "Art does not seek to describe but to enact" (*SW*, 61).

Already, one paradox has become obvious, although admirers of Olson do not remark on it. Here is a poet who claims that he will settle for nothing but the hurly-burly of experience itself, without evading the full turmoil of "the going-on" by flight into abstraction, logic, or classification, and yet takes his marching orders for poetic form from mathematicians and physicists. Topology relieves geometry of the need to correspond to the physical world; the spaces considered in topology can be purely imaginary (they can have seven dimensions, say, instead of three). The refinements of quantum mechanics rest for their evidence on the behavior of subatomic particles completely undetectable without instruments. What has all this to do with direct sensory experience of the physical world? Olson appears to think that poetic form must justify itself by an analogy to the macrocosm, as some (but by no means all) Renaissance poets asked it to do. And if so, is that not itself a prime instance of allegorical thinking? If the discussion of topological congruence in "Equal, That Is, to the Real Itself" is not simply a category mistake, an illegitimate attempt to derive value from fact, what is it but an extended metaphor, an allegory against allegory? And what are the various -*isms* that proliferate in Olson's prose ("Projectivism," "Objectism," "particularism") but abstractions by which to slay abstraction?

In rejecting the entire Western heritage from Plato down to the nineteenth century, Olson manages to make his heroes—Keats and Melville in literature, Lobachevsky and Riemann in mathematics, Heisenberg and Wiener in science, Whitehead in philosophy—appear to have emerged from no tradition and to have broken entirely with the preceding 2,500 years. To read Olson, you would think that the main achievement of these thinkers and writers was to recover the wisdom of the pre-Socratic philosophers, or better still, the Maya. The fact is, of course, that they all arose in western civilizations, that it would have been impossible to invent non-Euclidean geometry in a civilization such as the Maya that did not have Euclidean geometry to begin with, that Keats's idea of "negative capability" occurred to him as he contemplated the achievement of Shakespeare. Olson's attempt to rewrite intellectual history is absurdly ahistorical.

With his sense that the physical world in its uninterpreted self-exis-tence is the only true reality, Olson trusted that openness to that world would always lead to the same primal truths, whether one began as a Mayan or a modern. "There are no hierarchies, no infinite, / no such many as mass, there are only / eyes in all heads, / to be looked out of," he wrote in "Letter 6" (*MP I*, 33). Given his belief that "discourse" had become so habitual as to estrange even the most gifted moderns from experience, he seemed to think it surprisingly easy to throw off the tyr-anny of acculturation. "I don't believe in cultures myself," he said in response to a question after his Berkeley lecture (1965) on "Causal My-thology." "I think that's a lot of hung-up stuff like organized anything. I believe there is simply ourselves, and where we are has a particu-larity which we'd better use because that's about all we got." He went on to say that "we live so totally in an acculturated time that the reason why we're all here that care and write is to put an end to that whole thing" (*CM*, 35–36). If this is not simple self-contradiction, it must mean that culture is a mind-forged manacle: we are acculturated be-cause we believe in culture, and the minute we cease to believe in it, we will be free.

If Olson presents us with paradoxes in his abstract justification of particularism, his ahistorical reinterpretation of history and his thoughts on the relationship between process and result, inquiry and truth, are not paradoxical so much as simply confused. Von Hallberg tells us that Olson had "a moral conviction that certain information is verifiably true and should be known," yet goes on to observe that Olson ends his essay, "History,"

by renouncing truth altogether: "*Herodotus is looking for the evidence*—is it ever anything else that we such men who listen to Stories, *who make them up* are looking for? Is it now, or was it ever, 'truth?'—when each one of us *is* the only imaginable fact & 'truth' there could or can ever be? what more can any of us want than to assert the evidence of our own existence by means of that existence and by what evidence of it others give us, alive or dead, any others whom we find relevant to ourselves?" In the absence of an absolute to aim at, Olson affirms the existential value of action, self-assertion for its own sake.[11]

But Olson can also exclaim, in a more sanguine moment, "I believe in truth!" ("Letter to Elaine Feinstein," *SW*, 27).

Attempts to arrive at truth by logic or classification inevitably falsify, according to Olson, by distancing us from the real. But total immersion in the real, conceived of as process, makes it impossible to see where the process is heading. "Truth" thus had to be defined as ourselves in the act of searching for "the evidence" (evidence for what, we are not told) or asserting "the evidence of our own existence." The end toward which the process leads "is never more than this instant, than you on this instant, than you, figuring it out, and acting, so. If there is any absolute, it is never more than this one, you, this instant, in action" ("Human Universe," *SW*, 55). In this passage, Olson appears to assume that an end separable from means must be an "absolute," just as in the passage from "History" he tries to replace "truth" with "evidence," although the definition of "evidence," "the data on which a judgment or conclusion may be based, or by which proof or probability may be established," sends us back to the "judgment or conclusion"—in short, to the "truth"—for which the evidence has been offered.

Olson did not invent a poetics of process out of nothing; a rhetoric of process had become increasingly prominent in poetry since the romantic period. But it makes a great deal of difference whether one conceives of process as "a continuous and regular action or succession of actions, taking place or carried on in a definite manner, and leading to the accomplishment of some result . . ." (*Oxford English Dictionary*, definition 6), or as simply "the fact of going on or being carried on" (*Oxford English Dictionary*, definition 1). When we think of process as leading to a result, we plunge into indeterminacy trusting that we can work through it toward greater determinacy. (Not necessarily an absolute determinacy; Olson writes as if the only alternative to his position were faith in absolutes.) But if process is merely "the fact of going on," then indeterminacy will lead to more of the same. In nineteenth-century rhetorics of process, tied as they often were to notions of progress, Hegelian dialectic, or Darwinian evolution, process still leads toward a result, even if only as toward a limit approached but never attained. Olson still wants to think of process as leading to a result, to verifiable knowledge or to poetic form. But his own premises afford him no reason for supposing that it will. There is no bridle for his Proteus; there is only the present moment emptying its fullness into the next. If "END . . . is never anything more than this instant, than you on this instant, than you, figuring it out, and acting, so," then the quest is its own object, the means are their own end.

From Olson's doctrine of total immediacy comes an astonishingly naïve conception of language. He wanted to use language "as the act of the instant" and not as "the act of thought about the instant" ("Human Universe," *SW*, 54), but this distinction becomes fuzzier and fuzzier the more one thinks about it. Language is inescapably temporal. Even a single word takes up more than an instant, and when one begins a sentence, one is already thinking ahead to the continuation. In conversation, one improvises continually, and one may rely on tone of voice and gesture to convey meaning. But the good conversationalist, like the good writer, wishes to choose the right word and takes some trouble over the timing of an anecdote or the logical continuity of an argument. Good improvisation requires spontaneity, but it also requires control over long stretches of time, the ability to judge the cumulative effect of decisions taken at each moment. After years of practice, one can make such decisions very rapidly, even unconsciously. But language does not work automatically. That one is excited and responding to the impulses of the moment does not guarantee that the resulting language will convey the excitement or evoke the moment for someone else. Olson was a nominalist and a realist at once. He believed that the very grammatical categories of language reflect a false ontology, the imposition of taxonomies and essences on the flux of reality. Language as it lay ready to hand would never do. At the same time, he believed that if one were in a state of grace with the real, one could simply talk poetry—as he claimed he was doing in his poetry reading (or non-reading) at Berkeley in 1965, with disastrous results.[12]

Moving from Olson's epistemology to his remarks about poetry, one is dismayed by the abstractness, generality, and inarticulateness of the language in which Olson pleads for concreteness, specificity, and exactness. One cannot derive from "Projective Verse" any advice about how to engage in "composition by field," apart from the general injunction to "keep it moving" and not pause for second thoughts or grammatical difficulties. The famous slogan, "FORM IS NEVER MORE THAN AN EXTENSION OF CONTENT" ("Projective Verse," *SW*, 16), however loudly shouted in upper case letters, is useless; if each content determines its own form, and the content of each poem is unique, then each poem has a unique form. How can we know when the form it has is not the best one for that content, when the content is only available to us through whatever form the poet happens to have made?

If Olson can only point, in the most vaguely prospective manner, to a derivation of poetic technique from his allegedly revelatory epistemology, does he succeed any better in deriving a politics? Von Hallberg argues that there is an "objectivist politics" implicit in objectivist poetics; Olson, following Whitehead, distrusts individualism because "the individual has a reliance upon, and hence a responsibility to, a common world of sense."[13] Immersed together in the processes of the physical world, we are in community whether we like it or not.

If our reliance on a common world of sense binds us together, estrangement from that common world of sense threatens community. In *The Maximus Poems*, especially the first volume published in 1960, the fishermen of Gloucester are figures of the unestranged self. Olson was much impressed, during his stint as a crew member on the swordfishing vessel *Doris M. Hawes*, with the fishermen's acuity in responding to their environment; he idealizes their physicality and toughness:

Fishermen are, like gulls, tough ones. There's a muscularity about them, not of the biceps, but of the whole stuff of man, the gut. . . . There's a command and thus a dignity about them over this thing we introverts grapple with and miss and call life; they don't bother to name it but they've got it.[14]

And yet the modern fisherman, distracted by advertising and the "musick" of mass culture, is threatened with loss of the intimate connection with natural process that his work instills:

how shall you strike,
o swordsman, the blue-red back
when, last night, your aim
was mu-sick, mu-sick, mu-sick
and not the cribbage game?

(*MP I, 7*)

Olson envisions the conflict between the fisherman, standing in a right relation to natural process, and the corrupting temptations of mercantilism, which would subordinate fishing to profit-making, as dating from the very origin of Gloucester. *The Maximus Poems* treat the early history of Gloucester as a struggle for the national character. In the conflict between Miles Standish and one Captain Hewes over the fishing stage at Cape Ann in 1625, Olson found

the whole engagement against (I) mercantilism

(cf. the Westcountry men and Sir Edward Coke against the Crown,

in Commons, these same years—against Gorges); and (2) against

nascent capitalism except as it stays the individual adventurer

and the worker on share—against all sliding statism, ownership

getting in to, the community as, Chambers of Commerce, or
theocracy;

or City Manager

(*MP I, 105*)

"Was it puritanism, / or was it fish?" Olson asks in Letter 10 (*MP,* 49); Puritanism, as "theocracy" and "nascent capitalism," won out almost immediately. The new world stayed new only for a moment.

Just as western culture was spoiled at what most people consider its outset, when Plato and Aristotle directed attention away from the process of physical reality toward disembodied ideas and systems of classification, colonial New England was no sooner begun than spoiled:

> one's forced,
> considering America,
> to a single truth: the newness
>
> the first men knew was almost
> from the start dirtied
> by second comers. About seven years
> and you can carry cinders
> in your hand for what
>
> America was worth.
>
> (MP I, 136–37)

The fishermen, if left to themselves, would presumably have been immersed in the process of the real, only concerned with living in the here and now, rather than with building up their modest trade into a profitable enterprise. They were immediately threatened by the economic ambitions of those who wanted to get rich from the new world and by the theocratic ambitions of the Puritans—ambitions which could co-exist within the same people, as Max Weber famously demonstrated.

The villains of American history, for Olson, are those who direct the New England economy "away from primary production and trade," as he put it in Letter 16 (MP I, 76); thus one of Nathaniel Bowditch's misdeeds is founding insurance companies, while Stephen Higginson is a "son of a bitch" partly for writing to Vice President Adams, in 1790, in praise of the fishermen of Cape Cod, who unlike those of Gloucester "applied their gains to increase their Business" (MP I, 79), thus taking the first step from fisherman to capitalist. The Olsonian hero is the "individual adventurer," sustained by capitalism perhaps but not primarily motivated by it so much as by the love of adventure; such men are, like the Maya of "Human Universe," hot for the world we live in. John Smith

> changed
> everything: he pointed
> out
> Cape Ann,
>
> named her
> so it's stuck,
> and Englishmen,

who were the ones
who wanted to,

sat down, planted
fisheries
so they've stayed put,
on this coast, from Pemaquid
to Cape Cod.

("Some Good News," *MP I*, 128)

Smith, as Olson presents him, is concerned with the land (Cape Ann) and with fishing, with the direct physical struggle to get a living from the earth. In contrast,

we do it all
by quantity and
machine. The subjective
hides, or runs riot
("vainglorious",

they put Smith down
as, and hire a Standish
to do corporative
murder: keep things clean,
by campaigns,

drop bombs.

(*MP I*, 129)

In his idealization of the independent fisherman struggling against "nascent capitalism," Olson reminds one of the C. Wright Mills of *White Collar*, who laments the decline of the small business and its replacement by enormous corporate bureaucracies; his objection to "corporative / murder" and the "clean" dropping of bombs sounds like the New Left on the war in Vietnam, but "Some Good News" was completed in 1958;[15] the "bombs" Olson had in mind were doubtless the ones Truman dropped on Japan.

Despite the fragmentation and recondite allusions of *The Maximus Poems*, Olson's point about history and politics turns out to be simple, indeed almost simplistic, and very conventional. He is for the hardworking fisherman, wise in his physical relatedness to the world, against the abstract-minded capitalist, who cares nothing for the physical qualities of the world except insofar as they yield profit. His indictment of capitalism is everybody's indictment: Mills at his most conventional, the New Left at its most sentimental. A similar content, extended (since Olson would put it thus) into a more satisfactory form, can also be found in a few poems in *Lord Weary's Castle* and a great many essays by Ransom and Tate. Olson shares with e. e. cummings a righteous obsession with the evils of advertising—an easy satirical target, and one that represents effects rather than causes.

Olson's ideas about poetry do not, of course, entirely determine the course his poetry takes. But it should not surprise us that a poet at war with syntax, logic, and classification, who understands truth as immersion in the immediacy of experience rather than predications about experience, should have difficulty writing about history and politics. For causality cannot be discerned as imminence; one only infers it by inductive comparison, from the tendency of certain experiences to follow others. One must stand back from "the going-on" long enough to reflect on it before one has much chance of understanding why it is going on. Olson's thinking about politics in his poetry ironically resembles that which the odious ad-man wishes to provoke concerning his product. One is to be swayed by an image or emblem, by a Fenollosan ideogram bringing together desirable (or undesirable qualities): a pretty woman getting into a car is an ideogram for "buy this car"; the mention of Miles Standish along with corporations and bombs is an ideogram for "despise the heritage of Puritanism, capitalism, and militarism in American history." There is not much value in this kind of political "thinking."

A few of Olson's poems, in significant ways, run counter to the theory, or are simply irrelevant to it, out of its clutches. Such poems as "Maximus, to himself" and "Maximus, from Dogtown—I" both acknowledge the possibility that process can veer into misdirection or failure: the first, by acknowledging, in the poet's own experience, a difficulty in achieving the desired relation to the real, and hence the need for effort as well as openness; the second, by acknowledging that a spontaneous action can also be a wrong action.

"Maximus, to himself" is probably the most straightforward of the Maximus poems; it does not resort to collage, self-disruption, and other devices for challenging the reader's ontologies. Instead of writing a poem that thrashes confusedly about, Olson writes a controlled meditation on the experience of thrashing confusedly about. He resigns himself to "language as the act of thought about the instant" rather than "language as the act of the instant." And instead of presenting himself as the self-assured bard rousing his contemporaries from the sleep of Western culture since Plato, he speaks as one who has trouble following his own advice:

I have had to learn the simplest things
last. Which made for difficulties.

Even at sea I was slow, to get the hand out, or to cross
a wet deck.
The sea was not, finally, my trade.

(*MP I*, 56)

Olson admits to lacking the qualities he most admires:

the sharpness (the *achiote*)
I note in others,
makes more sense
than my own distances. The agilities
they show daily
who do the world's
businesses
and do nature's
as I have no sense
I have done either.

(*MP I*, 56)

The seamanlike agility of response and sharpness of vision that Olson
says he lacks are essential not only to a fisherman, but also to a poet:
"even at my trade, at it, I stood estranged." Even the true establishing
of human community depends on these qualities, if we are to believe
Letter 6, which begins "polis / is eyes" and illustrates that proposi-
tion by describing fisherman at work, with the poet as a "greenhorn"
amongst them.

In its very confession of inadequacy, however, "Maximus, to himself" achieves greater "sharpness," finer "agilities" of thought, than
most of Olson's poems that claim to be caught up in the inspiration of
"process." Its relatively detached manner permits a firmer sense of response to a clearly defined situation than the more passionate churn-
ings of a poem like "I, Maximus of Gloucester, to You," which opens
the sequence. In short, "Maximus, to himself" raises the possibility,
whether unwittingly or consciously, that detachment can enable as well
as inhibit response. And it suggests that "process" is not pure immanence, ready to enfold us if we offer ourselves up. To develop the
sharpness and agility required to keep pace with the "businesses" of
"the world" and "nature" demands continual effort, and this effort,
moreover, is likely to fail. In Olson's prose writings, he usually speaks as
one who has found the way and seeks to convert others; in "Maximus,
to himself" he speaks as one who struggles to change himself.

"Maximus, from Dogtown—I" narrates the story of a young sailor,
James Merry, who in a drunken impulse to "show off," met his death

fighting a bull in Dogtown, Massachusetts in 1892.[16] Like many of the Maximus poems from the second and third books, this one frames the event of local history in a cosmic mythology, touching upon Hesiod's account of creation, the Egyptian divinities Nut and Geb, and the earth personified as mother and wife. Olson portrays Merry's foolhardy deed more as an act of self-conscious vanity than as a truly spontaneous act; Merry is a "braggart man" who "raised himself to fight / in front of people, to show off his / Handsome Sailor ism" (*MP II*, 172); he deliberately "sought to manifest / his soul" (*MP II*, 173) In a sense, then, Merry dies of lyrical interference of the ego; Olson rebukes him for lacking the proper humility before nature, of which the bull is a local respresentative. "The stars / manifest their souls" (*MP II*, 173), but it is impious for men to do so.

And yet, Olson treats the event as a tragic sacrament; he clothes Merry in the robes of myth, treating him not as a fool but as a tragic figure:

> Merry
> had a wife
> She is the heavenly mother
> the stars are the fish swimming
> in the heavenly ocean she has
> four hundred breasts [.]
>
> (*MP II*, 174)

After his death, Merry is sexually united to the earth. While he was alive, his vanity stood in the way of this union, but now his body and consciousness dissolve, merging into the processes of nature:

> Then only
> after the grubs
> had done him
> did the earth
> let her robe
> uncover and her part
> take him in [.]
>
> (*MP II*, 176)

This poem, then, recognizes as few of Olson's works do, that surrendering of the ego to the workings of process can be dangerous as well as liberating. And it recognizes the difficulty of distinguishing between spontaneity and a more calculated sort of flamboyance like Merry's, which looks very much like spontaneity at first glance and indeed partakes of spontaneity as well as calculation. In Olson's portrait of Merry, there is youthful exuberance, the athlete's desire to test his skill, as well as presumption.

"Maximus, to himself" and "Maximus, from Dogtown—I" stand out for their intellectual honesty, their recognition of the dangers entailed in a poetics—and morality—of process. Since I also find them preeminent among Olson's poems for clarity and resonance of language, I am tempted to argue that the distinction of their language arises out of the deeper honesty of thought and feeling that informs them. But to do so would require an extensive discussion of his poetry, which the present occasion will not accomodate. In any case, such acknowledgment of process poetry as inherently problematic occurs too rarely in Olson's poems and almost never in his essays. I should now like to turn from Olson to Denise Levertov and Robert Duncan, and more specifically, to their poetry about the Vietnam war. In this poetry, as Altieri has observed, the limitations of a poetics of process force themselves on the poets' attention.

Process and Politics: Denise Levertov

Asked in 1966 for a contribution to an anthology of antiwar poems, *Where Is Vietnam*, Olson responded, "Oh *that* I don't believe I have anything to add to."[17] But several of the poets influenced by Olson—most notably Denise Levertov and Robert Duncan—felt compelled to write directly about the war.

Several critics have argued that the limitations of this antiwar poetry have something to do with the limitations of some contemporary theories of poetry. Von Hallberg, noting the weakness of political poems by Levertov and Duncan in *American Poetry and Culture, 1945–1980*, is inclined to blame the problems on modern rather than postmodern theories: the example of Pound "made a poetic of juxtaposition and image seem unavoidable."[18] As we have seen, von Hallberg credits Olson with reviving the possibilities of statement, as well as extending Pound's use of juxtaposition and image, although we have observed Olson arguing by juxtaposition in *The Maximus Poems*. By relying on juxtaposition and image, von Hallberg implies, Levertov and Duncan fail, in their war poetry, to follow Olson far enough. Charles Altieri, however, locates part of the difficulty in the branch of contemporary poetics for which Olson is the most influential apologist. Altieri, having praised the poetry of the sixties as "highly sophisticated" in "metaphysical or religious meditation," nonetheless concedes that it "fails miserably in handling social and ethical issues." He considers Levertov's antiwar poetry representative of "the most basic weaknesses of the contemporary aesthetic." Levertov shares with Olson, Bly, O'Hara, Snyder, and Duncan an "aesthetics of presence," or "immanence," according to which order and value can be discovered in the world as it presents itself, if we are only receptive to what it presents. But when the war comes into Levertov's poetry,

What she knows can no longer suffice because she is now confronted with two problems her aesthetics of presence cannot handle. With the war so dominant a fact of experience, especially for the poet whose sensitivity now becomes a kind of curse, she perceives in the present at least as many inescapable reminders of suffering and pain as causes for awe and religious acceptance. Second, the war brings home the poet's helplessness. What mystery she does perceive in the present is too personal and too particular to help her either judge or transform the suffering.[19]

And so, in "The Cold Spring" (*RA*, 5–6)[20] Levertov asks herself "what do I know" and can respond only with a passage of natural description, which she finds wanting: "It's not enough." In discussing Berryman, Lowell, and Plath, I have traced one kind of response to the poet's belief that aesthetic "sensitivity" had become "a kind of curse"; these poets believed that in order to bear witness to the suffering of their time, they had to receive it into themselves, even if they risked being destroyed by it. Confessional poetics, as I interpret it, is in effect a tragic version of Altieri's "aesthetics of presence." Levertov's response, though obviously not confessional, shares the same premise: that the madness of the nation reaches deep into the psyche, distorting the very processes of thought, feeling, and perception. As Cary Nelson has remarked, Olson "associates open form with an Adamic childlike, innocent perceptiveness";[21] but what happens when "process" becomes demonic, the content of perception no longer innocent?

One can see Levertov struggling with these problems in "Life at War," part of the closing section of *The Sorrow Dance* (1966) in which she writes about the war for the first time. She begins by lamenting her own inability to respond: "The disasters numb within us" (*SD*, 79). Since the war is far away, and we know of it only through pictures and news accounts of "the disasters," one has trouble making it present to the imagination. In a sense, the Vietnam war is but a particular instance of an omnipresent war. Not only the conflict in Vietnam, but all instances of violent cruelty can occur only because of a failure of imagination:

The same war

continues.
We have breathed the grits of it in, all our lives,

our lungs are pocked with it,
the mucous membrane of our dreams
coated with it, the imagination
filmed over with the gray filth of it.

(*SD*, 79)

In this passage, "war" in the larger sense is in the air we breathe. Considering the importance of "breath" in Olsonian poetics, the reflection that we have breathed the contaminated air of war "all our lives" becomes even more melancholy. The rhythm of the breath was to have shaped the lineation of poetry, joining "the HEART . . . to the LINE" (*SW*, 19). Moreover, breathing is Olson's central emblem both of the continual interchange between self and environment and of the bond between poetry and the life of the body: "breath is man's special qualification as animal" (*SW*, 25). Levertov, in this passage, gives us a fallen version of Olsonian process, its Adamic innocence poisoned by "war." She cannot fathom why "delicate man, whose flesh / responds to a caress, whose eyes / are flowers that perceive the stars" (*SD*, 79), nonetheless

still turns without surprise, with mere regret
to the scheduled breaking open of breasts whose milk
runs out over the entrails of still-alive babies,
transformation of witnessing eyes to pulp-fragments,
implosion of skinned penises into carcass-gulleys.

(*SD*, 80)

The problem, then, is that by breathing the war in daily, by becoming used to "scheduled" brutalities, we lose our capacity to grasp the brutalities as such. The imagination becomes "filmed over," unable to respond with anything more than "mere regret."

There is surely some validity to this understanding of how the American public condoned the war; Godfrey Hodgson remarks on the government's use of statistical quantification to lend a "pseudorational" logic to its arguments;[22] statistics also treat abstractly what those in Vietnam experienced concretely, in their own flesh. And yet, Levertov's poem itself shows a failure of imagination, most of all in its very preoccupation with imagination. However sincere its expression of outrage against the war, the poem seems finally more preoccupied with the consequences of the war for Levertov's poetics than with the war itself.

"Life at War" ends by lamenting that "nothing we do has the quickness, the sureness, / the deep intelligence living at peace would have"

(*SD*, 80). By closing with these lines, Levertov fixes our attention not on the plight of the Vietnamese, but on the way the war spoils life at home—the war is bad because it is bad for us. The images from Vietnam, torn from any context and programmatically lurid, protest too much. Instead of testifying to an imaginative grasp of the war, they betray an imagination flogging itself to respond. One sees the same unwitting lyrical interference of the ego (Olson's term describes quite precisely what is wrong) in "Advent 1966," which appeared in *Relearning the Alphabet* (1970). Instead of Southwell's visionary Burning Babe, "prefiguring / the Passion upon the Eve of Christmas," Levertov sees in photographs from Vietnam that same image "multiplied" and robbed of its promise of transcendence, "wholly human." "Because of this," she says,

> my strong sight,
> my clear caressive sight, my poet's sight I was given
> that it might stir me to song,
> is blurred.
>   There is a cataract filming over
> my inner eyes. Or else a monstrous insect
> has entered my head, and looks out
> from my sockets with multiple vision. . . .
>
> (*RA*, 4)

Here, the motif of poisoned consciousness, which we have already met with in so much poetry and social criticism of the period, manages to upstage the political content of the poem; along with compassion for the burned flesh of the Vietnamese, Levertov conveys (unwittingly, one presumes) a good deal of self-pity. Her "poet's sight," presumably clearer and more "caressive" than that of benighted nonpoets, has been "blurred" by the untoward events.

It is not fair to blame all of Levertov's faults on Olsonian theory—or to ascribe her virtues to that theory either, since Levertov at her best has a visual imagination superior to Olson's and indeed sometimes appears to be influenced more by Williams in his imagist phase than by Olson. Nonetheless, Olson's emphasis on the value of the poetic process, rather than on the poem as a made thing, feeds the contemporary myth of the poet as special person, the "implied premise," as Wendell Berry put it, "that poets are of a different kind from other people."[23] Ironically, the very emphasis on "openness" of perception to a changing world that was supposed to prevent egotistical pride of craftsmanship from distorting the truth of consciousness ends by defining the poet's gift not as the shaping of language but as superior perception of reality. "[T]he others are as good as he, only he sees it and they do not," said Whitman of the poet in his "Preface" to *Leaves of Grass* (1855).[24] With Levertov, democratic equality between poets and non-poets becomes lost. In "From a Notebook, October '68–May '69," prophecy modulates into the bleat of egotism when, after informing us that the young radical Chuck Matthei "travels the country / a harbinger," she adds:

And on his journeyings bears
my poem 'A Man'
to prisoners in the jails,

having "found in it / a message for all who resist war, / disdain to kill, / try to equate / 'human' with 'humane' (RA 103–4). In "Tenebrae," she writes of suburbanites as if she were observing some lower phylum:

Their parents at night
dream and forget their dreams.
They wake in the dark
and make plans. Their sequin plans
glitter into tomorrow.
They buy, they sell.
They fill freezers with food.
Neon signs flash their intentions
into the years ahead.

(*RA*, 13–14)

To which the reader is irked to reply, What do you know of their dreams, their plans, or their lives? Levertov's suburbanites are not specifically enough described to reveal whether they belong to the upper middle class or to Agnew's blue-collar "silent majority; in either case, the poem treats them with a class prejudice too intense to be bothered with careful observation, let alone imaginative comprehension.[25]

Projectivist theory, by diverting attention from the poem to the process of making, and by minimizing the role of self-criticism and self-consciousness in that process, does not offer a poet much help in resisting the tug of egotism. But Olson's proscription of distance between self and object, and of "separating out" some events from their interaction with others in the field of perception, has an even more serious consequence for public poetry. If one is responding immediately to events as they unfold within the field of perception, one has no way of tracing sources of influence outside that field which, though not immediately given in experience, are necessary to any but the most naïve interpretation of those events. Thus Levertov's poem "In Thai Binh (Peace)

Province" attempts to argue by the immediate presence of images. "I've used up all my film on bombed hospitals, / bombed village schools, the scattered / lemon-yellow cocoons at the bombed silk factory," she begins, continuing with an image of "yet another child with its feet blown off." Her grief spent, she resolves to use her "dry burning eyes"

> to photograph within me
> dark sails of the river boats,
> warm slant of afternoon light
> apricot on the brown, swift, wide river,
> village towers—church and pagoda—on the far shore,
> and a boy and small bird both
> perched, relaxed, on a quietly grazing
> buffalo.   Peace within the
>   long war.

(FD, 35)

"It is that life, unhurried, sure, persistent," she declares, "I must bring home when I try to bring / the war home"; it is where "the future, fabled bird / that has migrated away from America, / nests, and breeds, and sings" (*FD*, 35). Certainly the massive air war that the United States brought into Vietnam increased the amount of suffering far beyond what had been imaginable before American intervention, and yet Levertov's vision of the essential Vietnam as an untroubled village scene, a boy "relaxed" and at one with nature, is sentimental, willfully false. There *was* after all, a civil war already in progress when the United States intervened, a violence of Vietnamese against other Vietnamese. Levertov's argument by juxtaposition of images leaves the motives of the Vietnamese themselves entirely out of account, not to mention those of the Johnson administration. However arrogant and mistaken our leaders were, they did not undertake the war in Vietnam simply because they enjoyed bombing schools and hospitals, or because they couldn't leave simple folk perched on their buffaloes in peace. The poem, which derives from a visit to North Vietnam, may indeed be faithful to the field of perception and the flow of consciousness on the occasion that generated it, but as an attempt to bring home the meaning of the war to the American imagination, it is woefully shallow.

   To function historically, the imagination must include analytical intelligence. It must also attend to that which is real but impossible to experience directly, being in the past (the previous history of Vietnam, or of the Cold War) or else present to others in their experience but not in one's own. Although in theory projectivism imagines an intricate

confluence of forces, in practice both Levertov and Olson himself conceive only of a duality that must be mediated: myself and *my* environment, my field of perception. That is quite different from depicting the
self among other selves, which are, no less than the poet's own, centers
of perception and response. Other willing, perceiving subjects dissolve
into the undifferentiated welter of what Robert Duncan calls "It in
travail" (*BB*, vii), the world unfolding itself before the poet's sovereign
gaze. As a result, projectivism encourages a self-absorption more naïve
(and therefore more damaging) than that of confessional poetics, in
which self-absorption can at least be recognized as such.

Robert Duncan

Even if one grants that Levertov's antiwar poetry on the whole fails as
poetry, and does so in part because of weaknesses inherited through
Olson's influence, one must consider the prominent alternative of
Robert Duncan. In "Santa Cruz Propositions" (1968; *GW*, 36–46),[26] he
sharply criticized Levertov for the self-righteousness of her antiwar
writings, portraying her as the death-goddess Kali or, less mythologi-
cally, as "Madame Outrage of the Central Committee." He explained
to James Mersmann that he finds, in the unconscious associations of
Levertov's poetry, an unwitting "sadism, and masochism," so that the
image of the flayed penis in "Life at War" connects with earlier images
of "stripped stalks of grass": "Suddenly you see a charged, bloody, sexual image that's haunting the whole thing, and the war then acts as a
magnet, and the poem is not a protest though she thinks she's protesting."[27] Not only Duncan himself, but also some of his critics, find a redemptive difference between his response to the war and Levertov's.
Altieri, for all his objections to Levertov's antiwar poetry, claims that
Duncan

is the only contemporary poet successfully to include the sufferings of the
war in Vietnam within his myth . . . Combining Heraclitus's view of experience as based on strife, with the erotic urge to incorporate strife into community, Duncan can envision the war as a productive darkness. Underwrit-
ten beneath the war and the exiles it has created is the myth of Christmas
and natural myths of dying and redeeming gods.[28]

If Altieri's claim on behalf of Duncan is justified, then Levertov's failure
cannot be ascribed to the shared legacy of Olsonian poetics.

But if Duncan's antiwar poetry avoids (most of the time, at least) the
temptations of self-righteous harangue, it falls prey to others. The limitations of Duncan's political poetry arise from the fact that although he

shares Olson's poetics of process, he does not share Olson's materialism, his sense that "a man himself is an object, whatever he may take to be his advantages . . ." (*SW*, 24), and that consequently, "The meeting edge of man and the world is also his cutting edge . . ." (*SW*, 62). Duncan tries to reconcile what modern science has told us of the world with an essentially religious conception of reality. Poetry of process is for him reconcilable with an almost neo-Platonic faith in spiritual hierarchies and symbolic correspondences. In the "Introduction" to *Bending the Bow*, his most politically engaged volume of poetry, Duncan maintains that God "seeks in His Creation intensifications of Its orders"; poetry still has recourse to "the old doctrine of correspondences" (*BB*, viii, ix). He trusts that "all orders have their justification finally in an order of orders only our faith as we work addresses" (*BB*, ix).

When Duncan addresses the problem of the war, then, he has recourse to the classic religious response to the problem of evil, which is to regard it as a subordinate part of a larger, beneficent design. But Duncan's appeal to this argument is complicated by the fact that his religion has been stripped of doctrine. It is essentially a Jungian psychologized religion in which there is religious experience, but no binding interpretation of that experience and no prescription for ethical conduct. Moreover, he sometimes implies that God is still making himself, so that out of "the dance of the particles" and the evolution of species come

the Trinity of Persons we creatures know, within which the Son, "He," is born and dies, to rise as the morning forever announces, the Created Self, Who Proclaims the Father, first known as He named Himself to be Wrath, Fiery Vengeance and Jealousy, to be made or revealed anew as Love, the lasting reason and intent of What Is. . . .

(*BB*, vii)

This passage, despite its un-Olsonian theological cast, has the hallmark of Black Mountain prose: the attempt to conceal a crucial evasion of thought beneath a flurry of verbal "energy" and gaudily vague syntax. Whether God is "made . . . anew" or "revealed anew" makes an enormous difference; if the former, then he does not have a lasting essence and is to that extent assimilated to the flux of his creation.

Duncan, then, must somehow gather the evil of the war into a larger providential design. But he cannot profess, as those who claim the guidance of a church or a revealed scripture might, to have any reliable hint as to God's ultimate intentions; indeed, God himself may be only half-created as yet, and may therefore not yet know his own ultimate intentions. Moreover, the lack of scripture and moral doctrine makes the appeal to ultimate intentions all the more necessary. One cannot ground moral decisions in the absolute authority of scriptural commandment, and so one must try to see their place in the evolving *grand collage*, as Duncan calls it (*BB*, vii). As Peter Michelson justly objects, "How can we *know*, in the welter of quotidian confusions, what complements and what confounds the Grand Design?"[29] Duncan continually asserts that process is teleological, but the content of that teleology remains extremely vague, an ultimate resolution of strife in "love." The instrument of that resolution is poetry, which for Duncan does not so much replace religion as become the most adequate form of religious experience. "It in travail" writes the poem of the Grand Design; the poet records his partial experience of that Design unfolding in the world, as discernible within the field of his perception.

Duncan's essay, "Ideas of the Meaning of Form" (1961) provides a useful gloss on the antiwar poetry he was to write later in the decade. He begins with the widely shared position (illustrated in the first chapter with a quotation from Galway Kinnell) that a formal prosody is repressive, whereas free verse is allied with the repressed. "There is marshalled," he writes,

an imposing company of arbiters and camp followers, lady commandoes of quatrains right! and myrmidons of the metaphysical stanza, holding the line against any occurence of, much less the doctrines of, poetic genius or romantic imagination. . . .

Duncan condemns formal poetry by describing it in military metaphors. Such poetry, then, is defensive, trying to ward off or kill that which it would not admit. But his own

longing moves beyond governments to a co-operation; that may have seeds of being in free verse or free thought, or in that other free association where Freud led men to re-member their lives, admitting into the light of the acknowledged and then of meaning what had been sins and guilts, heresies, shames and wounds. . . .[30]

Free verse, then, means free association, free thought, and "co-operation"—a concept which takes on both political and religious implications in "Up Rising Passages 25," where the American soldiers in Vietnam act "in terror and hatred of all communal things, of communion, of communism" (*BB*, 81).

But if there is a bad poetry that resembles war, there is also a good warfare that resembles poetry and participates, like poetry, in religious "communion." Warfare, like poetry, has been corrupted by the Enlightenment. Just as the poetry of the Enlightenment becomes rationalized, so too

in military arts, manoeuvres and disciplines occupy the conscious mind. Men are drilled in order that there be an authority, removing them from immediate concern in the acts of killing and destruction involved. A Frederick the Great may be on the edge of knowing that his wars are devastations, not drills. But to such modern triumphs of the conventional mind as Roosevelt or Eisenhower decisions are matters of reason and plan. . . . Wrathful inspiration (divine or demonic) will not move our rulers to war, nor will some romantic drive to power or suicidal imagination: it is convention, what reasonable men agree upon, that will decide all. War, too, becomes rational.[31]

Wrathful inspiration can be divine as well as demonic, and even suicidal imagination is still imagination, and thus preferable to pure convention or rationality.

"Passages 26: The Soldiers" makes a sustained analogy between war and poetry. The soldiers must

> take their souls in the war
> as the followers of Orpheus   take soul in the poem
> the wood to take fire from that dirty flame!

On both sides, they "have no other / scene to make" (*BB*, 112). The American leader, Johnson, is "making it badly"; he is "no inspired poet" and is merely "amassing his own history in murder and sacrifice / without talent" (*BB*, 113). The war itself is "the bloody verse America writes over Asia" (*BB*, 113). Those on the revolutionary side, however, such as the Viet Cong or, earlier, Mao fighting "to liberate the New China," belong to a different sort of army:

> *Solidarius* : solderd   this army having its sodality
>
> in the common life,   bearing the coin or paid in the coin
>
> *solidum,* gold emblem of the Sun
>
>   tho we fight underground
>
> from the heart's volition,   the body's inward sun,
>
>   the blood's natural
>
>   uprising   against tyranny

And from the first it has been communism,   the true

Poverty of the Spirituals   the heart desired . . .

(BB, 113–14)

The poet not only condemns the American intervention—here one can follow him—but takes the side of the Viet Cong, idealizing them out of all resemblance to the Viet Cong as a Vietnamese peasant, let alone an American soldier, might have to encounter them. Having decided that the Viet Cong represent "sodality" and the communal ideal, he can write that "America, the secret union of all states of Man, / waits, hidden and challenging, in the hearts of the Viet Cong." Instead of appealing to any knowledge of events in Vietnam, or even any imaginative vision of what life in Vietnam must be like, he is off tracing the etymologies derived from *solidarius.* Duncan has assimilated the war to his myth, as Altieri would have it, at the cost of abstracting war from the literal, nonmythical suffering that occasioned his initial protest. It is one thing to ascribe the origin of an unjust war to a failure of imagination, another to interpret the conflict between the United States and the Viet Cong as an unequal contest between inspired and uninspired poets.

Here I can only note the irony that Duncan, having criticized non-projective verse for walling out experience, nonetheless allowed himself, in his political poetry, to lose sight of experience more completely than most of the formal poets did. The war, as experienced by anyone who had to fight it, or even by a noncombatant trying to comprehend it, simply disappears beneath the cosmic drama of "It in travail," with its baggage of mythical iconography. In "The Multiversity Passages 21," the administrators and trustees of Berkeley are "not men but heads of the hydra," the scales of which "are men officized" (*BB,* 70). This is like something out of Blake's Prophetic Books, but without the precision of Blake's indictment. In "Earth's Winter Song," the face of a war-protesting "girl is a fresh moon / radiant with the Truth she loves, / the Annunciation, the promise / faith keeps in life"; the opposition of the young to the war shows that although things are bad, "the new / lord of the true life, of Love // we remember, was always born, / as now, in a time of despair . . ." (*BB,* 93–94). Here, the war has been upstaged by a Christmas allegory.

Granted, sentimentality about the young protesters, idealizations of the Viet Cong, melodramatic metaphors of the corporation as the Hydra, and comparisons of Johnson to Hitler and Stalin ("Up Rising Passages 25") were commonplace when these poems were written, and it is perhaps unfair to criticize Duncan for taking up the *lingua franca* of the New Left. The poems I have been quoting are far from being his best. But it is surprising that poets like Duncan and Levertov, whose poetics make such a point of casting off convention, should have responded to the greatest political crisis of the postwar era in such conventional ways. In their struggle for poetic self-definition, their quarrel was with the conventions of formalism and rationalism; the conventions of irrationalism, just then emerging, appear to have caught them unprepared.

10

Warpless and Woofless Subtleties: John Ashbery and "Bourgeois Discourse"

John Ashbery appears, on the face of it, a less likely candidate for inclusion in this book than a number of poets who have been omitted. In a book on psycho-politics and poetry, here is a poet whose conception of self, according to John Koethe, "is not primarily a psychological one" and whose attitude toward politics, as described by David Lehman, is a skeptical disengagement, leaving him "at home with an essential homelessness among ideologies and programs."[1] Moreover, although Ashbery achieved national prominence early with the Yale Younger Poets Prize for *Some Trees* (1956), he has reached his present position as the most admired living American poet only recently. His third major collection, *Rivers and Mountains*, generally regarded as the one in which Ashbery found his mature voice,[2] appeared in 1966, but the literary climate in which Ashbery has been most admired did not arrive until the 1970s. Even though Ashbery was born in the same year as Galway Kinnell, W. S. Merwin, and James Wright, three years before Gary Snyder, and five years before Sylvia Plath, in an important sense he is historically later, by a few years, than any of these contemporaries.

Nonetheless, there is a good reason for including a study of Ashbery. If Lowell and Plath were the poets most enthusiastically endorsed by influential criticism in the early and mid-sixties, while Wright, Merwin, Kinnell, Snyder, and Bly appealed most to readers of the early seventies, the next repository of the spirit of the age would seem to be Ashbery. To read him in the context of the immediate past can tell us much about ourselves. His work helps us measure the extent to which we have really said goodbye to all that I have been describing in the preceding chapters, and the extent to which we are still playing out the permutations of the old ideas and attitudes.

In addition to this large reason, there is a smaller one: Ashbery shares some of the same premises, and some of the same historical context, as the Black Mountain poets discussed in the previous chapter.

The abstract expressionist painters from whom Ashbery drew inspiration were also represented at Black Mountain College in the days when Charles Olson was there. Like Olson, Ashbery appears to have profited by their example of an art that reveals the processes by which it is made and avoids conveying either the sense of a finished artifact or the assurance of a determinate, representational content. (A great deal of modern art is content with developing new conventions of representation rather than insisting on the disappearance of the object altogether.) One can understand Ashbery's poetry as an alternative to Olson's conception of process poetry. Whereas Olson wanted to capture the flux of perception before it had been falsified by thought, Ashbery often seems bent on catching the movement of thought alone with itself, the first stirrings of meditation before they can be shaped into meditations. He offers, in short, an idealist rather a materialist version of the poetics of process.

Unlike Lowell, Plath, Wright, and Merwin, whose careers have been interpreted as conversion narratives, Ashbery has held a fairly steady course, at least after the experimentation with disjunctive textures in his second book, *The Tennis Court Oath* (1962). From *Rivers and Mountains* through his tenth and most recent volume, *A Wave* (1984), there is a continuity of style; indeed, a disenchanted reader might complain that most of the poems sound too much alike. Therefore, the chronological overview, useful in some earlier chapters of this book, is of limited help in understanding Ashbery. I therefore propose to treat his work as a continuous whole and to consider three main questions: how can one most accurately describe that work; what are its characteristic accomplishments and limitations; and what does Ashbery's current high reputation imply about our relationship to the immediate literary past?

One must begin, of course, with the problem of accurate description. There have been, among Ashbery's admirers, two main versions of him. The first, best represented by Helen Vendler's essay, "Understanding Ashbery," Harold Bloom's "John Ashbery: The Charity of the Hard Moments," and David Kalstone's discussion in *Five Temperaments*,[3] gives us a poet rooted in the English romantic tradition, but concerned less with Shelleyan unacknowledged legislating than with Keatsian soul-making. For this Ashbery, art is all; he is not concerned with cultural strife but with the epiphanic "hard moments" of poetic vision. Yet his modern skepticism tells him that the epiphanic moments by which his nineteenth-century predecessors charted their spiritual progress may be only exquisite illusions. As Bloom the psychoanalyst of influence points out, he must also be wary of falling into the no longer viable elevated styles of his precursors and so is driven into a chastened "counter-sublime" of his own. As a result, Ashbery is intensely self-conscious and distrustful about his own romantic yearnings for transcendence and must hedge them about with self-deflating ironies—a strategy already prominent in Stevens, but now taken to far greater lengths. The critics I have named differ in their emphases, but they have in common their sense of Ashbery as essentially a poet of the inner life, considered as a realm unto itself, abstracted from its relations with a social world.

There is, however, a minority report. Douglas Crase would present Ashbery "not as our most private poet, but as our most public one," and Alan Williamson remarks on his "social and historical intelligence."[4] The most fully developed case for the public implications of Ashbery's work can be traced in David Shapiro's *John Ashbery* and, still more clearly, in Keith Cohen's essay, "Ashbery's Dismantling of Bourgeois Discourse." These critics read Ashbery as, at least in part, a socially engaged and adversarial poet, corrosively striking at what Shapiro calls "our degraded public naturalisms" and mounting what Cohen describes as "a very serious attack . . . on basic assumptions, institutions, and modes of thought in contemporary America."[5] This subversive Ashbery has ancestors in the French literary tradition rather than the Anglo-American; behind him stands Rimbaud, rather than Keats, Whitman, or Stevens, and he has something in common with Roland Barthes, Michel Foucault, and Jacques Derrida in his attempt to unmask the socially shared illusions embedded within language itself. The parody that Ashbery turns against himself when his poetry seems about to throw off its obliquity and arrive at a moment of moral wisdom or lyrical transcendence must then be understood not as a protective gesture shielding the vulnerable core of his sensibility, but as a weapon of attack. And the glimmerings of moral wisdom or lyrical transcendence must be understood as instances of false consciousness, as objects of that attack.

Cohen's description of the "bourgeois discourse" that Ashbery's work allegedly dismantles provides some clues to the continuity between his style and the adversarial styles of the recent past, and also, as we shall see, to a resolution of the disparity between the Keatsian Ashbery of Vendler or Kalstone and the deconstructionist Ashbery of Shapiro or Cohen himself. Cohen, borrowing from Barthes' analysis of Balzac, claims that the traits of bourgeois discourse "that seem clearly to apply to Ashbery's critique are the utility of referential orientation, structural continuity, and closure of form."[6] By claiming to be referential, bourgeois ideological pronouncements mask their arbitrariness and appear to derive from the objective structure of reality; by maintaining structural continuity and closure of form, they appear to unfold with the necessity of logical demonstrations, proceeding from one step to another toward a conclusion. Any poetry, therefore, which severs the reference of word to thing, and which refuses continuity and closure, undermines the habits of consciousness that allow people to accept bourgeois ideology without questioning it.

This argument is by now a familiar staple of deconstructive criticism. We have also encountered similar beliefs in Ginsberg's poetry, in Galway Kinnell's animadversions against order and certainty, and to some extent in the poetry of James Wright as well. And in Olson's advocacy of projective verse, one finds a similar argument that closed form betokens a closed consciousness. But Ashbery, as every reader of his poetry must have noticed, does not so much refuse reference, continuity, and closure as engage in a continual approach and avoidance game with them. He teases the reader into expecting all of these qualities, only to frustrate the expectation. As one reads his poetry, one is constantly aware of a highly nuanced syntax, anxious to make the finest distinctions, seemingly intended as the complex qualification of a rigorous argument. The rhythms of his sentences are those of the thinker at work upon a problem. And yet often, just when these rhythms have lulled us into the reassuring sense that resolution of the suspended syntax is approaching, we realize that some while back, we have lost track of the pronoun reference, or that while the grammar is formally coherent, the semantic content is irretrievable because the language is full of category mistakes; Noam Chomsky's example of a grammatically coherent but nonsensical sentence, "colorless green ideas sleep furiously,"[7] would be perfectly at home in Ashbery's poetry.

Cohen interprets this linguistic strategy as a subversion of bourgeois discourse, but as he himself admits,

the voice of the poems seems at one moment to be mouthing the discourse, at the next moment to be mocking it. It is often difficult to pinpoint where the rote repetition stops and the critical distancing begins. In a sense, these two activities are seldom distinguished. It is like trying to differentiate between a well-molded graduate from Harvard Business School and a comedian's impression of a businessman. Indeed, throughout Ashbery's work there is this problem of where the ax falls.[8]

Perhaps the discrepancy between the Bloom-Vendler-Kalstone Ashbery and the Shapiro-Cohen Ashbery results from a critical disagreement about "where the ax falls." Around what looks to Bloom or Vendler like Ashbery's hard-won spiritual wisdom, another reader may discern the ironic quotation marks of self-parody. Ashbery's self-parody is his way of registering his suspicion, shared with the culturally radical poets of the immediate past, that most pronouncements of hard-won spiritual wisdom are inauthentic, that rational coherence and formal closure mask rather than clarify truth. He also has some of the culturally radical poets' contempt for the socially shared world as a realm of dead works. If, for Ginsberg, that world was Moloch, for Ashbery it would appear in some more farcical guise. To Ginsberg, the face of contemporary America looked like that of a devouring Sphinx; to Ashbery it looks more like the face of a blathering salesman.

We have already seen the degree to which political protest in the poetry of the sixties and early seventies could be turned inward. The cure of consciousness, which was to have been the prelude to social change, became more and more an end in itself as the hope of radical social change diminished. Political rebellion was thus transformed into a version, coarsened perhaps in most instances, of Keatsian soul-making. Thus Vendler's approach and Cohen's presume different interpretations of the same observation, namely, that Ashbery's poetry seldom connects itself unequivocally to any external occasion or context. That disconnection can be understood either as political protest against a corrupt externality or as aesthetic disdain of a vulgar externality.

But there is, beyond the question of where the ax falls, ground for reasonable doubt about the usefulness of the term "bourgeois discourse" as defined by Cohen. For the admiration of referentiality, structural continuity, and formal closure goes back to pre-bourgeois periods of history. These ideals can be traced back to medieval rhetoric and beyond, to the traditions of ancient Greece and Rome; similarly, "the venerating of the past," which Cohen also identifies as a bourgeois trait,[9] can be found throughout western tradition and in many oriental and tribal societies as well.

Any definition of "bourgeois discourse" must identify features that are uniquely bourgeois. Moreover, if we are to have any clarity on the matter, we must renounce the use of "bourgeois" as an epithet to hurl at people we don't approve of and use it neutrally, to describe the culture of societies dominated by a bourgeois class, the class to which, like it or not, most contemporary poets and their readers belong. And the main characteristic of bourgeois discourse, I think, is its predication of a world in which *not much happens*, apart from the private events of falling in and out of love, forming and dissolving friendships, and eventually having to face one's own death. (Marriage and child-rearing, perhaps the most socially implicated parts of bourgeois experience, are not included in Ashbery's poetic world.) This privatized world, of course, still includes a great deal, but it rests on very large exclusions. Within it, one is unlikely to encounter hunger, violence, or injustice, the elemental suffering that makes the lives of the poor seem a rebuke to middle-class comfort. Neither is one likely to become fabulously rich, decide the fate of a large business, or become intimate with the great and powerful. That is the prerogative of the upper class. High-flying adventures are as unlikely as descents into the lower depths; for the person of imagination, then, the task is to find a worthy necessity within the pleasant but rather undifferentiated expanse of adult, middle-class life, which becomes, in one's skeptical moments, a vast featureless plain on which no destination looks worth a pilgrimage. Life in this situation becomes, to borrow a phrase from "The New Spirit," a tissue of "warpless and woofless subtleties" (*TP*, 29)[10] with no differentiation of texture. This way of conceiving the task simultaneously attenuates the sense of poetic occasion—since all occasions are really only the one occasion of consciousness meditating on its own frustrations—and focuses attention on a subject so featureless it might as well be no subject at all. As Ashbery writes in "The Painter," "Finally all indications of a subject / Began to fade, leaving the canvas / Perfectly white" (*ST*, 55). With very few exceptions, Ashbery's poems are meditations on an epistemological blankness, portraits of the whale's forehead.

It goes without saying, after seventy years of the artist as alienated consciousness, that Ashbery has an adversarial relationship with "bourgeois discourse" to some degree; what is less obvious but equally true is that he is also at home within bourgeois discourse, and that his own style is partially *of* it. Indeed, some of his best work might be described as bourgeois discourse raised to the level of poetry. And at the core, I believe, Ashbery's thinking and sensibility are surprisingly close to what the average bright, well-meaning, and slightly muddled middle-class person most deeply thinks and feels.

Helen Vendler is, I believe, the critic whose assumptions are most nearly identical to those I discern in Ashbery himself. Her explications presume a faithful band of sympathetic readers—whom she refers to as "we"—who receive the sad wisdom of Ashbery's texts:

> "Haunted Landscape" tells us that we all enter at birth a landscape previously inhabited by the dead. We all play Adam and Eve in the land; we then suffer uprootings and upheaval. We are all—as Ashbery says, quoting Yeats—"led . . . / By the nose" through life; we see life and ourselves dwindle into poverty, and it is only our naïveté (some would say stupidity) that lets us construct castles in the air, which of course collapse. Life is both

a miracle and a non-event. At the end, we die, and become part of the ground cover and the ground; we become ghosts, as we are told by an unknown herald that it is time to go. The transformation takes place without our knowing how, and our history becomes once again the history of earth's dust.[11]

You can hear the catch in the breath in this passage, as the critic dons the poet's mantle for a moment. But, I submit, this flight of eloquence will sound to future readers (and to the unconverted among present readers) much the way an earnest Victorian appreciation of Robert Browning would sound to us now. (Whether Ashbery, like Browning, will survive his admirers is of course another question.)

Still, Vendler has Ashbery's central preoccupations accurately mapped. Almost all of the poems could be glossed with the observation that "it is only our naïveté . . . that lets us construct castles in the air, which of course collapse." The Ashbery speaker, caught in his flat though comfortable world where nothing happens, and where all illusions have long since been investigated and unmasked, nonetheless cannot resist the dim intimation that amid all this exhausted familiarity, some transcendent revelation may flash upon him and change everything, if only he is attentive enough to receive it. Again and again, the moment seems at hand, but when his abortive epiphanies trail off into nonsense or banality, he keeps his balance and regards the puncturing of his latest illusion with urbane detachment. "The Instruction Manual," perhaps Ashbery's only 'easy' poem, is absolutely characteristic in theme though not in manner: the speaker takes us on an imaginary tour of Guadalajara, but even as we accompany him we know that we have not really gone anywhere, and that the entire journey is a fantasy indulged as an escape from the boredom of writing an "instruction manual on the uses of a new metal" (ST, 14).

Ashbery's most characteristic (and perhaps overused) effect is the momentous revelation that trembles on the threshold of articulate statement, only to veer off into non sequitur or self-parody, as in this passage from "Pyrography" (HD, 10):

That way, maybe the feeble lakes and swamps
Of the back country will get plugged into the circuit
And not just the major events but the whole incredible
Mass of everything happening simultaneously and pairing off,
Channeling itself into history, will unroll
As carefully and as casually as a conversation in the next room,
And the purity of today will invest us like a breeze,

Only be hard, spare, ironical: something one can
Tip one's hat to and still get some use out of.

These lines take off from a flat plain of colloquial diction ("That way,"
"get plugged into"), rise to the more elevated "Channeling itself into
history," and reach their apogee with "the purity of today will invest us
like a breeze," which is almost, by the chastened standards of contemporary poetry, a purple patch. Having just touched the edge of sentimentality, Ashbery pulls back; purity may "invest us like a breeze,"
but with the difference that it will be "hard, spare, ironical." And with
the last line and a half, the momentous culmination becomes trivialized;
most things to which one respectfully tips one's hat turn out to be no
good at all, and one is left with the diminished hope of getting "some
use out of" this one.

One can understand the appeal of Ashbery in recent years as partly
a reaction against the programmatic zeal, the earnestness about "experience," in so much of the poetry that held center stage just a little
while ago. His tolerant amusement at the persistence of false consciousness contrasts with the fierce desire, present in every other poet
we have discussed so far, to be changed utterly, to set one's foot on the
rock of the authentic and hold that ground against all comers.

One way of reconciling the soul-making Ashbery of Vendler with the
political Ashbery of Cohen or the prophetic Ashbery of Douglas Crase
is to argue that the featureless landscape of Ashbery's poetry, with its
constant light-show of dissolving illusions, is really the landscape of our
shared cultural predicament. Crase argues that Ashbery is "our most
public poet" in part because he has found a way to represent in art our
culture's turn toward narcissism:

[I]f clinical narcissism is truly encouraged by some general cultural event
that has overtaken our society, then that event is going to affect the rest of
us in the same direction, if not to the same degree. We may not all require
the couch; but we must all understand ourselves within the confines of a
common cultural aspect. The poet who shows us where those confines are,
via his context, has indeed brought accurate notice of our commonwealth
and its predicament.[12]

Very well; but one reason why clinical narcissism is so intractable on
the couch, and why the "culture of narcissism" feels less like culture
than the impoverishment of culture, is that narcissism by its nature
withholds libido from any possible object; there is no cathexis (to use
the Freudian term), only the constant putting forth and withdrawal of
pseudopods of desire. Ashbery's essential method, which is to preserve

free-floating detachment from occasion or theme, while continually putting forth provisional epiphanies that then collapse, is indeed analogous to narcissistic object-relations, but can we call this a "public" poetry? The irony is that the community of readers (Ashbery's "we," the "we" of Crase and Vendler) is thus constituted by the common sense of belonging to no community, of lacking authentic public experience altogether. "We" all sit off by ourselves building collapsing castles, waiting for the "unknown herald" who will appear to us while remaining invisible to the others. Cohen's definition of "bourgeois discourse," as I have argued, is too broad, and what is valid in it is out of date, describing a work-driven and moralistic nineteenth-century middle class. What Crase labels "our narcissistic predicament" seems to me much closer to describing middle-class American life as one now finds it.

The cumulative impression of sameness in most of Ashbery's poems results, I think, from the refusal of occasion. It is true that the tone and diction vary spectacularly within single poems. Ashbery is characteristically, as he puts it in "These Lacustrine Cities," "tender and insouciant by turns" (*RM*, 9). But the rapid shifts quickly begin to cancel each other out; they signal provisional responses, tried out a moment to see how they sound, and then cast aside. Despite the brilliance of phrasing in individual lines, the style often dissolves into arabesque, and one gets the sense of Reading Ashbery Again rather than of encountering a new poem by Ashbery, with a particular character of its own.

What, then, does Ashbery offer at his best, and what makes his best poetry different from his other work? To answer that question, I shall try to look closely at two of Ashbery's best poems (by my estimation and that of others as well). Even though only very few of his poems, in my judgment, show him at or near this level, some of these are rather long, and even the shorter ones require an intricacy of critical response answering to their own difficulty. Better to discuss two attentively than to race through six or seven. Moreover, since Ashbery's work is less various, in texture and thematic preoccupations, than that of any other comparably gifted poet I can think of, one does him less injustice than might at first appear by allowing two poems to illustrate the more general assessment with which the chapter will end.

Despite the similarity of Ashbery's poems, the best ones are not all of the same kind; they fall into two distinct and indeed contrasting groups. These groups correspond roughly to the alternatives, proposed in "The New Spirit," of putting everything in and leaving everything out (*TP*, 3). Although "Soonest Mended" provides a fine short example, the poems that put everything in tend, as one might expect, to be long: "The Skaters" and "The System" strike me as the most impressive of these. In these poems, the only "subject" to be found is that of the consciousness itself as it puts forth its provisional explanations, epiphanies, pseudopods of desire. As Robert Pinsky remarks in *The Situation of Poetry,* "the problem of Ashbery's artfully 'destroyed' language is the reader's potential boredom with the virtual absence of denotation."[13] In the few poems that stand out, in my judgment, as his best, denotation has not been quite so completely banished as elsewhere. These poems, though difficult and susceptible to conflicting interpretations, are determinate enough to support an interpretation that relates all the parts to each other and to the whole. They escape tedium and formlessness to the degree that the predicament of that consciousness becomes at least implicitly thematized: we are not watching a procession of dissolving illusions, or at least not that only; rather, we participate in the perceiving mind's reflection on its own processes. "This is a poem in the form of falling snow," says Ashbery in "The Skaters" (*RM,* 39), but he proposes, as an additional analogy, the "figure eight" (*RM,* 47) that the skaters trace on the ice. As the mind skates, returning on itself in its cyclical pattern, the snow is falling around it; one of the questions it ponders is why it perceives the world as having no more plot than the falling of snow.

The other kind of successful poem results from the few occasions when Ashbery—who, like Whitman, resists anything better than his own diversity—manages to put up some resistance for a change. The reader who has learned better than to expect farm implements and rutabagas just because the title mentions them will be relieved to find that "Evening in the Country" actually delivers "birds and trees," "surrounding fields and hills." Although this poem is more overtly concerned with morning than with evening, one gradually realizes that it is infused with prospective anxiety about the arrival of evening, which has its traditional symbolism of death. The speaker is trying to enter, like Wordsworth or Coleridge, into complete communion with the natural world around him, as

> the eidolon
> Sinks into the effective "being" of each thing,
> Stump or shrub, and they carry me inside
> On motionless explorations of how dense a thing can be,
> How light.
>
> (*DDS,* 33)

He remains troubled, however, by the knowledge that the night will eventually arrive, despite his hope that "the new sign of being" in him will "close late," and his slightly too cheerful declaration that anxieties about the "forces" of the night "eventually take care of themselves / With rest and fresh air and the outdoors, and a good view of things" (*DDS*, 33). The poem is not easy, but once the reader has discerned its theme and its occasion, the entire poem, to a degree unusual in Ashbery, falls into place around them. The longest and most ambitious example of this kind of poem is, of course, "Self-Portrait in a Convex Mirror"; others include "These Lacustrine Cities" and "Syringa," and several less ambitious short poems (e.g., the love poem "Nightlife" in *Shadow Train*).

As an example of the sort of Ashbery poem that tries to put everything in, without the exclusions demanded by occasion, I shall discuss "Soonest Mended," the shortest distinguished example I can find, and reluctantly decline to discuss "The Skaters" and "The System," which strike me as the finest of Ashbery's rudderless long poems. Of the few Ashbery poems that do steer by the rudder of occasion, I choose "Self-Portrait in a Convex Mirror," which has been singled out for extended critical discussion by a number of critics already.[14] Not only does the poem deserve its reputation as one of Ashbery's best, it raises the question of how much its rootedness in occasion has to do with its popularity among the critics—and with its intrinsic merits.

"Soonest Mended," by far the shortest of the three poems to be discussed here, provides a compact example of the most usual sort of Ashbery poem, which might borrow as its generic title Wallace Stevens's "How to Live. What to Do." In such poems, Ashbery confronts this problem head-on, without the exclusions and narrowed focus afforded by occasion. "Soonest Mended" opens with a statement about the modern condition; the complaint is familiar and couched, at first, in deliberately hackneyed language, but the third line introduces a sardonic complication:

> Barely tolerated, living on the margin
> In our technological society, we were always having to be rescued
> On the brink of destruction, like the heroines in *Orlando Furioso*
> Before it was time to start all over again.
>
> (*DDS*, 17)

From Shelley's time to ours, we have heard the lament that an increasingly mechanistic society has exiled us (especially the more poetic types who are likely to read *Orlando Furioso* or, for that matter, "Soonest Mended") to "the margin." From this marginal position we must be "rescued," but by whom, Ashbery does not say. Not only Shelley, but such modern poets as W. B. Yeats or Allen Tate as well, would say: by the artistic imagination. But Ashbery's simile complicates the cliché: to be in the modern situation is to be "like the heroines in *Orlando Furioso.*" In short, the post-romantic analysis of the marginal individual imprisoned within "our technological society" is itself a piece of mythmaking, and the myth it produces, moreover, is a bit silly and overwrought. The situation has become familiar enough to lose its *frisson* of self-pity; the rescue operation has been carried out many times already, and in each case it proves futile, as one must "start all over again."

The poem goes on to criticize, as deluded and self-important, the desire to be playing out some role in a quest romance. "Angelica, in the Ingres painting," is beyond terror or longing for rescue; she feels little menace from "The colorful but small monster near her toe" and seems to be "wondering whether forgetting / The whole thing might not, in the end, be the only solution" (*DDS*, 17). The monster is smaller than we thought; perhaps our aspirations must shrink accordingly: "This was our ambition: to be small and clear and free," rather than to be knights and damsels out of *Orlando Furioso*. Not Ariosto or Ingres but comic-book art may provide the image—and the deflating tone—by which to recognize ourselves: "there always came a time," says Ashbery after describing Angelica's disillusionment, "when / Happy Hooligan in his rusted green automobile / Came plowing down the course, just to make sure everything was O.K" (*DDS*, 17). Instead of regarding life as a book, wherein each change brings us to "another chapter," and ourselves as designers of its plot acting on our interpretation of the "latest piece of information," we must ask:

> Weren't we rather acting this out
> For someone else's benefit, thoughts in a mind
> With room enough and to spare for our little problems (so they began
>   to seem),
> Our daily quandary about food and the rent and bills to be paid?
>
> (*DDS*, 17)

After the inflated vision of danger and rescue, this deflated notion of selfhood seems more comforting than disappointing, as the reassuring phrase "room enough and to spare" implies.

Even though "ambition" has been disabused of the cloudy dreams of grandeur that make our actual reduced condition seem unfree, Ashbery cannot help regretting the disillusionment:

> Alas, the summer's energy wanes quickly,
> A moment and it is gone. And no longer

May we make the necessary arrangements, simple as they are.
Our star was brighter when it had water in it.
Now there is no question even of that, but only
Of holding on to the hard earth so as not to get thrown off.

(DDS, 17)

Our energy and unselfconscious ability to "make the necessary arrangements" have vanished along with the illusion that "Our star . . . had water in it." And yet—here the typical Ashbery situation emerges completely in this poem—even in our disillusionment, there is

an occasional dream, a vision: a robin flies across
The upper corner of the window, you brush your hair away
And cannot quite see.

(DDS, 18)

The unclarity, and the unfree sense that something beyond what can be clarified is nonetheless "what you wanted to hear," persist despite all disillusionment. One talks, explains, clarifies, and yet "underneath the talk lies / . . . the loose / Meaning, untidy and simple like a threshing floor."

The knowing "we" of the poem have recognized this situation, in which we can live neither with our illusions nor without them, for some time. Still,

Though we knew the course *was* hazards and nothing else,
It was still a shock when, almost a quarter of a century later,
The clarity of the rules dawned on you for the first time.

(DDS, 18)

This final disillusionment, reserved for middle age, some twenty years after the arrival of the first, entails the recognition of a passivity even more profound than that of a heroine waiting to be rescued, who at least has a destiny within the plot. This consolation Ashbery denies us: "*They* were the players, and we who had struggled at the game / Were merely spectators." Once this final disillusionment arrives, the last vestiges of control over our own lives, of a continual progress to "another chapter" in a narrative of our own making, must be replaced by something far more provisional and tentative:

The being of our sentences, in the climate that fostered them,
Not ours to own, like a book, but to be with, and sometimes
To be without, alone and desperate.

But the fantasy makes it ours, a kind of fence-sitting
Raised to the level of an aesthetic ideal.

                                                      (*DDS*, 18)

Although life is still our writing, we cannot "own" the "sentences" once
we have written them; moreover, the other meaning of "sentences"
confirms the suspicion that we act unfreely, condemned to be spectators of our own lives, while the other meaning of "own" suggests that
we do not acknowledge our own acts as our own; the confessional poet's
assumption of the continuity of identity is no longer viable. One is left
with "fence-sitting," the attempt to believe in a consoling fantasy of
meaning against the evidence of experience. I take Ashbery's "fence-
sitting" to be like the equivocations between skepticism and faith in
Santayana and Stevens, or like Vaihinger's philosophy of "As if." One
has a psychological need to believe what seems to be false, and so one
tries to create the psychological aura of belief without the substance of
any doctrine. The ambition "to be small and clear and free" proves
harder to fulfill than it seemed at first.

Because the apparent coherence of identity, and with it the apparent solidity and narrative shape of experience, are doomed to dissolve,
perhaps it is best to refuse to "struggle at the game," to withhold in-
vesting one's emotions in its possible outcomes, or one's attachments in
any person or thing:

> These were moments, years,
> Solid with reality, faces, namable events, kisses, heroic acts,
> But like the friendly beginning of a geometric progression
> Not too reassuring, as though meaning could be cast aside some day
> When it had been outgrown. Better, you said, to stay cowering
> Like this in the early lessons, since the promise of learning
> Is a delusion.

                                                      (*DDS*, 18)

The "I" of the poem quickly "agree[s]" with the "you" and concludes
that "probably thinking not to grow up / Is the brightest kind of maturity for us, right now at any rate" (*DDS*, 19). This passage describes an
essentially narcissistic strategy of response that has powerful appeal to
Ashbery: hold back, remain "in the early lessons," resisting the down-
stream movement from detachment to engagement, from fantasy to experience, from speculation to belief. (Even the decision not to grow up
is provisional, valid only for the moment.) The part of the self that
would take this advice remains locked in an essentially static tension
with the part that strains to catch sight of the robin as it flies past the

window, that wants to believe that *this* vague glimmering of romantic vision, unlike all the others, will not disappoint him, will at last tell him how to live and what to do.

The advice not to grow up, however attractive, of course proves impossible to implement entirely. The poem leaves us with a portrait of maturity as deadening habituation to the routines of the disillusioned life:

> the avatars
> Of our conforming to the rules and living
> Around the home have made—well, in a sense, 'good citizens' of us,
> Brushing the teeth and all that, and learning to accept
> The charity of the hard moments as they are doled out.
>
> (*DDS*, 19)

Within the good citizen, however, there is an imprisoned romantic who yearns for "the charity of the hard moments" and must uneasily resign himself to the meager portions in which these are "doled out." As a social being, one leads an impoverished life of timid domesticity ("living / Around the home") and "conforming to the rules." The realm of the social is a realm of automatism, in which one unthinkingly performs habitual actions like "Brushing the teeth." For that matter, the inner life, if we are really "spectators" rather than "players," is equally automatic, its promise of choice and meaning only an illusion. And yet, the self lives for the epiphanic moments, "hard" and painful though they may be, because they renew hope that the inner life is not entirely a sham, and allow some respite from despair and utter paralysis:

> For this is action, this not being sure, this careless
> Preparing, sowing the seeds crooked in the furrow,
> Making ready to forget, and always coming back
> To the mooring of starting out, that day so long ago.
>
> (*DDS*, 19)

These lines ask, by their tone, to be taken unironically. Magnificently written and uncharacteristically impassioned though they be, they strike me as somewhat forced in their grandeur, coming as they do at the end of a poem that has resisted the blandishments of grandeur on principle. One might treat them as an extreme example of the kind of smuggled-in elevated style that Pinsky describes when he says that in certain poems of Hardy, Ransom, and Berryman, the poet ironically deflates the pretensions of magniloquence so that he may also, without being accused of sentimentality, "use the style which annoys or embarrasses him, but which for some tasks he needs—needs more or less for its original, affirmative purposes."[15] But Ashbery's affirmation rings subtly false. If action is "careless / Preparing," and "this" refers to the situation described in the poem so far, "this not being sure," then "this," Ashbery's assertion notwithstanding, cannot be action, for there has been nothing "careless" in the rueful self-consciousness of Ashbery's meditation; the last lines lay claim to a heroic impetuousness that is not rightfully theirs and which the poem up to this point has taught us to distrust. Similarly, "coming back / To the mooring of starting out" sounds like a grand statement of the myth of eternal return, until one remembers the advice "not to grow up," never to leave the mooring of starting out in the first place.

"Soonest Mended" is one of Ashbery's most closely written, coherent, and passionate explorations of his obsessive central theme, and yet even here his style strikes me as overrefined and attenuated in its extreme self-consciousness; if the reader for one moment ceases to cooperate, opens the door and lets in the vulgar light of day, the poem vanishes into thin air. One would like to catch just a glimpse of those "moments, years, / Solid with reality, faces, namable events, kisses, heroic acts"; but Ashbery rests content with a one-line summation of them; he views them either from the perspective of the beginning, before he had surrendered any of his detachment to any of them, or conversely from the elegiac perspective of disillusionment, after meaning has been "outgrown" and "cast aside." Why bother to dwell attentively on faces, events, and acts that have become meaningless? With Ashbery as with Olson, the identification of freedom with fluidity and process divests the world of the very fullness that a poetics of process was supposed to protect. It is Ashbery's distinction and also his limitation to have invented a style simultaneously haunted by the desire to confront the authentic within experience directly, and by a horror of directness, as if there were something sentimental and even vulgar about that desire. As a result, his poetry repeats, however varied its costuming, essentially the same ritual of approach and avoidance, and seldom does he allow any "subject" drawn from experience to displace, as the central concern of the poem, his fastidious positioning of himself in relation to that subject.

"Self-Portrait in a Convex Mirror" is the longest of the few poems in which the "subject," as well as the speaker's dance of approach and avoidance, commands the reader's sustained attention. Not only does Parmigianino's portrait serve Ashbery as a center for his meditation, it suggests a comparison between Parmigianino's art and Ashbery's own, and even between Parmigianino's cultural situation and our own. According to Arnold Hauser,

The path that led to the revaluation of mannerism was laid by modern expressionism, surrealism, and abstract art, without which its spirit would have remained basically unintelligible; and at the same time these modern developments repeated the mannerist revolution by bringing to an end a preceding growth of naturalism which in both cases had lasted for several centuries.[16]

And the charges that once were brought against mannerist art—that it is too artificial, too self-conscious, and too preoccupied with style divorced from mimetic or expressive motivation—have also been brought against Ashbery's poetry. Finally, Ashbery's choice of a portrait that gives at first the illusion of looking in a mirror, rather than at someone else's image, invites us to compare our own way of looking at reality with that expressed in the painting. The poem has the same title as the picture: we look into the convex surface of Ashbery's self-portrait, which shows him meditating upon the convex surface of Parmigianino's—and since Parmigianino used his reflection in an actual mirror as his model, even "the portrait / Is the reflection once removed" (*SPCM*, 68). The mannerist fascination with ingenious artifice is certainly akin to Ashbery's intimation of distorted reflections within distorted reflections.

If preoccupation with ingenious distortion is typical of Ashbery, his willingness in this instance to organize the poem around one central occasion (contemplation of Parmigianino's painting) is almost unique; only "The Instruction Manual" has a similar coherence, and it is far less ambitious. Ashbery's poem about mannerism turns out to be his nearest approach to classicism, which according to John Shearman can be distinguished from mannerism by its preference for "direct treatment of the matter" and for adhering to rather than inverting the precept *Rem tene, verba sequuntur*.[17] Ashbery's "Self-Portrait," to a greater degree than his other poems, subordinates style to "the matter" of occasion and denotative meaning. If it remains preoccupied with style, it is atypical in being a meditation *on* style. Rather than displaying style for its own sake, it treats style as the subject of its discourse, though the poem gradually works loose from its moorings as it evolves, returning less and less frequently to the central symbol of the portrait.

Parmigianino's portrait is, among other things, a technical *tour de force*, an assertion of virtuosity, but the self presented in the portrait, as interpreted by Ashbery, is as reticent as he is assertive. "The right hand, / Bigger than the head, thrust at the viewer" is also "swerving easily away, as though to protect / What it advertises." The face, too, "swims / Toward and away" (*SPCM*, 68). Parmigianino, like Ashbery himself, is negotiating an uneasy response to his audience and to the surrounding world; like Ashbery, he seems torn between the desire to approach and the desire to avoid. The technique of the painting, also, gives mutually contradictory impressions of frozen artifice and immediacy; the painter's image is "Glazed, embalmed, projected at a 180-degree angle." Despite the fixity and artificiality suggested by these adjectives,

> The time of day or the density of the light
> Adhering to the face keeps it
> Lively and intact in a recurring wave
> Of arrival.
>
> (*SPCM,* 68)

If the distortion of the mirror embalms, the painter's mimetic skill in depicting the play of light and shadow keeps the face "Lively." But, by a further turn of irony, this naturalistic illusion of liveliness is itself an embalmer's trick, a stay against the destructive power of time, as we are reminded by the word "intact."

In these early lines of the poem, Ashbery's description of the portrait is strikingly clear and straightforward; he even versifies a passage from Vasari, as he will later quote from Sydney Freedberg. And although Ashbery's initial account of the portrait reveals its contradictory qualities, it suggests that the contradictions have been, if not reconciled, then mastered and held in harmonious balance: the face, though it "swims / Toward and away" is also "in repose." Parmigianino's style seems to reconcile the qualities of permanence and liveliness, the "glazed, embalmed" timelessness of the masterpiece and the "recurring wave / Of arrival" that makes the masterpiece live again at each fresh encounter with it. Both the poem and the painting seem less problematical at first than they soon afterwards become.

The first notable instance of Ashberian syntactic slippage coincides with a disturbing complication in the poet's interpretation of the painting:

> The soul establishes itself.
> But how far can it swim out through the eyes
> And still return safely to its nest? The surface
> Of the mirror being convex, the distance increases
> Significantly; that is, enough to make the point
> That the soul is a captive, treated humanely, kept
> In suspension, unable to advance much further
> Than your look as it intercepts the picture.
>
> (*SPCM,* 68–69)

The characteristic slippage occurs in the phrase "the distance increases"—what distance, one wants to ask? Surely not the distance the soul can travel while safely returning, since the point is rather that it can't travel far at all. Ashbery seems to mean that the surface of the painting itself recedes from the viewer, toward the plane of the wall, as the viewer's gaze moves away from the center. Since Parmigianino's face occupies the center, to move away from the center is also to move outward from his eyes. The portrait does not proclaim the artist's godlike mastery of a difficult technical problem, but rather his imprisonment within the artifice of his painting. Art

> is life englobed.
> One would like to stick one's hand
> Out of the globe, but its dimension,
> What carries it, will not allow it.
>
> (*SPCM*, 69)

Artificiality, within art, is like a Kantian category, like space itself: the space of the painting is curved, and so the hand, however much it may wish to reach out for a direct encounter with reality, "must join the segment of a circle, / Roving back to the body." Although one longs to strike through the mask, past the superficial and the illusory, the eyes of the face in the portrait "proclaim that everything is surface. The surface is what's there / And nothing can exist except what's there" (*SPCM*, 70). Whatever essence things may have is inexpressible except as surface, which, if we could only find words for what it is, would prove "not / Superficial, but a visible core" (*SPCM*, 70). To abandon the quest for something behind the surface is to renounce an illusion, but is also to affirm an almost mystical acceptance of reality as it is directly given. Ashbery here manages to reconcile the mannerist insistence on artifice with a Whitmanian faith in the absolute adequacy of things as immediately given to perception.

The relationship between the entrapped image of the painter and the world beyond the studio window that appears as a sliver of light on the edge of the painting becomes an explicit theme of the poem from the moment when Ashbery calls it "a globe like ours." The world itself shares with the portrait a contradictory sense of stability "within / Instability"; it seems "secure" though it rests "On a pedestal of vacuum" and is fragile as "a ping-pong ball" (*SPCM*, 70). Like the portrait, it gives assurance of its coherence and its absolute presence, but on closer examination this self-evident quality proves to be a *trompe-l'œil* illusion. And yet this illusion is desirable, even necessary; the portrait preserves the sense of "uncharted" possibility that every day seems to promise, only to disappoint us every time:

> Some day we will try
> To do as many things as are possible
> And perhaps we shall succeed at a handful
> Of them, but this will not have anything
> To do with what is promised today, our
> Landscape sweeping out from us to disappear
> On the horizon. Today enough of a cover burnishes
> To keep the supposition of promises together
> In one piece of surface, letting one ramble
> Back home from them so that these
> Even stronger possibilities can remain
> Whole without being tested.
>
> (SPCM, 72)

The burnishing "cover" that keeps the dispersing promises "to-gether / In one piece of surface" is the art of Parmigianino; the portrait, then, recommends art as a way of keeping possibility from "being tested" by experience; in the terms of "Soonest Mended," it is a way of remaining forever "in the early lessons." Otherwise, one moves forward to the inevitable disappointed epiphany.

Even the portrait, however, contains hints that experience will not support its illusion of repose and stability. The painter's face seems to meditate serenely on a secret withheld; it seems, also, an expression of Parmigianino's soul, which at once "establishes itself." But on second perusal the secret turns out to be "that the soul is not a soul, / Has no secret, is small, and it fits / Its hollow perfectly" (SPCM, 69). The portrait seems a triumph of artifice and order over the randomness of experience. But Ashbery, wondering if any artist's hand controls "the turning seasons and the thoughts / That peel off and fly away at breathless speeds," finds in that thought only

> the chaos
> Of your round mirror which organizes everything
> Around the polestar of your eyes which are empty,
> Know nothing, dream but reveal nothing.
>
> (SPCM, 71)

The portrait has been organized around an empty center; it confesses that its order is only an arbitrary imposition on a disorderly reality. What remains is only "the fascination of self with self," the ability of the self to create ingenious if arbitrary patterns. But the self can "Know nothing" and it looks out through "empty" eyes.

The more Ashbery looks at the portrait, the less securely ensconced within its hemisphere it seems. It lies open to a random and fleeting experience that it can only mirror without quite understanding. Although "The skin of the bubble-chamber's as tough as / Reptile eggs," it admits the world: "everything gets 'programmed' there in due course" (*SPCM*, 72), and the room in which Parmigianino is depicted, painting himself, "contains this flow like an hourglass" (*SPCM*, 73). The world, in its turn, has an adversary relation to the portrait. "The shadow of the city injects its own / Urgency" (*SPCM*, 75); not only "Rome, where Francesco / Was at work during the Sack," but also Vienna, where the portrait now hangs, and New York, Ashbery's own city, enter into the poet's response:

> Our landscape
> Is alive with filiations, shuttlings;
> Business is carried on by look, gesture,
> Hearsay. It is another life to the city,
> The backing of the looking glass of the
> Unidentified but precisely sketched studio. It wants
> To siphon off the life of the studio, deflate
> Its mapped space to enactments, island it.
>
> (*SPCM*, 75)

Art and life engage in a mutual siphoning by which they steal from each other's sources of energy. The referent of Ashbery's "it" is characteristically vague, but I take "business" to be the other "life to the city," which, vampirelike, "wants / To siphon off the life of the studio." The surrounding business activity of the city threatens to "island" or isolate the activity of the artist. Thus the strong sense of enclosure within the round surface of the portrait, the seemingly impermeable "reptile-egg" toughness, must be understood as a defensive countermeasure against the business world's insidious "siphoning" of its life. The painting has managed, for its part, to siphon off the sense of movement, of "filiations" and "shuttling" that belong to the everyday business of the city. It proclaims the artist's mastery over the transitory chaos of experience, but it is mastery by an arbitrary and highly self-conscious formalization that remains empty of any knowledge, either of the world or of the self. All the portrait can do is preserve the transience of the day on which Parmigianino created it, in all its incomprehensible immediacy, for "Today has no margins, the event arrives / Flush with its edges, is of the same substance, / Indistinguishable" (*SPCM*, 79). It sends us back to "the present we are always escaping from / And falling back into" (*SPCM*, 78), just as Parmigianino's hand and face, in the portrait, swim "Toward and away" in their "recurring wave / Of arrival."

The attempt of the city's "business" to "siphon off the life of the studio," to defeat art by its distracting randomness, has been "temporarily stalled," but, as Ashbery warns Parmigianino,

> something new is on the way, a new preciosity
> In the wind. Can you stand it,
> Francesco? Are you strong enough for it?
>
> (*SPCM*, 75)

This "something new" appears to be modern self-consciousness, an "inertia that once / Acknowledged saps all activity, secret or public," or "a chill, a blight / Moving outward along the capes and peninsulas / Of your nervures" (*SPCM*, 75). Rightly or wrongly,[18] early mannerist painting such as Parmigianino's has been taken to mark the beginning of modern self-consciousness. But Ashbery's Parmigianino seems unaware of the incipient "blight" about to overwhelm both life and art. Quoting Sydney Freedberg, Ashbery points out that "The forms retain / A strong measure of ideal beauty" (*SPCM*, 73) and finds that "The consonance of the High Renaissance / Is present, though distorted by the mirror" (*SPCM*, 74). Ashbery in effect asks Parmigianino whether his art is strong enough to survive the reinterpretation that a modern viewer, inclined to look for anxiety, "chill," and "blight," will inevitably give it.

Toward the end of the poem, Ashbery affirms the durability of Parmigianino's self-portrait by asserting that the modern response unfolds a meaning of the painting beyond Parmigianino's intentions, and that all art similarly evolves away from what its creator thought it meant. Inevitably, "the way of telling" must

> intrude, twisting the end result
> Into a caricature of itself. This always
> Happens, as in the game where
> A whispered phrase passed around the room
> Ends up as something completely different.
> It is the principle that makes works of art so unlike
> What the artist intended. Often he finds
> He has omitted the thing he started out to say
> In the first place. Seduced by flowers,
> Explicit pleasures, he blames himself (though

Secretly satisfied with the result), imagining
He had a say in the matter.

(SPCM, 80)

In these lines (which, like many of Ashbery's meditative passages, contain echoes of Eliot's *Four Quartets*), the artwork is completely severed
from the intention of the artist; Ashbery speculates that Parmigianino
"must have realized this," the "otherness / That gets included" in all
purposive activity, "tearing the matter / Of creation, any creation, not
just artistic creation, / Out of our hands" (*SPCM*, 81). And "This otherness," he concludes, "is all there is to look at / In the mirror" (*SPCM*,
81). Creation, in art and in life, is thus a matter of obeying, without
understanding, some process that is not controlled by our intention; as
in Plato's *Ion*, the artist uncomprehendingly obeys a daemon. What
separates Ashbery from Plato, of course, is his fascination with artistic
creation as a commentary on itself: the poem is a mirror in which to see
Parmigianino's painting, which itself is "the reflection once removed"
of the painter's face. Finally the sense of the painting as stable artifact,
so overwhelming upon first encounter with it, dissolves as the portrait
becomes only an imperfectly "frozen gesture," mutable as the air:

Aping naturalness may be the first step
Toward achieving an inner calm
But it is the first step only, and often
Remains a frozen gesture of welcome etched
On the air materializing behind it,
A convention. And we have really
No time for these, except to use them
For kindling. The sooner they are burnt up
The better for the roles we have to play.
Therefore, I beseech you, withdraw that hand.

(SPCM, 82)

Here, Ashbery comes full circle, returning to the gesture of the hand
that first caught his attention. Having used the portrait "for kindling,"
he withdraws from it, suffering now from

the 'it was all a dream'
Syndrome, though the 'all' tells tersely
Enough how it wasn't.

(SPCM, 82)

Leaving the portrait behind, as one might turn to the work of the day
after a vivid and revealing dream that was nonetheless only a dream,

Ashbery turns to an analogous metaphor for his own artistic creation. The city around him becomes a convex surface like that of the portrait, or the mirror from which Parmigianino "set himself . . . to copy all that he saw":

> We have seen the city; it is the gibbous
> Mirrored eye of an insect. All things happen
> On its balcony and are resumed within.

> (*SPCM*, 82–83)

Like Parmigianino imprisoned within his sphere, "One feels too confined, / Sifting the April sunlight for clues." Ashbery's own self-portrait ends with the recognition that

> The hand holds no chalk
> And each part of the whole falls off
> And cannot know it knew, except
> Here and there, in cold pockets
> Of remembrance, whispers out of time.

> (*SPCM*, 83)

We are returned to immersion in transience and forgetfulness, redeemed only by occasional epiphanic "whispers out of time."

In the two poems I have analyzed in detail, and in perhaps a dozen others, Ashbery has given us poetry of real distinction. But his limitations of wraithlike insubstantiality and thematic single-mindedness remain, even in his best work. The best of his poems have just enough substance to exert a gravitational pull against the dispersive energies of his style, providing them with anchorage in experience. The presence of a thematic center—even if the theme is that of the impossibility of defining themes, the inevitable dissolution of identity in flux and solipsism—draws most, if not all, of the parts into relation with each other. (Paradoxically, this most antidiscursive of poets, by systematically destroying the sustained relationships of image and metaphor that might convey meaning indirectly, forces the reader to place all the more weight on the fragmentary assertions embedded within the poems.)

One ought to be able to recognize the value of Ashbery's best poems while firmly resisting David Lehman's suggestion that they point the way to "the most significant and attractive aesthetic strategy available to an American poet today."[19] One must resist, too, Harold Bloom's influential thesis that the central line of post-romantic American poetry runs from Emerson and Whitman through Stevens and thence through Ashbery. In this revision of literary history, Eliot, Pound, and Lowell become minor figures; Frost, though he fares better, is secondary; Stevens and Ashbery remain to tower over the landscape. To follow Bloom and Lehman is to advocate an increasingly self-conscious poetry, self-devouringly fixated on its own processes rather than drawing energy from sustained encounter with that which is not itself.

And if we follow Bloom and Lehman, it is only a matter of time before the next generation of poets begins crying for a "breakthrough back into life," and the next pageant of the bleeding heart begins. Instead of evolving a more inclusive poetics that diverges not by will but by some inherent necessity from the past, we will simply swing back to the other pole of the same oversimplified dichotomy, in a sterile Empedoclean strife of opposites. One can reject neither artifice nor experience; each needs the other if poetry is to offer anything beyond shallow elegance or blundering sincerity. Without this recognition, brilliance and originality have nothing to build on; the very ground is cut out from under them. If poetry cannot be, in Lowell's phrase, "words meat-hooked from the living steer,"[20] neither can it be a "shadow train." Not, at least, if passengers are expected.

Notes

Abbreviations

See first citation in notes for bibliographical information

AG	Allen Ginsberg, *The Collected Poems of Allen Ginsberg 1947–1980*
BB	Robert Duncan, *Bending the Bow*
BPT	James Wright, *To a Blossoming Pear Tree*
CF	W. S. Merwin, *The Compass Flower*
CM	Charles Olson, *Causal Mythology*
DDS	John Ashbery, *The Double Dream of Spring*
FD	Denise Levertov, *The Freeing of the Dust*
FFBP	W. S. Merwin, *The First Four Books of Poems*
FTUD	Robert Lowell, *For the Union Dead*
GW	Robert Duncan, *Ground Work: Before the War*
H	Robert Lowell, *History*
HD	John Ashbery, *Houseboat Days*
JW	James Wright, *The Collected Poems of James Wright*
L	W. S. Merwin, *The Lice*
LS	Robert Lowell, *Life Studies*
LWC	Robert Lowell, *Lord Weary's Castle*
MPI	Charles Olson, *The Maximus Poems* (1960)
MPII	Charles Olson, *Maximus IV, V, VI* (1968)
MT	W. S. Merwin, *The Moving Target*
NB II	Robert Lowell, *Notebook* (1970 edition, revised and expanded)
NO	Robert Lowell, *Near the Ocean*
OH	W. S. Merwin, *Opening the Hand*
PT	Charles Olson, *Poetry and Truth: The Beloit Lectures and Poems*, edited and transcribed by George F. Butterick
RA	Denise Levertov, *Relearning the Alphabet*
RM	John Ashbery, *Rivers and Mountains*
SD	Denise Levertov, *The Sorrow Dance*
SP	Sylvia Plath, *The Collected Poems*, edited by Ted Hughes
SPCM	John Ashbery, *Self-Portrait in a Convex Mirror*
ST	John Ashbery, *Some Trees*

SW   Charles Olson, *Selected Writings of Charles Olson*, edited by Robert Creeley

TC   James Wright, *Two Citizens*

TJ   James Wright, *This Journey*

TP   John Ashbery, *Three Poems*

WUA   W. S. Merwin, *Writings to an Unfinished Accompaniment*

Introduction

1. Sir Karl Popper, *The Open Society and Its Enemies*, vol. I (Princeton: Princeton Univ. Press, 1966), ix.

2. Paul Roazen, *Freud: Political and Social Thought* (New York: Vintage, 1968), 10.

3. I take this phrase from Louis Simpson's title, *A Revolution in Taste: Studies of Dylan Thomas, Allen Ginsberg, Sylvia Plath, and Robert Lowell* (New York: Macmillan, 1978).

4. Paul Zweig, "The New Surrealism," *Salmagundi* 22–23 (Spring–Summer 1973): 269.

5. Charles Olson, *Selected Writings*, edited by Robert Creeley (New York: New Directions, 1966), 46.

Chapter One

1. Frederick Seidel, "Interview with Robert Lowell," *Paris Review* 25 (Winter–Spring 1961): 56–95; reprinted in Robert Boyers, ed., *Robert Lowell: A Portrait of the Artist in His Time* (New York: David Lewis, 1970), 269. Lowell was not the first to use this term; cf. Malcolm Cowley, *The Literary Situation* (New York: Viking, 1954), 12: " . . . we are living in an Alexandrian or late-Roman age of lowered creative vigor."

2. Scott Chisholm, interview with Donald Hall, in *Goatfoot Milktongue Twinbird: Interviews, Essays, and Notes on Poetry, 1970–76* (Ann Arbor: Univ. of Michigan Press, 1978), 22.

3. Robert Bly, "The Dead World and the Live World," *The Sixties*, no. 8 (Spring 1966): 4–5.

4. Galway Kinnell, "Poetry, Personality, and Death," *Field: Contemporary Poetry and Poetrics*, no. 4 (Spring 1971): 67.

5. "Talking with Adrienne Rich," *Ohio Review* (Fall 1971): 43–44; quoted by Wendell Berry in "The Specialization of Poetry" [1975] which was reprinted in *The Poet's Work: 29 Masters of 20th Century Poetry on the Origins and Practice of Their Art*, edited by Reginald Gibbons (Boston: Houghton Mifflin, 1979), 146. Rich concedes that Yeats is "a poet whom I still love very much," but the tone of her remarks fluctuates uneasily between grudging respect and dismissive condescension.

6. Godfrey Hodgson, *America in Our Time* (New York: Randon House, 1978), 19–20.

7. Daniel Bell, *The End of Ideology: On the Exhaustion of Political Ideas in the Fifties* (New York: The Free Press, 1960), 373. See also, Hodgson, *America in Our Time*, 67–98.

8. So Gabriel Kolko argued, announcing his thesis in his introduction to *Wealth and Power in America* (New York: Frederick A. Praeger, 1962), 3: "Most recent studies of American society assume that since the end of the Great Depression, in 1939, the nation's wealth has been redistributed and prosperity has been extended to the vast majority of the population. . . . But this assumption is nonetheless fallacious, for despite the obvious increase in prosperity since the abysmal years of the Great Depression, the basic distribution of income and wealth in the United States is essentially the same now as it was in 1939, or even 1910."

9. C. Wright Mills, *White Collar: The American Middle Classes* (New York: Oxford Univ. Press, 1951), 131–36; *The Power Elite* (New York: Oxford Univ. Press, 1956), 218–19.

10. David Riesman, Nathan Glazer, and Reuel Denney, *The Lonely Crowd: A Study of the American Character* (New Haven: Yale Univ. Press, 1950), 49.

11. R. D. Laing, *The Politics of Experience* (New York: Ballantine Books, 1967), 74.

12. Herbert Marcuse, *One-Dimensional Man: Studies in the Ideology of Advanced Industrial Society* (Boston: Beacon Press, 1964), 10–11.

13. Riesman, Glazer, and Denny, *The Lonely Crowd*, 84, 302.

14. Mills, *White Collar*, 110.

15. Harold Rosenberg, *The Tradition of the New* (New York: Grove Press, 1961), 276.

16. Carl Oglesby, "The Idea of the New Left," in *The New Left Reader*, edited by Carl Oglesby (New York: Grove Press, 1969), 5.

17. Bruno Bettelheim, "Individual and Mass Behavior in Extreme Situations," *The Journal of Abnormal and Social Psychology*, 38 (October 1943); reprinted and abridged in *The 1940's: Profile of a Nation in Crisis*, edited by Chester E. Eisinger (Garden City, NY: Doubleday, 1969), 123, 125. Much of this article is incorporated, in revised form, into Bettleheim's *The Informed Heart: Autonomy in a Mass Age* (Glencoe, IL: The Free Press, 1960).

18. Hodgson, *America in Our Time*, 183, 211.

19. Denise Levertov, "Statement for a Television Program," in *The Poet in the World* (New York: New Directions, 1973), 123–24.

20. Eldridge Cleaver, *Soul on Ice* (New York: Dell, 1968), 82.

21. Truman Nelson, *The Right of Revolution* (Boston: Beacon Press, 1968), 44.

22. Ruth Benedict, *Patterns of Culture* (Boston: Houghton Mifflin, 1934), 24.

23. Sigmund Freud, *The Ego and the Id*, in vol. 19 of *The Standard Edition of the Complete Psychological Works of Sigmund Freud*, edited and translated by James Strachey (London: The Hogarth Press, 1964), 54, 52.

24. See, for instance, the closing sentences of Lecture 31 in *New Introductory Lectures on Psychoanalysis*, vol. 22 of *The Standard Edition*, 80.

25. Karen Horney, *The Neurotic Personality of Our Time* (New York: W. W. Norton & Co., 1937), 18.

26. Philip Rieff, *Freud: The Mind of the Moralist*, 3d ed. (Chicago: Univ. of Chicago Press, 1979), 213.

27. Harry Stack Sullivan, "The Illusion of Personal Individuality" (1950), reprinted in *The Fusion of Psychiatry and Social Science* (New York: W. W. Norton & Co., 1964), 198–226.

28. Herbert Marcuse, *Eros and Civilization: A Philosophical Inquiry Into Freud* (Boston: Beacon Press, 1955), 256.

29. Clara Thompson, *Psychoanalysis: Evolution and Development* (New York: Hermitage House, 1950), 215.

30. Karen Horney, *New Ways in Psychoanalysis* (New York: W. W. Norton & Co., 1939), 178–79.

31. Horney, *Neurotic Personality of Our Time*, 242–47.

32. Erich Fromm, *Man for Himself: An Inquiry Into the Psychology of Ethics* (New York: Rinehart & Co., 1947), 151, 158, 60–61.

33. "What characterizes Freudian technique is just this imputation of rationality, this enterprise of recovering the irrational for the rational—beginning with the reduction of behavior to emotive statement, and proceeding through a more or less set sequence of ingeniously rational interpretations" (Rieff, *Freud: The Mind of the Moralist*, 125–26).

34. Marcuse, *Eros and Civilization*, 37; Freud, *The Ego and the Id*, vol. 19 of *The Standard Edition*, 54.

35. Norman O. Brown, *Life Against Death* (Middletown, CT: Wesleyan Univ. Press, 1959), 86.

36. Marcuse, *Eros and Civilization*, 168, 171, 169.

37. Ibid., 130, 164, 173.

38. Marcuse, *One-Dimensional Man*, 239; 247.

39. Herbert Marcuse, *Counter-Revolution and Revolt* (Boston: Beacon Press, 1972), 93–94; 101.

40. Ibid., 104, 105, 129.

41. Norman O. Brown, *Love's Body* (New York: Knopf [Vintage], 1966), 253.

42. Herbert Marcuse, "Love Mystified: A Critique of Norman O. Brown," *Commentary* 43, no. 2 (February 1967): 73.

43. Norman O. Brown, "A Reply to Herbert Marcuse," *Commentary* 43, no. 3 (March 1967): 83.

44. Theodore Roszak, *The Making of a Counter Culture: Reflections on the Technocratic Society and Its Youthful Opposition* (Garden City, NY: Doubleday, 1969), 84–123.

45. Among the books that have assisted me in arriving at this conclusion are Gil Green, *The New Radicalism: Anarchist or Marxist?* (New York: International Publishers, 1971); Irving Howe, ed., *Beyond the New Left* (New York: The McCall Publishing Co., 1970); Christopher Lasch, *The Agony of the American Left* (New York: Random House, 1969); Michael W. Miles, *The Radical Probe: The Logic of Student Rebellion* (New York: Atheneum, 1971); and

Nigel Young, *An Infantile Disorder? The Crisis and Decline of the New Left* (Boulder, CO: Westview Press, 1977).

46. C. Wright Mills, "Letter to the New Left," *New Left Review* (September–October 1960); reprinted in Priscilla Long, ed., *The New Left: A Collection of Essays* (Boston: Porter Sargent, 1969), 14–25. For an analysis of the class constituency of the New Left, see Miles, *The Radical Probe*, 88–108 and 275–93.

47. Robert Lowell, *For the Union Dead* (New York: Farrar, Straus & Giroux, 1964), 72.

48. Sacvan Bercovitch, *The Puritan Origins of the American Self* (New Haven: Yale Univ. Press, 1975), 135.

49. "Preface to the 1855 edition of *Leaves of Grass*," *Walt Whitman: Complete Poetry and Collected Prose*, edited by Justin Kaplan (New York: The Library of America [Viking], 1982), 5.

50. Freud, *The Interpretation of Dreams*, vol. 5 of *The Standard Edition*, 608.

51. Ibid., 541, 562. [The same volume number as in the preceding note.]

52. Freud, *Introductory Lectures on Psychoanalysis*, 9, vol. 15 of *The Standard Edition*, 145–46.

53. Marcuse, *Eros and Civilization*, 218; Wilhelm Reich, "Dialectical Materialism and Psychoanalysis" [1934], in Reich, *Sex-Pol: Essays, 1929–1934*, edited by Lee Baxandall (New York: Vintage, 1972), 55.

54. Paul Christensen, *Charles Olson: Call Him Ishmael* (Austin, TX: Texas Univ. Press, 1979), 28–30.

55. Richard King, *The Party of Eros: Radical Social Thought and the Realm of Freedom* (1969; reprint, New York: Dell Publishing Co., 1973), 95.

56. Paul A. Robinson, *The Freudian Left: Wilhelm Reich, Geza Roheim, Herbert Marcuse* (New York: Harper & Row, 1969), 24–25.

Chapter Two

1. Allen Ginsberg [with Robert Duncan], "Early Poetic Community" [1971], in *Allen Verbatim*, edited by Gordon Ball (New York: Graw Hill, 1975), 133–36.

2. Robert von Hallberg, *American Poetry and Culture, 1945–1980* (Cambridge: Harvard Univ. Press, 1985), 14.

3. Richard Wilbur, "Speech for the Repeal of the McCarran Act" and "The Beacon," in *Things of This World* (1956), reprinted in *The Poems of Richard Wilbur* (New York: Harcourt, Brace & World, 1963), 100, 81–82. Howard Nemerov, "The Dancer's Reply" and "The Sunglasses," in *Mirrors and Windows* (1958), reprinted in *The Collected Poems of Howard Nemerov* (Chicago: Univ. of Chicago Press, 1977), 206–7, 144. Elizabeth Bishop, "Argument" and "The Bight," in *A Cold Spring* (1955), reprinted in *Elizabeth Bishop: The Complete Poems 1927–1979* (New York: Farrar, Straus & Giroux, 1983), 81, 60–61.

4. Quotations from Ginsberg's *Collected Poems 1947–1980* (New York:

Harper and Row, 1984) are cited by the abbreviation *AG*, followed by page number.

5. Allen Ginsberg, *To Eberhart From Ginsberg: A Letter About* "Howl" *1956* (Lincoln, MA: Penmaen Press, 1976), 21.

6. Richard Kostelanetz, "Conversation with John Berryman," *Massachusetts Review* 11, no. 2 (Spring 1970): 345.

7. Peter Michelson, "The Blinding Lights of Contrariety: A Dialogue Concerning Ginsberg, Buddhism and Reality," *Rolling Stock* (Univ. of Colorado, Boulder), 1 (no. 1): 12–13.

8. Ginsberg, *To Eberhart*, 11.

9. Jane Kramer, *Allen Ginsberg in America* (New York: Random House, 1969), 16–21.

10. *Writers at Work: The Paris Review Interviews, Third Series*, introduced by Alfred Kazin (New York: Viking, 1967), 317.

11. Tom Clark, *The Great Naropa Poetry Wars: With a copious collection of germane documents assembled by the author* (Santa Barbara, CA: Cadmus Editions, 1980), 21.

12. Ibid., 53, 60, 63.

13. Ibid., 54.

14. Ibid., 65.

15. Ibid., 67.

Chapter Three

1. M. L. Rosenthal, *The New Poets: American and British Poetry since World War II* (New York: Oxford Univ. Press, 1967), 25.

2. Ibid., 15.

3. A. Alvarez, *The Savage God: A Study of Suicide* (London: Weidenfeld and Nicolson, 1971), 213–14.

4. Steven Gould Axelrod, *Robert Lowell: Life and Art* (Princeton: Princeton Univ. Press, 1978), 4, 173.

5. Edward Butscher, *Sylvia Plath: Method and Madness* (1976; reprint, New York: Washington Square Press, 1977), 278.

6. Wallace Stevens, *The Necessary Angel: Essays on Reality and the Imagination* (New York: Vintage, 1951), 36.

7. John Berryman, *His Toy, His Dream, His Rest* (New York: Farrar, Straus & Giroux, 1968), ix.

8. Ibid., 316.

9. Frederick Seidel, "An Interview with Robert Lowell," *Paris Review* 25; reprinted in *Robert Lowell: A Portrait of the Artist in His Time*, edited by Michael London and Robert Boyers (New York: David Lewis, 1970), 272.

10. Quoted in Sylvia Plath, *The Collected Poems*, edited by Ted Hughes (New York: Harper & Row, 1981), 293.

11. Hawthorne's *The Scarlet Letter* and Dostoyevsky's *Crime and Punishment* are, among other things, explorations of the tension between these

senses of "confession," which (as Lawrence Lipking pointed out to me) could be traced back to Augustine's distinction between *confessio peccati* and *confessio laudus.*

12. Robert Lowell, *Life Studies* (New York: Farrar, Straus & Giroux, 1959), 55.

13. Richard Sennett, *Authority* (New York: Vintage, 1980), 28.

14. Robert Lowell, *History* (New York: Farrar, Straus & Giroux, 1973), 118.

15. Ezra Pound, "The Teacher's Mission" [1934], in *Literary Essays of Ezra Pound,* edited by T. S. Eliot (New York: New Directions, 1968), 58.

16. Charles O. Hartman, "Condensation: The Critical Vocabulary of Pound and Eliot," *College English* 39, no. 2 (October 1977): 181.

17. Arthur Mizener, "To Meet Mr. Eliot," reprinted in *T. S. Eliot: A Collection of Critical Essays,* edited by Hugh Kenner (Englewood Cliffs, NJ: Prentice-Hall, 1962), 20 [quoted in Hartman, "Condensation," 182].

18. T. S. Eliot, *The Use of Poetry and the Use of Criticism* (1933; reprint, London: Faber & Faber, 1964), 148.

19. T. S. Eliot, *Selected Essays of T. S. Eliot,* rev. ed. (New York: Harcourt, Brace & World, 1950), 8.

20. Marjorie G. Perloff, *The Poetic Art of Robert Lowell* (Ithaca, NY: Cornell Univ. Press, 1973), 86–88.

21. Seidel, "Interview," in London and Boyers, *Robert Lowell,* 290; Robert Lowell, "A Symposium on 'Skunk Hour,'" in *The Contemporary Poet as Artist and Critic,* edited by Anthony Ostroff (Boston: Little, Brown & Co., 1964), 108.

22. Seidel, "Interview," in London and Boyers, *Robert Lowell,* 270, 285.

23. T. S. Eliot, "The Perfect Critic," in *The Sacred Wood* (1920; reprint, London: Methuen, 1960), 11.

24. Eliot, *The Use of Poetry,* 146.

25. Allen Tate, "The Man of Letters in the Modern World," in *Essays of Four Decades* (London: Oxford Univ. Press, 1970), 7–8.

26. Axelrod, *Robert Lowell,* 92.

27. Ian Hamilton, *Robert Lowell: A Biography* (New York: Random House, 1982), 237.

28. Peter A. Stitt, "The Art of Poetry XVI: John Berryman 1914–1972," *The Paris Review* 14, no. 53 (Winter 1972): 207.

29. Richard Kostelanetz, "Conversation with John Berryman," *Massachusetts Review* 11, no. 2 (Spring 1970): 344–45.

30. Sylvia Plath, *Ariel,* "Foreword" by Robert Lowell (New York: Harper & Row, 1966), x.

31. Robert Lowell, *For the Union Dead* (New York: Farrar, Straus & Giroux, 1964), 63–64.

32. John Berryman, *77 Dream Songs* (New York: Farrar, Straus & Giroux, 1964), 6.

Chapter Four

1. Alan Williamson, *Pity the Monsters: The Political Vision of Robert Lowell* (New Haven, CT: Yale Univ. Press, 1974), 2–4; Robert von Hallberg, *American Poetry and Culture, 1945–1980* (Cambridge, MA: Harvard Univ. Press, 1985), 173–74. Williamson places Lowell as a psycho-political thinker "somewhere between Freud and the radical Freudians."

2. Citations of Lowell's poetry in this chapter use the following abbreviations: *LWC, Lord Weary's Castle* (1946; reprint, Cleveland: World Publishing Co. [Meridian Books], 1961); *LS, Life Studies* (New York: Farrar, Straus & Giroux, 1959); *FTUD, For the Union Dead* (New York: Farrar, Straus & Giroux, 1964); *NO, Near the Ocean* (New York: Farrar, Straus & Giroux, 1967); *NB II, Notebook*, Revised and Expanded Edition (New York: Farrar, Straus & Giroux, 1970); *H, History* (New York: Farrar, Straus & Giroux, 1973).

3. Walt Whitman, "Song of Myself," section 20, in *Walt Whitman: Complete Poetry and Selected Prose*, edited by Justin Kaplan (New York: Library of America, 1982), 206.

4. R. P. Blackmur, "'Nothing Loved'" [1945], reprinted in *Robert Lowell: A Portrait of the Artist in His Time*, edited by Michael London and Robert Boyers (New York: David Lewis, 1970), 3.

5. Irvin Ehrenpreis, "The Age of Lowell" [1965], reprinted in London and Boyers, *Robert Lowell*, 162.

6. Ian Hamilton, *Robert Lowell: A Biography* (New York: Random House, 1982), 157.

7. Ehrenpreis, "The Age of Lowell," in London and Boyers, *Robert Lowell*, 174.

8. Mark Rudman, *Robert Lowell: An Introduction to the Poetry* (New York: Columbia Univ. Press, 1983), 65.

9. Williamson, *Pity the Monsters*, 60.

10. Stephen Yenser, *Circle to Circle: The Poetry of Robert Lowell* (Berkeley: Univ. of California Press, 1975), 136–37.

11. Charles Molesworth, *The Fierce Embrace: A Study of Contemporary American Poetry* (Columbia, MO: Univ. of Missouri Press, 1979), 20.

12. Robert Lowell, "On 'Skunk Hour,'" in *The Contemporary Poet as Artist and Critic*, edited by Anthony Ostroff, (Boston: Little, Brown & Co., 1964), 109–10.

13. Richard Wilbur, "On Robert Lowell's 'Skunk Hour,'" in Ostroff, *The Contemporary Poet*, 86. Among other critics, only David Kalstone, *Five Temperaments* (New York: Oxford Univ. Press, 1977), 51, and Mark Rudman, *An Introduction*, 90, consider the possibility of projection rather than correspondence; neither traces the general implications of that possibility for the interpretation of Lowell's autobiographical poetry.

14. Rudman, *An Introduction*,

15. Williamson, *Pity the Monsters*, 108–9.

16. Rudman, *An Introduction*, 132.

17. Allen Tate, "The Man of Letters in the Modern World," in *Essays of Four Decades* (London: Oxford Univ. Press, 1970), 10.

18. Steven Gould Axelrod, *Robert Lowell: Life and Art* (Princeton, NJ: Princeton Univ. Press, 1978), 170; Philip Cooper, *The Autobiographical Myth of Robert Lowell* (Chapel Hill, NC: Univ. of North Carolina Press, 1970), 73–101; Jonathan Crick, *Robert Lowell* (Edinburgh: Oliver & Boyd, 1974), 92; Williamson, *Pity the Monsters*, 106.

19. Williamson, *Pity the Monsters*, 121.

20. The book of Genesis, chap. 34 (allusion noted by Williamson, *Pity the Monsters*, 123).

21. Norma Procopiow, *Robert Lowell: The Poet and His Critics* (Chicago: American Library Association, 1984), 271–73.

22. Kalstone, *Five Temperaments*, 66.

23. von Hallberg, *American Poetry and Culture*, 158.

24. Ibid.

25. Williamson, *Pity the Monsters*, 164.

26. Hamilton, *A Biography*, 203–4.

27. Williamson, *Pity the Monsters*, 96–101.

28. Robert Bly, in "Robert Lowell's *For the Union Dead*" [1966], reprinted in London and Boyers, *Robert Lowell*, 74, criticized Lowell generally for having "always had a poor grasp of the inner unity of a poem." See also Hayden Carruth, "A Meaning of Robert Lowell" [1967], reprinted in London and Boyers, *Robert Lowell*, 234–35, for a critique of Lowell's "inability to sustain the long units of poetry," despite "his great talent for the short units."

29. Williamson, *Pity the Monsters*, 164–65; von Hallberg, *American Poetry and Culture*, 152.

30. Donald Hall, "Robert Lowell and the Literature Industry," *The Georgia Review* 32, no. 1 (Spring 1978): 7–12.

Chapter Five

1. "If we reject the simplistic notion of objective sexual oppression as the cause of Plath's suicide, we must also deny that her death resulted from heroic self-revelations of the poetry itself" (John Rosenblatt, *Sylvia Plath: The Poetry of Initiation* [Chapel Hill, NC: Univ. of North Carolina Press, 1979], 10). "To approach Plath as a poet rather than to use her as an image of a poet one must confront her work in its own terms, which is to say, as literature. In these terms, the fact, for example, that she killed herself is irrelevant to the consideration of the meaning of her work" (Judith Kroll, *Chapters in a Mythology: The Poetry of Sylvia Plath* [New York: Harper and Row, 1976], 1).

2. Kroll, *Chapters*, 2.

3. *The Journals of Sylvia Plath*, edited by Ted Hughes and Frances McCullough (1982; reprint, New York: Ballantine Books, 1983), 250–51, 320, 292, 314, 305, 299.

4. Sylvia Plath, *Letters Home: Correspondence 1950–1963*, edited by Au-

relia Schober Plath (New York: Harper & Row, 1975), 460, 488, 491 (ellipses *sic*).

5. The suicidal thesis is, of course, old business by now. See A. Alvarez, *The Savage God: A Study of Suicide* (London: Weidenfeld and Nicolson, 1971), 31–33; M. L. Rosenthal, *The New Poets: American and British Poetry Since World War II* (New York: Oxford Univ. Press, 1967), 86–87; George Steiner, "Dying Is an Art," in *The Art of Sylvia Plath*, edited by Charles Newman (1970; reprint, Bloomington: Univ. of Indiana Press, 1971), 211–18. For Rosenblatt, the theme of rebirth is central, as he explains at the outset (*Sylvia Plath*, ix). See also Kroll, *Chapters*, 3 ("in Plath's poetry there is one overriding concern: the problem of rebirth or transcendence"); and Leonard Sanazaro, "The Transfiguring Self," in *Critical Essays on Sylvia Plath*, edited by Linda W. Wagner (Boston: G. K. Hall, 1984), 87–97.

6. All citations of Sylvia Plath's poetry are from *The Collected Poems*, edited by Ted Hughes (New York: Harper and Row, 1981), abbreviated as *SP*.

7. Kroll, *Chapters*, 19.

8. T. S. Eliot, *The Complete Poems and Plays 1909–1950* (New York: Harcourt, Brace, and World, 1958), 119.

9. Edward Butscher, *Sylvia Plath: Method and Madness* (1976; reprint, New York: Washington Square Press, 1977), 12.

10. Irving Howe, "The Plath Celebration: A Partial Dissent," in *Sylvia Plath: The Woman and the Work*, edited by Edward Butscher (New York: Dodd, Mead and Co., 1977), 232–33. (I follow Howe's lead in rejecting the defense of "Daddy" as a dramatic monologue.)

11. W. H. Auden, "September 1, 1939," in *The English Auden: Poems, Essays, and Dramatic Writings*, edited by Edward Mendelson (New York: Random House, 1977), 245.

12. Hugh Kenner's satirical analogy is all too just: "As who should say, 'The price of absorption is pornography is an incremental deadening of the spirit, an attenuation of an already frail belief in the sanctity of personhood. I shall now show you a pornographic film'" ("Sincerity Kills," in *Sylvia Plath: New Views of the Poetry*, edited by Gary Lane, [Baltimore: Johns Hopkins Univ. Press, 1979], 35).

13. So Alvarez argues convincingly, *The Savage God*, 31.

14. Ted Hughes, "Notes on the Chronological Order of Sylvia Plath's Poems," in Newman, *The Art of Sylvia Plath*, 194.

15. Kroll, *Chapters*, 44.

16. Steiner, "Dying Is an Art," in Newman, *The Art of Sylvia Plath*, 211, 218.

Chapter Six

1. Symptomatic of this disenchantment are Adrienne Rich's criticism of Lowell's three books of blank sonnets, especially *The Dolphin*, in the final installment of her column, "Carayatid," *The American Poetry Review* 2, no. 5 (September/October 1973): 42–43 ("Finally, what does one say about a poet who, having left his wife and daughter for another marriage, then titles a book

with their names, and goes one to appropriate his ex-wife's letters written under the stress and pain of desertion, into a book of poems nominally addressed to the new wife?"); and Donald Hall's "Robert Lowell and the Literature Industry," *Georgia Review* 32, no. 1 (Spring 1978): 7–12, which summed up Lowell's career, half a year after his death, as "the corruption of a great poet"; Hall continues to value Lowell's work through *Life Studies*, but sees decline thereafter.

2. Paul Zweig, "The New Surrealism," *Salmagundi* 22–23 (Spring–Summer 1973): 269–84. Jonathan Holden makes a useful distinction between deep-image surrealism and a surrealism of the "abstract image" whose best exponent is John Ashbery. See his *Style and Authenticity in Postmodern Poetry* (Columbia: Univ. of Missouri Press, 1986), 58–72.

3. Richard Howard, "A Note on Charles Simic," in Charles Simic, *Dismantling the Silence* (New York: Braziller, 1971), xii; "Crunk," "James Wright," *The Sixties*, no. 8: 77; Mark Strand, quoted on the back cover of the paperback edition of James Tate, *Absences* (Boston: Little, Brown & Co., 1972).

4. W. S. Merwin, *The Carrier of Ladders* (New York: Atheneum, 1970), 65.

5. James Atlas, "Diminishing Returns: The Poetry of W. S. Merwin," in *American Poetry Since 1960: Some Critical Perspectives*, edited by Robert B. Shaw (Cheadle, England: Carcanet, 1973), 78–79.

6. James Wright, *Collected Poems* (Middletown, CT: Wesleyan Univ. Press., 1971), 78–79.

7. Charles Simic, "Knife," in *Dismantling the Silence* (New York: Braziller, 1971), 56–57.

8. Robert Bly, *The Light Around the Body* (New York: Harper & Row, 1967), 57.

9. C. G. Jung, *Memories, Dreams, Reflections*, rev. ed., edited by Aniela Jaffé, translated by Richard and Clara Winston (New York: Vintage, 1965), 159.

10. Sigmund Freud, *The Interpretation of Dreams*, vol. 5 in *The Standard Edition of the Complete Psychological Works of Sigmund Freud*, edited and translated by James Strachey (London: The Hogarth Press, 1964), 541, 562.

11. Freud, vol. 15 of *The Standard Edition*, 181.

12. C. G. Jung, "The Practical Use of Dream Analysis," vol. 16 in *The Collected Works of C. G. Jung*, edited by Herbert Read, Michael Fordham, and Gerhard Adler (New York: Pantheon/Bollingen Foundation, 1957), 149.

13. See Jung, "Conscious, Unconscious, and Individuation," vol. 9 in *The Collected Works of C. G. Jung*, i, 288.

14. Marvin Bell, "Homage to the Runner" (column), *American Poetry Review* 4, no. 3 (May–June 1975): 11–12; Robert Pinsky, *The Situation of Poetry* (Princeton, NJ: Princeton Univ. Press, 1976), 162–66.

15. Pinsky, *The Situation of Poetry*, 162.

16. Robert Bly, *Silence in the Snowy Fields* (Middletown, CT: Wesleyan Univ. Press, 1962), 25.

17. W. S. Merwin, *The Moving Target* (New York: Atheneum, 1963), 78.

18. Simic, "Sleep," in *Dismantling the Silence*, 19.

19. Mark Strand, "The Stone," in *Darker* (New York: Atheneum, 1970), 31.

20. Gregory Orr, "A Final Aubade," in *Burning the Empty Nests* (New York: Harper & Row, 1973), 47.

21. Galway Kinnell, *The Book of Nightmares* (Boston: Houghton Mifflin, 1971), 52.

22. Pinsky, *The Situation of Poetry*, 163.

23. Kinnell, *Nightmares*, 4.

24. James Richardson, "Encyclopedia of the Stones: A Pastoral," in *Reservations* (Princeton: Princeton Univ. Press, 1977), 13–24; Charles Simic, *Somewhere Among Us a Stone Is Taking Notes* (Santa Cruz: Kayak Press, 1969); "Stone," in *Dismantling the Silence*; Tom Clark, "Summer Open," in *Stones* (New York: Harper & Row, 1969), 30; James Wright, "Confession to J. Edgar Hoover," *Collected Poems*, 163–64.

25. Jung, *Memories, Dreams, Reflections*, 42.

26. Galway Kinnell, "An Interview with A. Poulin, Jr., and Stan Sanvel Rubin" (1971), reprinted in *Walking Down the Stairs: Selections from Interviews*, edited by Galway Kinnell (Ann Arbor: Univ. of Michigan Press, 1978), 23.

27. Mark Strand, "Keeping Things Whole," in *Reasons For Moving* (New York: Atheneum, 1968), 40.

28. James Tate, *Absences*, 16.

29. Merwin, *The Carrier of Ladders*, 124.

30. Bly, "The Dead World and the Live World," *The Sixties*, 8: 4–5.

31. Gary Snyder, "Poetry and the Primitive: Notes on Poetry as an Ecological Survival Technique" [1967], in *Earth House Hold* (New York: New Directions, 1969), 122.

32. Snyder, *Earth House Hold*, 91.

33. Alan Williamson, *Introspection and Contemporary Poetry* (Cambridge: Harvard Univ. Press, 1984), 66.

34. As early as 1970, W. H. Pritchard identified a "somnambulistic school," including James Dickey and Donald Justice along with Bly, Wright, Merwin, and Strand, whose poems present "an 'I' that is above, or at the point of transcending, the agonies and strifes of human hearts, in a relatively toneless mode" ("Wildness of Logic in the Modern Lyric," in *Selected Papers from the English Institute*, edited by Reuben Brower [New York: Columbia Univ. Press, 1970], 127–50).

35. Wright, *Collected Poems*, 121–22.

36. Bly, *The Light Around the Body*, 9–10.

37. Freud, *The Ego and the Id*, vol. 19 of *The Standard Edition*, 15.

38. Philip Rieff, *The Triumph of the Therapeutic: Uses of Faith After Freud* (New York: Harper & Row, 1966), 139.

39. C. G. Jung, "The Practical Use of Dream Analysis," vol. 16 in *The Collected Works of C. G. Jung*, 153.

Chapter Seven

1. W. S. Merwin, "Act of Conscience: The Story of *Everyman*," *The Nation* 195, no. 22 (29 December 1962): 463–80.

2. W. S. Merwin, letter to *The New York Review of Books* 16, no. 10 (3 June 1971): 41.

3. W. S. Merwin, "To Name The Wrong," *The Nation* 194, no. 8 (24 February 1962): 176.

4. Frank MacShane, "A Portrait of W. S. Merwin," *Shenandoah* 21, no. 2 (Winter 1970): 7–8.

5. W. S. Merwin, "Notes for a Preface," in *The Distinctive Voice*, edited by Louis Martz (Glenview, IL: Scott, Foresman & Co., 1966), 270.

6. Douglas Flaherty and James Bradford, "An Interview With W. S. Merwin," *Road Apple Review* 1, no. 2 (Spring 1969): 36.

7. Cary Nelson, *Our Last First Poets: Vision and History in Contemporary American Poetry* (Urbana, IL: Univ. of Illinois Press, 1981), 190.

8. Robert Hass, "Death Camps of the Free World," *The Nation* 207, no. 8 (16 September 1968): 254.

9. See Charles Altieri, *Enlarging the Temple: New Directions in American Poetry During the 1960s* (1979; reprint, London: Associated Univ. Presses [Bucknell], 1980), 194; Helen Vendler, "W. S. Merwin," in *Part of Nature, Part of Us* (Cambridge: Harvard Univ. Press, 1980), 233–34; Nelson, *First Poets*, 192, n. 8.

10. See Altieri, *Temple*, 195–96; Nelson, *First Poets*, 188.

11. Richard Howard, "W. S. Merwin: 'We Survived the Selves that We Remembered,'" in *Alone With America: Essays on the Art of Poetry in the United States Since 1950* [enlarged edition] (New York: Atheneum, 1980), 414.

12. In this chapter, the following abbreviations are used for citations of Merwin's poetry: *FFBP, The First Four Books of Poems* (New York: Atheneum, 1975); *MT, The Moving Target* (New York: Atheneum, 1963); *L, The Lice* (New York: Atheneum, 1967); *CF, The Compass Flower* (New York: Atheneum, 1977); *WUA, Writings to an Unfinished Accompaniment* (New York: Atheneum, 1980); *OH, Opening the Hand* (New York: Atheneum, 1983).

13. I follow Charles O. Hartman in preserving this distinction, discussed in his *Free Verse: An Essay on Prosody* (Princeton, NJ: Princeton Univ. Press, 1980), 111–17.

14. Howard, *Alone With America*, 432.

15. Ibid.

16. Vendler, *Part of Nature, Part of Us*, 235.

17. I am indebted to a Northwestern graduate student, Katherine Hoffman, for her discussion, in a seminar paper of June 1984, of the political implications of this poem.

18. W. S. Merwin, *Unframed Originals: Recollections by W. S. Merwin* (New York: Atheneum, 1982), 24.

Chapter Eight

1. James Wright, "The Pure Clear Word, An Interview" [30 September 1979], in *The Pure Clear Word: Essays on the Poetry of James Wright*, edited by Dave Smith (Urbana: Univ. of Illinois Press, 1982), 6.

2. The following abbreviations are used in citations of James Wright's poems: *JW, Collected Poems* (Middletown, CT: Wesleyan Univ. Press, 1971); *TC, Two Citizens* (New York: Farrar, Straus & Giroux, 1973); *BPT, To a Blossoming Pear Tree* (New York: Farrar, Straus & Giroux, 1977); *TJ, This Journey* (New York: Random House [Vintage], 1982).

3. See *JW*, 25–26 and 82–84 (George Doty); *JW*, 158 (Willie Lyons); *JW*, 139 (Charlie); *JW*, 20–21 (the "defected Savior"); *JW*, 50–51 (Mr. Bluehart); *BPT*, 9–10 (Homer Rhodeheaver); *BPT*, 14–16 (Ralph Neal).

4. So, for example, James E. B. Breslin: "Like so many of his contemporaries . . . Wright moved toward the dismantling of traditional technique, the cracking apart of a wall of formal control, a 'breakthrough back into life' which would permit evolution of a new language for poetry" (*From Modern to Contemporary: American Poetry 1945–1965* [Chicago: Univ. of Chicago Press, 1984], 189–90).

5. Peter Stitt, "The Art of Poetry XIX: James Wright," *Paris Review* 62 (Summer 1965): 47–48; "Something to Be Said For the Light: A Conversation with William Heyen and Jerome Mazzaro," edited by Joseph R. McElrath [24 September 1970], reprinted in *Collected Prose: James Wright*, edited by Annie Wright (Ann Arbor, MI: Univ. of Michigan Press, 1983), 156; "An Interview with Michael André" [1972], reprinted in *Collected Prose*, 145.

6. James Wright, "Poetry Must Think: An Interview with Bruce Henrickson" [1978], reprinted in *Collected Prose*, 180; Stitt, "The Art of Poetry XIX: James Wright," 51; Wright, "An Interview with Michael André," in *Collected Prose*, 134.

7. Wright, "An Interview with Michael André," in *Collected Prose*, 142.

8. Wright, "Something to Be Said For the Light," in *Collected Prose*, 158.

9. Wright, "Poetry Must Think," in *Collected Prose*, 180.

10. Robert Hass, "James Wright," in Smith, *Pure Clear Word*, 198.

11. Ibid., 200.

12. Michael Rossman, *The Wedding Within the War* (Garden City, NY: 1971), 30–45.

13. Stitt, "The Art of Poetry XIX: James Wright," 52.

14. See Herbert Marcuse, *Eros and Civilization: A Philosophical Inquiry Into Freud* (1955; reprint, New York: Vintage, 1962), 77–78.

15. As a young man, Wright himself played on "a sort of semi-pro team. There was a lot of that in the Ohio River Valley, where I grew up." In his interview with Dave Smith, he remarked that "The Football season . . . was very intensely a communal activity, a communal occasion" ("The Pure Clear Word, An Interview," in Smith, *Pure Clear Word*, 3.

16. Wright mentions his irritation with critical responses to this line in "An Interview with Michael André," 138. Alan Williamson, *Introspection and Con-*

temporary Poetry, (Cambridge: Harvard Univ. Press, 1984), 70, construes it as a quotation from Rimbaud's "Song of the Highest Tower" (*J'ai perdu ma vie*), but Wright's commentary in "Poetry Must Think," 184, implies that he was unaware of borrowing from any source.

17. "The Pure Clear Word, An Interview," in Smith, *Pure Clear Word*, 30.

18. "An Interview with Michael André," in *Collected Prose*, 145–46.

19. A. R. Davis, *Tu Fu* (New York: Twayne Publishers, 1971), 43.

20. Wright, "On the Occasion of a Poem: Bill Knott," *Collected Prose*, 321–22.

21. Williamson, *Introspection*, 68.

22. "The Pure Clear Word, An Interview," in Smith, *Pure Clear Word*, 38–39.

Chapter Nine

1. Robert Bly, "A Wrong Turning in American Poetry," *Choice* 3 (1963): 36; John Berryman, "In and Out," in *Love & Fame*, 2d ed., revised (New York: Farrar, Strauss & Giroux, 1972), 24. The first stanza of the passage quoted borrows from a sentence in an unsigned review of Creeley's *Poems: 1950–1965*, *Times Literary Supplement*, 1 December 1966, 22: "But in general, this fifteen-year bundle of almost 200 poems makes crushingly dull reading."

2. Robert von Hallberg, *Charles Olson: The Scholar's Art* (Cambridge: Harvard Univ. Press, 1978), 40.

3. See Thomas Merrill, *The Poetry of Charles Olson: A Primer* (Newark: Univ. of Delaware Press, 1982), 199–213.

4. The following abbreviations will be used for citations of writing by Olson: *MP I* for the portion of *The Maximus Poems* that appeared under that title in 1960, *MP II* for the portion that appeared in 1968 under the title *Maximus IV, V, VI*; both are cited in *The Maximus Poems*, edited by George Butterick (Berkeley: Univ. of California Press, 1983) where they are separately paginated; *SW, Selected Writings*, edited by Robert Creeley (New York: New Directions, 1966); *CM, Causal Mythology*, edited by Donald Allen (San Francisco: Four Seasons, 1969); *PT, Poetry and Truth: The Beloit Lectures and Poems*, transcribed and edited by George F. Butterick (San Francisco: Four Seasons, 1971).

5. Paul Christensen, *Charles Olson: Call Him Ishmael* (Austin: Univ. of Texas Press, 1979), 30.

6. Von Hallberg, *Charles Olson*, 2.

7. John Crowe Ransom, "Poetry: A Note in Ontology," in *The World's Body* (1938; reprint, Baton Rouge: Louisiana State Univ. Press, 1968), 116, 115; "The Mimetic Principle," in *The World's Body*, 206.

8. Allen Tate, "Three Types of Poetry," in *Essays of Four Decades* (London: Oxford Univ. Press, 1970), 177.

9. Ransom, "Forms and Citizens," in *The World's Body*, 38–39.

10. Merrill, *Poetry of Charles Olson*, 60.

11. Von Hallberg, *Charles Olson*, 113.

12. The transcript of this event, during which Olson talked extemporaneously for hours, reading a small number of poems along the way, has been published in *Muthologos: Charles Olson*, vol. 1, edited by George Butterick (Bolinas, CA: Four Seasons, 1978), 97–156.

13. Von Hallberg, *Charles Olson*, 121.

14. Merrill, *Poetry of Charles Olson*, 26.

15. George F. Butterick, *A Guide to the Maximus Poems of Charles Olson* (Berkeley: Univ. of California Press, 1978), 176. I am generally indebted to this book for information about people, places, and events obscurely mentioned in the *Maximus* sequence.

16. Ibid., 242.

17. Von Hallenberg, *Charles Olson*, 123.

18. Robert von Hallberg, *American Poetry and Culture, 1945–1980* (Cambridge: Harvard Univ. Press, 1985), 145.

19. Charles Altieri, *Enlarging the Temple: New Directions in American Poetry During the 1960s* (1979; reprint, London: Associated Univ. Presses [Bucknell], 1980), 230.

20. The following abbreviations will be used for citations of poems by Denise Levertov: *SD, The Sorrow Dance* (New York: New Directions, 1967); *RA, Relearning the Alphabet* (New York: New Directions, 1970); *FD, The Freeing of the Dust* (New York: New Directions, 1975).

21. Cary Nelson, *Our Last First Poets: Vision and History in Contemporary American Poetry* (Urbana: Univ. of Illinois Press, 1981), 139.

22. Godfrey Hodgson, *America in Our Time* (1976; reprint, New York: Vintage, 1978), 239.

23. Wendell Berry, "The Specialization of Poetry" [1975], reprinted in *The Poet's Work: 29 Masters of 20th Century Poetry on the Origins and Practice of Their Art*, edited by Reginald Gibbons (Boston: Houghton Mifflin, 1979), 142.

24. Walt Whitman, "Preface" to *Leaves of Grass* (1855), in *Walt Whitman: Complete Poetry and Selected Prose*, edited by Justin Kaplan (New York: Library of America, 1982), 10.

25. Von Hallberg (*American Poetry and Culture*, 134–38) observes the antisuburban, "class-oriented" quality of political poetry during the 1960s and cites this poem among his examples.

26. The following abbreviations will be used for citations of writings by Robert Duncan: *BB, Bending the Bow* (New York: New Directions, 1968), *GW, Ground Work: Before the War* (New York: New Directions, 1984).

27. James Mersmann, *Out of the Vietnam Vortex: A Study of Poets and Poetry Against the War* (Lawrence: Univ. of Kansas Press, 1974), 94, n.

28. Altieri, *Temple*, 168, n. 26.

29. Peter Michelson, "A Materialist Critique of Robert Duncan's Grand Collage," *Boundary 2*, 8, no. 2 (Winter 1980): 32.

30. Robert Duncan, "Ideas of the Meaning of Form," in *The Poetics of the New American Poetry*, edited by Donald Allen and Warren Tallman, (New York: Grove Press, 1973), 201, 196.

31. Ibid., 208.

Chapter Ten

1. David Lehman, "The Shield of a Greeting: The Function of Irony in John Ashbery's Poetry," in *Beyond Amazement: New Essays on John Ashbery*, edited by David Lehman (Ithaca, NY: Cornell Univ. Press, 1980), 126.

2. See Harold Bloom, "John Ashbery: The Charity of the Hard Moments," in *Figures of Capable Imagination* (New York: Seabury Press, 1976), 177; Marjorie Perloff, "Fragments of a Buried Life," in Lehman, *Beyond Amazement*, 78; Helen Vendler, "Understanding Ashbery," *The New Yorker*, 16 March 1981, 108; Alan Williamson, *Introspection and Contemporary Poetry* (Cambridge: Harvard Univ. Press, 1984), 124–25.

3. See Vendler, "Understanding Ashbery," 108–36; Bloom, *Figures*, 169–208; David Kalstone, *Five Temperaments* (New York: Oxford Univ. Press, 1977), 170–203.

4. Douglas Crase, "The Prophetic Ashbery," in Lehman, *Beyond Amazement*, 30; Williamson, *Introspection*, 137.

5. David Shapiro, *John Ashbery: An Introduction to His Poetry* (New York: Columbia Univ. Press, 1979), 2, 20, 159. Keith Cohen, "Ashbery's Dismantling of Bourgeois Discourse," in Lehman, *Beyond Amazement*, 128.

6. Cohen, "Bourgeois Discourse," in Lehman, *Beyond Amazement*, 134.

7. Noam Chomsky, *Syntactic Structures* (1957; reprint, The Hague, Netherlands: Mouton & Co., 1964), 15.

8. Cohen, "Bourgeois Discourse," in Lehman, *Beyond Amazement*, 138–39.

9. Ibid., 137.

10. The following abbreviations will be used for citations of Ashbery's poetry: *ST, Some Trees* (1956; reprint, New York: Corinth Books, 1970); *RM, Rivers and Mountains* (New York: Holt, Rinehart and Winston, 1966); *DDS, The Double Dream of Spring* (New York: E. P. Dutton, 1970); *TP, Three Poems* (New York: Viking, 1972); *SPCM, Self-Portrait in a Convex Mirror* (New York: Viking, 1975); *HD, Houseboat Days* (New York, Viking, 1977).

11. Vendler, "Understanding Ashbery," 130.

12. Crase, "Prophetic Ashbery," in Lehman, *Beyond Amazement*, 59.

13. Robert Pinsky, *The Situation of Poetry* (Princeton, NJ: Princeton Univ. Press, 1976), 81.

14. See David Kalstone, *Five Temperaments* (New York: Oxford Univ. Press, 1977), 176–85; Charles Altieri, *Self and Sensibility in Contemporary American Poetry* (Cambridge: Cambridge Univ. Press, 1984), 151–61; Williamson, *Introspection*, 141–45; Shapiro, *John Ashbery*, 4–10.

15. Pinsky, *Situation*, 36–37.

16. Arnold Hauser, *Mannerism: The Crisis of the Renaissance and the Origin of Modern Art*, vol. I (New York: Knopf, 1965), 4.

17. John Shearman, *Mannerism* (Harmondsworth, Middlesex, England: Penguin Books, 1967), 38.

18. Shearman (*Mannerism*, 19–21) disputes this view: "Modern aesthetic attitudes, at least those of sufficient maturity for us to be aware of them, are

quite as effective an obstacle to the appreciation of Mannerist works of art as were those of Ruskin's era. . . ."

19. Lehman, "The Shield," in *Beyond Amazement*, 103.

20. Robert Lowell, "The Nihilist as Hero," *History* (New York: Farrar, Straus & Giroux, 1973), 193.

Index

Acculturation, xiii, 8, 9–17, 33, 190; as adjustment, 10–14; as conformity, 3–7, 29; and language, 201, 213–14; as "one-dimensionality," 5, 16–18, 28–29, 127–28, 134, 153; as self-destructiveness, 42–44, 54–56, 68; and symbolism, 50–52, 64, 68
Agnew, Spiro T., 203
Altieri, Charles, 199–200, 205, 209
Alvarez, A., 42, 44, 57, 95, 103, 116, 127, 132, 246nn.5, 13
André, Michael, 158, 172
Arendt, Hannah, 7
Aristotle, 54, 185, 186, 194
Ashbery, John, xvi, xvii, 44, 211–35; as belated romantic poet, 212–13; and "bourgeois discourse," 213–16; and deconstruction, 213–14; and mannerism, 226–27, 232, 253n.18; and narcissism, 218–19, 224; as political poet, 213–16, 218–19; and projectivism, 212–13; self-canceling epiphany in, 217–19, 224–25; syntax of, 228–29, 231. Poems: "Evening in the Country," 220–21; "Haunted Landscape," 216; "The Instruction Manual," 217, 227; "These Lacustrine Cities," 219; "The New Spirit," 216, 219; "Nightlife," 221; "The Painter," 216; "Pyrography," 217–18; "Self-Portrait in a Convex Mirror," 221, 226–34; "The Skaters," 220, 221; "Soonest Mended," 219, 220–26; "Syringa," 221; "The System," 220, 221
Atlas, James, 120, 125
Auden, W. H., 105
Augustine, Saint, 243n.11
Axelrod, Steven Gould, 43, 64, 65, 73

Baraka, Amiri (LeRoi Jones), xvii, 1
Barthes, Roland, 213
Baudelaire, Charles, 55, 143
Bell, Daniel, 3

Bell, Marvin, 125
Bellow, Saul, 131
Benedict, Ruth, 9
Benedikt, Michael, 118
Bercovitch, Sacvan, 18
Berry, Wendell, 202
Berryman, John, 23, 44, 53, 56, 158; comic gift of, 57; and courtship of suffering, 55, 56, 58, 200; on Robert Creeley, 182; and elevated style, 225; reticence of, 45–46; on society and madness, 26, 56. Poems: "Dream Song # 4," 57; "In and Out," 182
Bettelheim, Bruno, 7
Bishop, Elizabeth, 23, 55, 66, 94
Blackmur, R. P., 62
Blake, William, xiii, 1, 55, 77, 209
Bloom, Harold, xii, 212–23, 214, 234–35
Bly, Robert, 79, 82, 118, 136, 211; and "aesthetics of presence," 200; antiformalism of, 159; on Robert Creeley, 183; and Jungian symbolism, xvi, 97, 125; on Robert Lowell, 131, 245n.28; and mysticism, 22; on poetry of "the dead world," 2, 131; as political activist, 1, 128; and symbolism of light and darkness in, 162; and James Wright, friendship with, 135, 159. Poems: "Moving Inward at Last," 123; "Unrest," 126; "Romans Angry about the Inner World," 134
Breslin, James E. B., 250n.4
Brown, Norman O., 9, 13–16, 59, 72
Browning, Robert, 45, 217
Burroughs, William, 40
Butscher, Edwin, 44

Carruth, Hayden, 245n.28
Chekhov, Anton, 53
Chessman, Caryl, 163
Chomsky, Noam, 214
Christensen, Paul, 184

Civil Rights Movement, 7, 72, 73, 90–92
Clark, Tom, 38–40, 129
Class, 36, 146, 172–74; and conflict,
    16–17, 194–95; and ego, 132; middle-
    class, 7, 16–17, 36, 128, 203, 213–16;
    presumed disappearance of in 1950s,
    3–4; working, 165, 168–69, 180–81
Cleaver, Eldridge, 8
Cohen, Keith, 213–15, 218, 219
Coleridge, Samuel Taylor, 54
"Confessional" poetry, xvi, 26, 42–58,
    96, 102–3, 110. See also Private/public
    dualism
Consensus politics, 3–4
Conventions (poetic): as constraint, 2; and
    experience, xv, 50–55, 101, 188,
    191–92, 234–35; in the 1950s, 140,
    141, 160; and poetic coherence in Mer-
    win, 116, 149; and private/public du-
    alism, 45–47, 103, 106–9; and the
    unconscious, xv, 2, 18–19, 120–27,
    132–33, 139, 148. See also Prosody;
    Symbolism; Syntax
Cooper, Philip, 73
Crane, Hart, 48–50, 61, 97, 113, 119
Crase, Douglas, 213, 218, 219
Creeley, Robert, 2–3, 182, 183
Crick, Jonathan, 73
cummings, e. e., 196

Dante, 140
"Deep-image" poetry, xvi, 97, 118–35,
    136, 157, 182
Denney, Reuel, 3
Derrida, Jacques, 213
Donne, John, 102, 140
Dorn, Edward, 182
Dostoyevsky, Fyodor, 242 n.11
Dramatic monologue: as alternative to
    confessional mode, 45–47, 50, 104, 109
Duncan, Robert, 79, 205–10, and "aes-
    thetics of presence," 200; and "Black
    Mountain" group, 182; critique of De-
    nise Levertov, 205; as political poet,
    183; 199; on prosody, 207; and religion,
    206–7; syntax of, 206; on war, 207–8.
    Essays: "Ideas of the Meaning of
    Form," 207–8; "Introduction" to Bend-
    ing the Bow, 206–7. Poems: "Earth's
    Winter Song," 209; "The Multiversity
    Passages 21," 209; "Passages 26: The
    Soldiers," 208–9; "Santa Cruz Proposi-
    tions," 205; "Up Rising Passages 25,"
    209

Eberhart, Richard, 25
Ego: as acculturated self, 14, 20–21, 25,
    128, 132, 148; and "adjustment," 14;
    and class structure, 132; and ego psy-
    chology, 10, 12; and id, 10, 83; "lyrical
    interference" of, 183; and radical
    Freudians, 14; and superego, 10, 12,
    102–3
Ego Psychology (Neo-Freudianism),
    10–14
Ehrenpreis, Irvin, 63, 64
Eisenhower, Dwight D., 133–34, 182
Eliot, T. S., 19, 40, 55, 97; and John Ash-
    bery, 233; and Bloomian canon, 235;
    and "dissociation of sensibility," 185;
    and W. S. Merwin, 138–40, 143; and
    Sylvia Plath, 102, 111; and symbolism,
    51–54; and James Wright's "The Jewel,"
    122
Emerson, Ralph Waldo, 86, 235
Erikson, Erik, 9
Everwine, Peter, 118

Flaubert, Gustave, 53
Flegg, H. Graham, 188
Ford, Ford Madox, 67
Foucault, Michel, 213
Freedberg, Sydney, 228, 232
Freud, Sigmund, 24, 44, 87, 218; on ego's
    role as mediator, 10, 239 n.24; and poli-
    tics, 11, 13, 20; on superego, 10, 12,
    102–3; on symbolism, 18–19, 123–25;
    on unchangeability of instincts, 11, 13,
    20; on the unconscious, 18–19, 121,
    123–25. See also Ego; Unconscious
Fromm, Erich, 10, 12–13
Frost, Robert, 91, 119, 157, 159, 235

Gestalt psychology, 20, 184
Gilbert, W. S., 109
Ginsberg, Allen, xvi, 3, 20, 22–41, 44,
    82, 128, 166, 214; and "confessional"
    poetry, 22, 25–26, 42, 44, 55; and in-
    stincts as authenticity, 24, 39, 60, 85,
    162; and madness, 23–24, 26–30, 42,
    44, 55; at Naropa Institute, 38–40; and
    "one-dimensional" society, 18, 29; as
    political activist, 1, 59; and private/
    public dualism, 26, 29–31, 61; and reli-
    gion, 25, 26, 31, 34; syntax of, 24–25;
    and Whitman, 24. Poems: "Contest of
    Bards," 39; The Fall of America,
    36–37; "The Green Automobile," 26;
    "Howl," 23–31, 33, 40, 42, 66, 85, 182,

215; "Kaddish," 25, 29–34; "Mind Breaths," 35; "Please Master," 39, 40; "Sunflower Sutra," 25; "Wales Visitation," 35; "Wichita Vortex Sutra," 31–33, 37–38, 42
Glazer, Nathan, 3
Goodman, Paul, 20, 184
Graff, Gerald, 27
Graves, Robert, 145
Green, Gil, 240n.45

Hall, Donald, 1–2, 93, 247n.1
Hamilton, Ian, 89
Hardy, Thomas, 157, 159, 225
Hartman, Charles O., 51, 249n.13
Hass, Robert, 138, 139, 142, 152, 153, 160–61
Hauser, Arnold, 226–27
Hawthorne, Nathaniel, 242n.11
Hegel, G. W. F., 16, 191
Hemingway, Ernest, 177
Heyen, William, 159
Hitler, Adolf, 7, 9, 40, 86, 89, 93, 104, 105, 110, 209
Hodgson, Geoffrey, 3, 7, 201
Hoffman, Katherine, 249n.17
Holden, Jonathan, 247n.2
Horney, Karen, 10–13
Howard, Richard, 118, 139, 142, 145
Howe, Irving, 105, 240n.45, 246n.10
Hughes, Ted, 98, 100

Jarrell, Randall, 55
Johnson, Lyndon Baines, 9, 79, 80, 204, 208, 209
Joyce, James, 19
Jung, Carl Gustav: and Robert Bly, xvi, 125; and the collective unconscious, 19–21, 123–25, 183–84; and "individuation," 125; and Charles Olson, xvi, 183–84; on relations of conscious and unconscious, 135; and religion, 134–35, 206; right-wing politics of, 19–20; "shadow," concept of, 154; and symbolism, 19, 123–25, 129–30

Kalstone, David, 81–82, 212–14, 244n.13
Kant, Immanuel, 14, 187, 229
Keats, John, 130, 189, 212, 213, 215
Kennedy, Robert, 37, 93
Kenner, Hugh, 246n.12
King, Martin Luther, 74, 90–92
King, Richard, 20

Kinnell, Galway, 97, 211, 214; antiformalism of, 2, 207; as "deep-image" poet, 118, 127, 129; and mysticism, 22; as political activist, 1, 128, 136; and symbolism, 130, 162
Koethe, John, 211
Kolko, Gabriel, 239n.8
Kroll, Judith, 95–96, 99, 101, 110–12, 245n.1, 246n.5
Kuzma, Greg, 118

Laing, R. D., 5, 9, 18, 29
Lamantia, Philip, 118
Lasch, Christopher, 240n.45
Lawrence, D. H., 39, 175, 186
Lehman, David, 211, 234, 235
Levertov, Denise, xvii, 199–205; and "aesthetics of presence," 200; and "Black Mountain" group, 182; and imagism, 199, 202; New Left rhetoric of, 8, 138; as political activist, 1; as political poet, 183, 199–205; and private/public dualism, 8, 43; and projective poetry, 199–203; on U.S. imperialism, 8. Poems: "Advent 1966," 202; "The Cold Spring," 200; "From a Notebook, October '68–May '69," 203; "In Thai Binh (Peace) Province," 203–4; "Life at War," 200–202; "Tenebrae," 203
Liberalism: and Robert Lowell, 59, 82–83, 87–89
Lincoln, Abraham, 93
Lipking, Lawrence, 243n.11
Locke, John, 88
Lowell, Robert, 41, 58–94, 103, 145, 158, 182, 235; on ancient history, 85–86; and Elizabeth Bishop, 66; and "confessional" poetry, xvi, 22, 43, 46, 56–57; and courtship of suffering, 55, 56; and Hart Crane, 48–50, 61; instability of tone in, 59, 62–63; instinct as authenticity in, 59–60, 82–83; instinct as violence in, 83–86; and liberalism, 59, 82, 87–89; and madness 49, 63–64, 68–70, 78; New Left in poetry of, 89–92; and "one-dimensional" society, 18, 79, 91; political activism of, 1, 59; and private/public dualism, 15, 43, 57, 64–65, 68–70, 74, 78, 81, 92; and radical Freudianism, 59, 71–72; and religion, 62, 72, 73, 77–78, 90; skepticism of, 59–60, 82–83; and symbolism, 55, 63–64, 78; syntax of, 80; visionary impulse in, 59–61; and Walt

Lowell, Robert (*continued*)
Whitman, 61. Prose memoir: "91 Revere Street," 65, 66, 67. Poems: "Abra-
ham Lincoln," 93; "At the Indian
Killer's Grave," 64; "Bishop Berkeley,"
60–62; "Caligula 2," 86; "Can a
Plucked Bird Live?" 93; "Che
Guevara," 92; "Christmas in Black
Rock," 62; "Clytemnestra 2," 86;
"Clytemnestra 3," 87; "Death of Alex-
ander," 86, 89; "Ezra Pound," 61;
"Fame," 85–86; "Father's Bedroom,"
66–67; "For Robert Kennedy
1925–68," 93; "For the Union Dead,"
18, 56, 70–74; "Hannibal 2. The Life,"
86; "History," 83; "Home After Two
Months Away," 60; "Leader of the
Left," 89–90; "Life and Civilization,"
87–89; "Man and Woman," 84–85;
"The March 1," 90; "The March 2," 90,
93; "Mexico," 61; "Mohammed," 85;
"Mr. Edwards and the Spider," 75; "My
Last Afternoon with Uncle Devereux
Winslow," 65, 67; "The Nihilist as
Hero," 235; "Non-Violent," 93; "The
Quaker Graveyard in Nantucket," 63;
"The Revolution," 89; "Sheep," 86;
"Skunk Hour," 66–70, 103, 107; "Small
College Riot," 90; "Soft Wood," 57;
"Thanksgiving 1660 or 1960," 90; "Two
Walls," 91–92; "Waking Early Sunday
Morning," 56, 60, 74–81; "West Side
Sabbath," 89; "Where the Rainbow
Ends," 23, 64; "Women, Children,
Babies, Cows, Cats," 90; "Words for
Hart Crane," 48–50, 57; "Xerxes and
Alexander," 86

Macauley, Thomas Babington, 46
McCarthy, Eugene, 93
McCarthy, Joseph, 4, 32
Machado, Antonio, 134
Madness: in Allen Ginsberg's poetry,
23–24, 26–34; as higher sanity, 29, 30;
as internalized social violence, 28–29,
32, 42–44; in Robert Lowell's poetry,
49, 63–64, 68–70, 78; in Sylvia Plath's
poetry, 95, 105, 107; and prophecy,
63–64; as protest, 27–28, 30; as sign of
sensitivity, 24, 54, 56; in James Wright's
poetry, 165
Mallarmé, Stéphane, 97, 143
Mannerism, 226–27
Mao Tse-tung, 208
Marcuse, Herbert, 9, 11, 19, 20, 59; on
acculturation, 11, 13; and conformity

critics, 4–6; on instincts as authen-
ticity, 13–14, 168; and "one-dimensional" society, 5–7, 17, 29, 79, 91,
153; on political role of art, 14–16
Marin, Peter, 38
Marxism, 7, 12, 16–17
Matthews, William, 118
Melville, Herman, 91, 189
Merrill, James, 141
Merrill, Thomas, 188
Mersmann, James, 205
Merwin, W. S., xvi, 97, 129, 135–56; and
absence, 130–31, 142; as "deep-image"
poet, 118–21, 126; and modernism,
138–39; and mysticism, 22; and Naropa
Institute, 38–40; and narrative,
150–51; as political poet, 138, 146,
152–54; as political activist, 1, 128,
136–37; prosody of, 140–41; private/
public dualism in, 138; and quotidian
experience, 140, 144–46, 154–56; and
regionalism, 145–46; and romantic
transcendence, 142–43; and symbolism, 128, 136, 145–46, 154–56;
syntax of, 132, 140–42, 144, 154–56.
Prose Memoir: *Unframed Originals*,
156. Poems: "Anabasis (I)," 142; "Anabasis (II)," 142; "The Annunciation,"
143; "The Asians Dying," 152–54;
"The Burning Mountain," 144; "By
Day and By Night," 146, 151; "Carol of
the Three Kings," 141; "City," 154;
"The Coin," 154–55; "Finally,"
147–49; "The First Darkness,"
130–31; "Grandmother Dying,"
144–45; "The Houses," 155–56; "The
Hydra," 150–51; "In the Gorge," 147;
"The Last One," 153–54; "Line," 154;
"The Mountain," 143; "The Native,"
146; "Ode: The Medusa Face," 141;
"The Night of the Shirts," 119–21;
"One-Eye," 144; "Over the Bier of the
Worldling," 141; "The Portland Going
Out," 144; "Rime of the Palmers,"
140–41; "Sailor Ashore," 144; "Saint
Sebastian," 142; "St. Vincent's," 154;
"The Search," 151–52; "The Station,"
143–44; "Their Week," 149–51
Michelson, Peter, 27, 28, 207
Miles, Michael W., 240 n.45, 241 n.46
Miller, Arthur, 131
Mills, C. Wright, 4, 6, 17, 195
Milton, John, 69
Mizener, Arthur, 51, 54
Modernism, 19; and John Ashbery,
221–22, 224–26, 233; and "confes-

sional" poetry, 50–55, 68, 97; and "deep-image" poetry, 119; and W. S. Merwin, 138–39; and projective poetry, 186–87, 196, 199
Molesworth, Charles, 66

Naone, Dana, 38, 39
Naropa Institute, 38–40
Nation, Carry, 31, 32, 38
Narcissism: and John Ashbery, 218–19, 224
Nazi extermination camps, 7, 78; in Sylvia Plath's poetry, 105–6, 108–9, 117
Nelson, Cary, 138, 152, 200
Nelson, Truman, 8–9
Nemerov, Howard, 23, 140, 141
New Left, 4–9, 14–17; and Robert Duncan, 209–10; and Allen Ginsberg, 29; and Denise Levertov, 203; and Robert Lowell, 79, 89–92; and W. S. Merwin, 136–38, 153–54; and Charles Olson, 195, 199; and poetry, 17–18; and James Wright, 163, 168
Nixon, Richard M., 9

Oglesby, Carl, 6
O'Hara, Frank, 2, 200
Olson, Charles, xv, xvi, 136, 182–99; and acculturation, 190; antirationalism of, 185–86, 189; on early New England history, 193–95; friendship with Allen Ginsberg, 22; and Gestalt psychology, 20; and language, 191–92; materialism of, 187; and modernism, 186; and New Critical poetics, 186–88; and non-Euclidean geometry, 188–89; as poet, 193–99; on poetry of process, 183–84, 191–92, 198; and private/public dualism, 15; on prosody, 188, 192; syntax of, 186, 191–92, 196; as theorist, 183–93; on truth, 190–91. Essays: "Causal Mythology," 190; "Equal, That Is, to the Real Itself," 188–89; "History," 190; "Human Universe," 185–86, 191; "Letter to Elaine Feinstein," 190; "Projective Verse," 187, 192. Poems: "Capt Christopher Levett (of York)," 194; "I, Maximus of Gloucester, to You," 193, 197; "The Kingfishers," 184; "Letter 6," 190, 197; "Letter 10," 193; "Letter 16," 184, 194; "Letter 23," 193; "Maximus, from Dogtown—I," 196–99; "Maximus, to Himself," 196–97; "Some Good News," 194–95

Orr, Gregory, 118, 126, 127, 129
Orwell, George, 7

Packard, Vance, 4
Perloff, Marjorie, 52
Pinsky, Robert, 125, 127, 220, 225–26
Plath, Sylvia, xvi, xvii, 22, 41, 53, 58, 95–117, 128, 182, 211; autobiography as myth in, 95–99; John Berryman on, 56; as "confessional" poet, 44, 95; and courtship of suffering, 95; and dramatic monologue, 46–47; and Ted Hughes, 98, 110; instability of tone in, 103, 105–10; and modernism, 97; Nazi motifs in, 103–6, 108–9; and Aurelia Plath, 113; and Otto Plath, 99, 103–4; and private/public dualism, 44, 95; prosody of, 106–7, 109; psychological absolutism of, 101, 111; and religion, 113–16; reticence of, 46–47; and self-transformation, 98–102; suicide of, 95, 108; symbolism in, 57, 99, 103–4, 109–13. Poems: "Ariel," 100, 102, 116; "The Bee Meeting," 101; "Berck-Plage," 116; "A Birthday Present," 99–100; "Black Rook in Rainy Weather," 102; "Daddy," 103–10, 116, 117; "The Earthenware Head," 100; "Fever 103°," 100; "Getting There," 100; "Kindness," 101; "Lady Lazarus," 100–103, 107–11, 116; "The Moon and the Yew Tree," 99, 110–17; "Moonrise," 99; "Nick and the Candlestick," 116; "The Night Dances," 116; "Poem for a Birthday," 100; "Poppies in October," 116; "Tale of a Tub," 101–2; "Totem," 116; "Words," 100
Plato, 185, 186, 194, 196, 233
Poe, Edgar Allan, 55, 109
Poetry of process, xvi, 1–2, 36, 81–82, 183–92, 196–200, 202, 203, 205–7, 211–12. See also Projective poetry
Popper, Sir Karl, xi
Pound, Ezra, 50–51, 60, 119, 136, 186, 199, 235
Pritchard, W. H., 248 n.34
Private/public dualism, "conflated," 8, 17–18, 31, 42–43, 50, 60–61, 64, 67–70, 74, 95, 103, 105, 127; and disappearance of public realm, 215–16, 219; maintained, 30, 39, 43–44, 56–57, 62–65, 67, 76, 81, 127, 138; as split between profane outer and sacred inner space, 121–22, 131, 167, 171–72, 184

Projective poetry, xvi, 183–92, 199–200, 202, 203, 205–7, 211–12. *See also* Poetry of process
prosody: in Allen Ginsberg's poetry, 24–25; in Robert Lowell's poetry, 53; in W. S. Merwin's poetry, 140–41; meter as constraint, 2, 53, 207; and Charles Olson, 192; and James Wright, 159, 178. *See also* Convention
Psychoanalysis: and the New Left, 1, 14–17; and popular culture, xiii; and romanticism, xiii, 1, 14, 16. *See also* Ego psychology; Radical Freudianism

Radical Freudianism, xiii–xiv, 5, 14–16, 20–21; and poetry, 17–18, 29, 59, 71, 72, 79, 168. *See also* Brown, Norman O.; Laing, R. D.; Marcuse, Herbert; Reich, Wilhelm
Reich, Wilhelm, 20–21, 39
Ransom, John Crowe, 158–59, 186–87, 196, 225
Rationality: as barrier to experience, 185–87; and poetic coherence, 146–47; and emotion in poetry, 3, 44; and Freudian analysis, 13, 44, 240 n.33; and liberal attitude, 87–88; as psychopolitical repression, 4, 6, 15, 27, 128, 201; as source of freedom, 13
Religion, 7; and "deep-image" poetry, 121; and Allen Ginsberg, 25, 26, 31, 34, 38–40; and Robert Lowell, 62, 72, 73, 77–78, 90; and W. S. Merwin, 149, 156; and Sylvia Plath, 113–16
Rich, Adrienne, xvii, 2, 140, 158, 246–47 n.1
Richardson, James, 129
Rieff, Philip, 11, 135, 240 n.33
Riesman, David, 3–6
Rimbaud, Arthur, 60, 61, 77, 97, 213
Roazen, Paul, xiii
Robinson, Edward Arlington, 157, 159
Robinson, Paul A., 20–21
Roethke, Theodore, 55
Romanticism: and John Ashbery, 220–21, 234–35; and contemporary poetry, 142, 191, 203, 212–13; and the New Left, xiii, 1, 14, 16
Rosenberg, Harold, 6, 11
Rosenblatt, Jon, 95, 245 n.1, 246 n.5
Rosenthal, M. L., 22, 42, 57, 95, 103, 116, 127, 132, 246 n.5
Rossman, Michael, 163
Roszak, Theodore, 16
Rudman, Mark, 64, 65, 70, 244 n.13

Sanazaro, Leonard, 246 n.5

Sanders, Ed, 38
Santayana, George, 224
Schiller, Friedrich, 14, 22
Schramm, Richard, 118
Schwartz, Delmore, 53, 55, 67
SDS (Students for a Democratic Society), 6
Sennett, Richard, 49
Sexton, Anne, 53, 95
Sexual instincts: and authenticity, 20–21, 24, 39, 61, 78–79, 91, 92, 128, 161–62; and violence, 78–79, 83, 85–86, 164, 168–69
Shakespeare, William, xv, 54, 116, 189
Shapiro, David, 213, 214
Shapiro, Karl, 55
Shaw, Robert Gould, 73–75
Shearman, John, 227, 253 n.18
Shelley, Percy Bysshe, xiii, 48–50, 90, 212, 221
Shils, Edward, 3
Simic, Charles, 118, 122–23, 126, 129
Simpson, Louis, 238 n.3
Snodgrass, W. D., 131
Snyder, Gary, 118, 128, 129, 132, 136, 200, 211
Socrates, 185
Stalin, Josef, 7, 93, 209
Steiner, George, 246 n.5
Stevens, Wallace, 44, 77, 213, 221, 224, 235
Strand, Mark, 118–19, 126, 128, 130
Suicide, 56, 95, 98–99, 107, 108
Sullivan, Harry Stack, 10, 11
Symbolism: and autobiography, 95–97, 99, 103–4, 111, 112; as formulaic vocabulary, 120, 125–27, 132, 141–42, 149; and Freudian dream interpretation, 18–19, 124–25, 128; and Jungian dream interpretation, 19, 124–25; and landscape, 68, 70–74; of light and dark, 133–34, 162–63; and madness, 78; and metonymy, 52; in modern and "confessional" poetry, 50–55; Charles Olson's critique of, 188–89; and private reference, 52, 103–4, 119; of self as representative victim, 42–45, 64; of stone, 129–30; and the unconscious, 18–19, 121–25, 134, 160–61, 171–72. *See also* Private/public dualism
Syntax: in John Ashbery's poetry, 214, 228–29; in "deep-image" poetry, 132–33; and Robert Duncan, 206; in Allen Ginsberg's poetry, 24–25; in Robert Lowell's poetry, 80; in W. S. Merwin's poetry, 132, 140–42, 144,

154–56; and Charles Olson, 186, 191–92, 196, in James Wright's poetry, 133, 134, 160, 176

Tate, Allen, 55, 72–73, 186–87, 196, 221
Tate, James, 118, 119, 130
Thomas, Dylan, 113
Thompson, Clara, 11
Truman, Harry S., 182, 195
Trungpa, Chogyam, 22, 38–40
Tu Fu, 174

Unconscious: as authentic part of self, 13–18, 20–21, 44, 102–3, 119, 121, 128–29, 131–32, 134, 148, 160–61, 167, 172, 183; and ego, 10–11, 18–19, 132, 134–35, 148, 150; Freudian, 18–19, 124; Jungian, 19–20, 123–25, 134–35; and poetic convention, 44–45, 120–27, 132–33, 139, 148; and pre-conscious, 19; and Wilhelm Reich, 20–21; and superego, 10–11, 102–3; as unviolated inner space, 171–72

Vaihinger, Hans, 224
Vendler, Helen, 152, 212–19
Vietnam War, 7–8, 31–32, 37, 38, 76, 78, 152–53, 195, 199, 200, 202, 204–5, 208–9
von Hallberg, Robert, 22, 59, 82, 88, 92, 93, 184, 190, 192, 199

Waldman, Anne, 38
Weber, Max, 194
Whitehead, Alfred North, 189, 192
Whitman, Walt, 24, 38, 48–50, 213, 220, 229, 235; and acculturation, 17–18; and equality of poet and reader, 203; and visionary poetry, 60–61
Whyte, William H., Jr., 4
Wilbur, Richard, 23, 69, 140, 141, 159
Williams, William Carlos, 77, 119, 136, 186, 202
Williamson, Alan, 59, 64, 71, 82, 92, 132, 136, 213, 244 n.1, 251 n.16
Wordsworth, William, xiii
Wright, James, 97, 136, 140, 157–82, 211, 212, 250 n.15, 250 n.16; and antiformalism, 158–59; and anti-rationalism, 160–62, 214; as "deep-image" poet, 118, 121–22, 129, 181; on formal poetry, 158–59; Horatian pose of, 158–59, 178; instincts as authen-ticity in, 160–62, 214; and W. S. Mer-win, 145–46; and nature vs. industrial landscape, 157, 167, 171; as political activist, 128; as political poet, 133–34;

regionalism of, 135, 145–46, 157–58, 166–67, 169, 171, 180–81; surrealism in 160–61; symbolism of light and darkness in, 133, 162–64; syntax of, 133, 134, 160, 176; and the uncon-scious, 134, 160, 171–72; and working-class life, 165-66, 168–69, 174–75. Poems: "American Twilights," 163–64; "At the Executed Murderer's Grave," 164–66, 176; "Autumn Begins in Mar-tins Ferry, Ohio," 167–70, 180; "Be-fore a Cashier's Window in a Depart-ment Store," 172–74; "A Blessing," 167, 169–70, 172; "Confession to J. Edgar Hoover," 129, 176; "Eisenhow-er's Visit to Franco, 1959," 133–34, 164; "Eleutheria," 162–63; "The First Days," 179; "The Flying Eagles of Troop 62," 180; "Honey," 180–81; "In Response to a Rumor That the Oldest Whorehouse in Wheeling, West Vir-ginia, Has Been Condemned," 166–67; "The Jewel," 121–22, 171–73; "A Little Girl on Her Way to School," 162; "Lying in a Hammock at William Duf-fy's Farm in Pine Island, Minnesota," 167, 170–72; "Many of Our Waters: Variations on a Poem by a Black Child," 160–61, 177; "May Morning," 159, 178; "The Minneapolis Poem," 160, 172, 176; "Morning Hymn to a Dark Girl," 163; "On Having My Pocket Picked at Rome," 178; "On Minding One's Own Business," 161–63; "Paul," 178; "A Poem about George Doty in the Death House," 162, 163; "Poem for Kathleen Ferrier," 162; "A Poem Writ-ten Under an Archway in a Discon-tinued Railroad Station, Fargo, North Dakota," 176; "The Poor Washed Up by Chicago Winter," 175–76; "Prayer to the Good Poet," 178; "The Quail," 160; "The Secret of Light," 179; "Speak," 176; "To a Hostess Saying Good Night," 162; "To the Muse," 176–77; "Two Mo-ments in Rome," 178; "Two Moments in Venice," 178–79; "Willy Lyons," 172, 174–76; "Written on a Big Cheap Postcard from Vienna," 178; "The Young Good Man," 177
Yeats, William Butler, 2, 112, 119, 221
Yenser, Stephen, 65
Young, Nigel, 241 n.45

Zweig, Paul, xiv, 118